D0776799

Praise for *People Operations*

"In many ways, now is the easiest and hardest time to be a small business in the US. The thesis of *People Operations* is that if small businesses master the emerging disciple of people operations, they will have a sustainable competitive advantage.

As someone who has studied human motivation and performance for my whole adult life, I couldn't agree more. *People Operations* is a practical must-read guide for small business owners. Have your to-do list handy when you're reading it, because you'll get a very long list of ideas you'll want to implement immediately."

—Neel Doshi, Co-author, *Primed to Perform*;
Co-Founder, The Vega Factor

"Regardless of your business's size, if you employ people, you want to empower them to create the most value they can for your customers and their fellow employees. That is the core of any business. But there are lots of other demands on your time that can take your eye off the ball, from compliance regulations to workforce benefits to a myriad of other things. *People Operations* shows you how you can use technology and tools to offload all that other stuff so you can focus your energies on the stuff that really matters."

—Geoffrey Moore, Author, *Crossing the Chasm*

"*People Operations* is critical reading for businesses of all sizes. The book expertly lays out an updated vision for what had traditionally been considered 'human resources' and makes clear that a new way of thinking about engaging with and managing employees is not just needed, it is critical for the success of businesses in the 21st century."

—Seth Levine, Co-author of *The New Builders*;
Partner and co-founder of Foundry Group

"*People Operations* provides a prescriptive and pragmatic playbook for going from paper work to people work, giving small businesses a competitive advantage by bringing the human back in the center."

—Pat Wadors, Chief Talent Officer, Procore

"*People Operations* is the playbook for small business entrepreneurs who want to win in the new world of work. This book upends the traditional approach to managing the workforce with insightful ideas and examples for creating a winning employee experience and organizational culture."

—John Suh, former CEO, LegalZoom

"Business leaders know that their only true competitive differentiator is their people. Knowing how to transform from traditional HR practices to an employee experience set of approaches means disrupting status quos without adversely impacting business outcomes. *People Operations* explains why the shift is important and provides the practical insights and tools that small business leaders can use to transform how their people experience work without risking business results."

—Patti Fletcher, CMO, Workhuman

"One of the biggest challenges for business owners today is attracting and retaining employees. *People Operations* will help you create a great employee experience, which will help you keep your staff and grow your business."

—Rieva Lesonsky, CEO, President & Founder at GrowBiz Media/Small Business Daily

PEOPLE
OPERATIONS

JAY FULCHER • KEVIN MARASCO • TRACY COTE

PEOPLE
OPERATIONS

AUTOMATE HR,
DESIGN A GREAT EMPLOYEE EXPERIENCE,
AND **UNLEASH YOUR WORKFORCE**

WILEY

Library of Congress Cataloging-in-Publication Data

Names: Fulcher, Jay, author. | Marasco, Kevin, author. | Cote, Tracy, author.
Title: People operations : automate HR, design a great employee experience, and unleash your workforce / Jay Fulcher, Kevin Marasco, and Tracy Cote.
Description: Hoboken, New Jersey : Wiley, [2021] | Includes bibliographical references and index.
Identifiers: LCCN 2021018709 (print) | LCCN 2021018710 (ebook) | ISBN 9781119785231 (hardback) | ISBN 9781119785309 (adobe pdf) | ISBN 9781119785316 (epub)
Subjects: LCSH: Personnel management—Data processing.
Classification: LCC HF5549.5.D37 F76 2021 (print) | LCC HF5549.5.D37 (ebook) | DDC 658.3/03—dc23
LC record available at https://lccn.loc.gov/2021018709
LC ebook record available at https://lccn.loc.gov/2021018710

Cover Design: Wiley
Cover Image: Business Woman: © Sorbetto/Getty Images
Multitasking Icons: © Rudzhan Nagiev/Getty Images

SKY10027064_051721

This book is dedicated to small business owners, hustlers, people who have dreams, and people who create opportunities for others to follow their dreams.

Contents

Preface: Leveling the Playing Field for the "Other 99 Percent"

One in five small businesses fail within their first year. One in two go out of business within five years. In 2020, that rate was even higher (Hannon 2020).

These aren't nameless, faceless statistics. Small businesses are the manifestation of the American dream. Ninety-nine percent of all businesses in the United States are "small" as defined by the Small Business Association's definition of employing 500 people or fewer. They're also the lifeblood of the US economy. Thirty-two million small businesses employ 47 percent of the US workforce, about 60 million people. And they have contributed 66 percent of all new jobs since 2000 (SBA Office of Advocacy 2018).

The good news is that even in the dire economic realities of the COVID-19 pandemic and globalization, small businesses in America are getting stronger. Although the average lifespan of a small business is 8.5 years, the failure rate (percent of year-over-year failures) is actually shrinking (Todd 2020).

Why? Small organizations are typically more creative. They're more in tune with their customers. They can move faster, and are more nimble. They have a better finger on the pulse of their employees. And now, they have newfound access to services, tools, and technology that let them do more—much more—with less. They're using these tools to better operationalize and automate their business processes. They're using these tools to turn adversity into advantage.

Perhaps the least operationalized business function—and the one with the most potential impact—is the people function. You know, the function that oversees a company's greatest asset, expense, and source of competitive advantage: its people.

This book is all about bringing that function into focus—and up to speed—to meet the massive shifts in the *new* world of work.

By "people function," do we mean HR? No, actually we don't. Human resources, formerly the personnel department or "policy police," might have worked in the twentieth century. It still might have worked before the 2020 pandemic. Actually, at best, it *might* have worked. At worst, it was strangely separate from the business—seen as a necessary evil, an overhead, and a hassle. Business leaders and employees often don't like HR, or their idea of HR. We agree. This book is about a new approach to a timeless challenge.

People Operations (People Ops, or POPS) is a people-centric business approach that emphasizes workforce empowerment to drive growth. POPS focuses on automating administration, using data to drive decisions, and delivering tangible results. When you empower your people to do their best every day, you build a more resilient culture that becomes a sustainable competitive advantage.

People Ops is the future of work. If you own, run, or work for a small business and are responsible for people in any capacity, this book is for you and your future.

We Get It: It's Hard to Be a Small Business

The playing field for *32 million* small businesses like yours is markedly stacked against you, as compared to fewer than *20 thousand* enterprise companies with workforces larger than 500 people (SBA Office of Advocacy 2020).

You don't have the big companies' budgets, departments, depth of sophistication, or tools they have access to. And you likely lack the benefits, perks, and employee experience to compete as effectively for the best talent.

What you do have is an equal amount of the same compliance overhead. There are 180 federal labor laws alone for businesses of all sizes to manage. Compound that with state and city ordinances, and that's where small business owners' sleepless nights begin.

You also share the challenge of employing, engaging and retaining five generations of workers with fundamentally different expectations from their employers. Seventy percent of them will be from the Millennial and Gen Z generations in 2025 (Lettink 2019). And they're in it for purpose over paycheck, for lifestyle over the corporate ladder, for inclusion and empathy over titles. They expect their work experience to include tech that's as easy to use as the apps on their iPhones.

And what you have even more of: costs for providing insurance coverage. On average, small businesses pay 8–18 percent more for healthcare insurance coverage per employee than large firms who can negotiate better rates with more people, ostensibly in exchange for lower risk to insurance carriers (Ferguson 2020). And that's on top of a more frightening reality: the average cost of healthcare for a US family of four in 2020 was $28,653 (Girod et al. 2020). That could equate to 38–100 percent of total family income, according to Brian Melanson at M4 Innovation. Therefore, it's scary, but not surprising, that less than half of small businesses offer health insurance.

Because salaries and benefits represent the top two costs for businesses, and labor compliance is one of your greatest risks, you cannot afford to manage your people function by "gut" or good intention with occasional swag and fun events. Profit leaks, regulatory risks, and people issues are among the top reasons for small and medium-sized business (SMB) failure, and you need to be on your game.

How This Book Helps Tilt the Advantage

First of all, as authors of this book, we absolutely subscribe to the notion in *The Hard Thing About Hard Things,* by Ben Horowitz (2014):

> There's no recipe for really complicated, dynamic situations. There's no recipe for building a high-tech company; there's no recipe for leading a group of people out of trouble; there's no recipe for making a series of hit songs; there's no recipe for playing NFL quarterback; there's no recipe for running for president; and there's no recipe for motivating teams when your business has turned to crap. That's the hard thing about hard things—there is no formula for dealing with them . . . [The most successful CEOs] . . . have the ability to focus and make the best moves when there are no good moves.

So we've established what we don't have. What is it that we do have? We have a pretty close and sober view of the realities facing small businesses.

We authors have each started and/or contributed to the growth, success, and profitable exits across a number of businesses—many of them focused on technology and automating people programs. Individually, and collectively, we've been motivated by solving hard problems. And you'd better believe we've learned a lot of hard lessons in the process.

Over the past decade, we've worked with more than 30,000 of the most successful small businesses across the country, leaning in and learning with them—and from them—about the market, social, demographic, environmental, political, mobile, health, and well-being dynamics that impact their people and therefore their businesses.

Most importantly, we've recognized the force multiplier of pairing an eyes-wide-open awareness of the dynamics of the new world of work, to better build, engage, and unleash a team of people against a hard problem or unexplored potential.

The keys: take the time to understand the changing market, business, and people dynamics, and their impact on your business. Then, continually challenge your assumptions.

Where to Start: With Your Advantage

The great thing about running a small business is your ability to adapt.

Throughout the pandemic we were awed by and grateful for how our own Zenefits team rose to the challenge and changes with grit, tenacity, and innovation. Instead of slowing our product development, we sped it up, delivering a host of products, features, and content geared directly at making it easier to manage during the crisis—from applying for Payroll Protection Program (PPP) loans, to supporting paid sick time off and managing related tax incentives and loan forgiveness criteria.

We were inspired to see the phenomenal bravery, determination, and humanity across our customer base finding new ways to exist, transform, and even grow in spite of the obstacles in front of them.

You, too, likely have access to easily tap these same tremendous small business advantages right now for better resilience:

- Speed: Your lack of size means fewer constraints to move quickly on new ideas.
- Agility: Your ability and appetite for continual iteration and improvement make your business more agile.
- Digital-readiness: Your scalable, cloud-based technologies allow you to connect, pivot, and communicate.
- People-first: You treat employees like customers, partners, and trusted counselors.

These are your strengths, and this is where you have the competitive edge over the lumbering big corporations.

The average S&P 500 company today is up to 20 years old (Sheetz 2017). Their supply chains and infrastructure that once gave them a competitive advantage have become a ball and chain that is immobilizing them. Meanwhile, smaller organizations like yours disrupt their business by providing easier and better ways for their customers to get greater value from you.

Technology is often the engine at the heart of that disruption. Technology has changed the potential for small businesses to start with significantly less capital, and continue with more ease. Software in the cloud has replaced prohibitively priced hardware and the tech staff needed to support it. High-speed internet allows your team to work from home—or increasingly, wherever—versus maintaining an expensive office space. And of course Zoom has become as ubiquitous as a lightbulb, connecting us in our digital Brady Bunch boxes.

Technology is also the catalyst that's helped build rigor and data to transform: your bookkeeping with financial operations; your customer acquisition with sales operations; your brand awareness with marketing operations. Now it's time to leverage your huge investment in finding, hiring, and training your people to accelerate their success and the success of your business with people operations.

For sure, technology is a piece of it. Automating the paperwork is a start. But there is a science, a practice, and practical changes required for your small business to unleash the potential of your people and your profit. And it's not a nice-to-have; it's a have-to-have.

The COVID-19 pandemic fast-tracked many concepts about the future of work—at warp speed—to the present. In 2020 you may have managed a remote team for the first time; you may have dealt for the first time with life-and-death health and safety decisions for employees and customers; you may have been truly afraid for the emotional well-being of yourself and your team.

Healthy people are critical for a healthy business.

It's the new world of work. Work has changed, and continues to change. Have you? That might be why you're here. We're glad you're here.

Our company mission—or noble purpose as we like to think of it—is to help take the stress, headache, and complexity out of difficult, perplexing (and sometimes frustrating) business processes.

We're in business to give small businesses like yours the right data in the right place, seamlessly. We enable you to easily shop for benefit options all in one spot to get the same coverage and capabilities that large companies have. To curate and democratize access to content and open resources for anything from health and well-being to mentoring and developing employees. You know—like big companies do.

Yes, we provide a people operations technology platform that supports onboarding, HR, payroll, and all levels of healthcare, engagement, performance, and well-being. And sure, we'd love you to become a customer. But more than that, we'd love you to succeed.

Through all of our work and our learning alongside the nation's community of small businesses—many of which grew up to be large businesses—we've noticed how they do work differently. This helped to shape our thinking about tech, strategy, practice, process, and the integral role of the right data for decision making. This puts you and your team in the best possible position to be successful.

All of this—and a deep passion for small business—informed this book.

We've consolidated the information in this book to offer you guideposts and mile-markers, questions, options, and real-world "POPS Star" examples so that you're prepared to make the best choices when there are no good ones. So you can build a team and business resilience to meet the future.

Here's to your success, and to your success with people operations.

Because your people are your business. And your success powers our economy.

We're in it, together.

PART I

The Rise of People Operations

CHAPTER 1

The Great Pivot:
The New Work Order!

People are the lifeblood of any organization.

They're so significant that intangible assets—things comprised of and created by people—make up 90 percent of all business value. There clearly would be no business without people. But managing them can be hard, especially in the *new* world of work.

In the new world of work, companies are running away from traditional working practices. In the new world of work, everything is changing. The workforce is changing. The workplace is changing. Work styles are changing.

Remember when . . . we had full-time employees who worked in offices? And all they really wanted was a paycheck? Do you remember walking into your boss's office on a Friday to get a paper check, and then going to the bank to deposit it just so you can use your own money? Ahh, the good old days! That was when work was just a job. That was before robots took over. That was before the COVID-19 pandemic transformed the workplace and business forever. That was then. This is now—the New Work Order.

This book is for not only managing—but embracing—the new world of work. Regardless of your role—be it a small business owner or CEO, CFO, COO, HR leader, or office manager, if you oversee your workforce or wear the hat of the HR or people leader of your business, this book is for you.

Our way of doing things has been able to get us to this point. But what got us *here* won't get us *there*. Not in the New Work Order. We believe that the idea of human resources as we've known it is broken, and it is time for a change.

The solution? It's a paradigm shift—a new approach called "people operations." People operations is designed for the new world of work. It champions technology, data, and the employee experience to accelerate business priorities. People operations is a competitive differentiator for any business, but especially small and midsize businesses looking to punch above their weight and do more with less. It allows you to better focus your time and effort on things that matter most to you: your people and your business.

Our goal with this book is to arm you with a step-by-step guide for implementing people operations in your organization. Your employees, leadership team, and shareholders will thank you for it.

If you're new to HR—perhaps a business owner, operating executive, or accidental HR person—pay close attention to Part II of the book, where you'll learn about a refreshing approach to an ageless challenge. You'll learn how to skip building out a traditional HR function—or worse yet, wasting your valuable time and resources on administrative busywork—and instead, lean on technology to advance your workforce productivity to the next level.

If you're an experienced HR pro or feel you have a solid HR foundation in place, you'll benefit most from Parts III and IV, where you will walk away with new ideas and techniques to unlock productivity and profits. These are things traditional HR playbooks have overlooked or dismissed. We believe the setup in Part I is a valuable context in either case, and we encourage you to read straight through, but feel free to skip around. After all, it's your book. With it, we're including several of our most popular guides, tools, frameworks, and checklists for free. These will be referenced through-out the book and are available online. You can find additional details and instructions for accessing the accompanying tools in the Appendix.

Thousands of companies are doing things differently. They're embracing people operations. They're changing the game and we hope you do too. Thanks for joining us on this journey.

Here Come the Robots

Let's cut to the chase. It's only a matter of time until a robot takes your job. Your job in its current form, that is.

I mean, think about it. We used to ride on horse and buggy, and that buggy was built by human craftsmen. But the buggy was replaced by the car—originally the "horseless carriage." Not only do machines build them cheaper and faster, they actually make them better. Machines provide a better user (driver, passenger) experience with things like air conditioning, entertainment systems, and panoramic sunroofs. They also make them safer with seat belts, airbags, and emergency braking. Finally, they unleash the full potential of transportation with fast, easy, mass production—putting automobiles within the reach of most households. And now, they drive themselves too (in many cases, once again . . . better than humans).

The human-machine relationship is quite an interesting one if you think about it: friend, foe, or subordinate? Perhaps it's all of the above. We used to compete exclusively with other humans at puzzles and games. Now, we play against computers. And, who usually wins? Today, computers can beat humans at even the most skilled games like chess, Go, and Jeopardy. Even in most video games, you can only win if you allow the machine to let you ("easy" level = let human win). (see Figure 1.1.)

Humans versus machines has been a long-running debate. Technology has been replacing jobs for hundreds of years. At the turn of the twentieth century, farms employed nearly half the US workforce. Today, they account for less than 1 percent. Buttons displaced elevator and telephone operators. ATMs replaced bank tellers. And, when was the last time you booked a trip using a travel agent?

According to Gartner, automation technology usually costs one-fifth the amount of a US employee—that's 20 cents on the dollar, and one-third the amount of an offshore employee (Gartner 2020). But cost savings aren't the only benefit of automation. Regardless of industry, technology also helps:

- Improve speed
- Improve accuracy
- Reduce risk and variance
- Enable 24/7 output or servicing ability

FIGURE 1.1 Robot intelligence versus human intelligence.
Source: Zenefits, 2021.

Prior waves of mechanization clearly brought productivity improvements. They also brought plenty of debate, disruption, and anxiety. In the early nineteenth century, English textile workers actually destroyed machines as part of the Luddite movement. *TIME* magazine ran a story titled "The Automation Jobless" in 1961. It raised fears of technology advancements, stating, "automation is beginning to move in and eliminate office jobs too."

It is true that these breakthroughs often brought some short-term job loss. But they also brought fresh opportunities. New jobs creating the machines and algorithms. New jobs overseeing and maintaining the machines. New jobs managing the additional output from the machines. New jobs to handle unforeseen impacts of the machines. New jobs to manage the new jobs. In the end, the innovations usually created more jobs than they displaced.

The transformation usually follows one of—and in many cases, a sequence of—the following scenarios:

1. **Evolution:** technology is introduced to automate manual tasks. Machines work alongside people. *Example: ATMs and bank tellers.*
2. **Displacement:** technology replaces an old job entirely. New categories of jobs emerge to manage machines and their downstream impacts. *Example: buttons replace elevator operators; now we need security guards and elevator technicians.*
3. **Reinvention:** technology automates lower-value activities, freeing up cognitive and physical capacity. People take on more meaningful work, increasing the value of the entire profession. *Example: once threatened by electronic trading systems, stockbrokers became wealth managers (cha-ching!).*

Digital transformation is profoundly impacting every profession and every industry. Advances in machine learning (ML), artificial intelligence (AI), and Robotic Process Automation (RPA) are bringing in a new age of automation. And it's changing the way we interact with our world.

So where do we go from here? If software is eating the world, the robots are hungry for more. Reports show that 50 percent of today's work can be automated (Manyika et al. 2017). That's half of all work. Half! Two-and-a-half-day workweek, anyone?

Economists predict that up to one in four workers—or 800 million people, globally—will lose their jobs to new technology over the next decade (Manyika et al. 2017). This was only accelerated by the COVID-19 crisis. Companies in survival mode have been forced to get creative. They're deploying technology anywhere and everywhere. To create cost efficiencies, yes, but also to deliver a safe, convenient, digital experience for their customers and employees. Let's take a look at the types of tasks machines do well, and others that they don't (yet). (see Figure 1.2.)

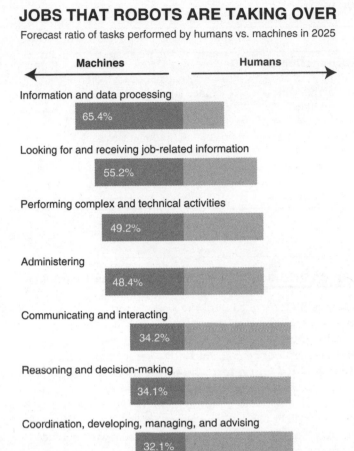

JOBS THAT ROBOTS ARE TAKING OVER

Forecast ratio of tasks performed by humans vs. machines in 2025

Machines ← → **Humans**

Information and data processing
65.4%

Looking for and receiving job-related information
55.2%

Performing complex and technical activities
49.2%

Administering
48.4%

Communicating and interacting
34.2%

Reasoning and decision-making
34.1%

Coordination, developing, managing, and advising
32.1%

FIGURE 1.2 The percent of jobs forecasted to be run by machines by 2025.

Source: World Economic Forum, "The Future of Jobs Report 2020," October 2020.

In short, robots free humans from repetitive, administrative (and often boring) tasks. The key for humans who still want a job? Embrace and manage the automation. This allows people to take up more meaningful and intellectually stimulating work. According to McKinsey & Company, "All workers will need to adapt as machines take over routine and some physical tasks and as demand grows for work involving socioemotional, creative, technological, and higher cognitive skills" (Lund et al. 2019). When technology is embraced, it actually increases the output, and value—worth and pay—of the work being performed. This ultimately makes companies more productive. (see Table 1.1.)

TABLE 1.1 Humans only versus humans plus computers.

THEN	NOW
People-Driven: Humans Only	**Technology-Driven: Humans + Computers**
People do all the work	People do higher-order work
People do repetitive, production tasks	Machines automate repetitive, production tasks
People manage front-line workers	People manage people and technology
Humans only for cognitive tasks	AI assists with cognitive tasks
Linear productivity gains	Exponential productivity gains

Source: Zenefits, 2021.

Human versus Machine: Five Jobs Taken Over by Robots

- **Scribes:** Before the Gutenberg press in the mid-1400s, books were handwritten. These jobs were replaced by movable type and the printing press, which were replaced by digital printing, computers, and desktop publishing. And now, we have 3D printers.
- **Switchboard Operator:** The invention of the telephone in 1876 disrupted the telegraph and other communication methods—and jobs. But it also created hundreds of thousands of *new* jobs operating the switchboards. Supervisors scooted around on roller skates just to keep up. Eventually, these jobs too were replaced entirely. From fax machines and pagers to email and mobile phones, jobs were continuously reinvented.
- **Knocker-Upper:** Until the 1920s, people used long sticks to wake people up. This job was replaced by wind-up clocks, which were replaced by alarm clocks, which are being replaced by smartphones and wearables.
- **Pinsetter:** Until the 1930s, people manually reset bowling pins to their correct position. They cleared fallen pins and returned balls to bowlers. This job was replaced by semi-automated, and then, fully automated mechanical pinsetters. Eventually, it all became part of integrated digital scoring systems.
- **Book Authors:** Until recently, people wrote books. Hopefully you didn't notice, but this book was written by a robot using AI. Okay, that's a joke. But as we write this, a writing assistant is managing the adverb volume, suggesting easier-to-read phrasing, correcting run-ons, and stating that 96 percent of sentences are easy to read with a total reading level of "8th grade."

Work is being reshaped. Business processes are being transformed. There are numerous benefits to automating the drudgerous parts of your job. From sipping on piña coladas beachside with your family to making more money by doing more valuable work . . . embracing automation has significant upside.

The takeaway? Robots kill jobs, but they create them too. Tomorrow's workers will have to adapt, change, and learn new skills. We *all* need to embrace a lifelong learning mindset that enables us to evolve. It allows us to grow our companies and our own careers too. As you read the rest of this book . . . we hope you do so with an open mind for change, progress, and growth. It's what will separate you from a robot. Robots want your job. Let them have it!

The Rise of the Fluid Workforce

Start. Stop. Pivot. If there's one lesson the first part of this century has taught us, it's our need to adapt. Quickly!

The digitization of our economy has dramatically changed who does what, and how. We've been forced to respond to volatile conditions— market, economic, and world events. Not just in business, but often on personal levels as well. The winners are the ones that take fast and meaningful action. With the pace of change accelerating, businesses need the ability to turn on a dime. One way to do this is by creating a more flexible, or "fluid workforce." A fluid workforce is one that combines and connects regular employees with contingent workers—including temps, freelancers, independent contractors, consultants, vendors/agencies, and more. (see Figure 1.3.)

In this new workforce model, technology connects, aligns, and manages these blended teams. Skills and capabilities are built around priorities and projects rather than traditional business functions. Blended teams replace traditional department silos. Flatter, collaborative organizational structures replace hierarchical organization charts. The fluid workforce is designed, ground-up, for agility. It embraces automation and change.

Today's most successful businesses are building fluid workforces to:

- Move and change quickly
- Scale up and down efficiently
- Find specific skills for specific priorities and projects

FLUID WORKFORCE

| Full Time | Part Time | Intern | Independent Contractor | Consultant | Temp | Vendor Employee | Volunteer | Robot |

Employees **Contingent Workers** **Robot**

FIGURE 1.3 An artful representation of the modern workforce.

Source: Zenefits, 2021.

- Tap a broader and more diverse "boundary-less" talent pool
- Reduce unnecessary costs (pay as you go/need)
- Reduce overhead costs (tax and benefit savings)
- Avoid unnecessary investment in reskilling workers

Experts estimate the cost savings in real estate space and office expenditures alone can reach $10,000 per year per employee (Hussain 2019). Beyond the clear business benefits, there are several factors driving this shift to the fluid workforce. One is an increasing volume and accessibility of freelancers, or "the gig economy." This creates newfound work opportunities in the form of project work, or gigs. The duration of work can range from days to months, or even years. Gig workers can help small businesses get through large projects or peak times, or become a long-term part of the team.

The gig economy brings work of all types and levels to people everywhere. Freelance workers can stitch together paychecks from several gigs to create the equivalent pay of a full-time job. They get the ultimate in flexibility, work/life balance, and control.

Freelancer platforms like Upwork connect workers with all types of gigs in seconds. These sites allow businesses to hire for a specific project or for ongoing work that doesn't justify a full- or even part-time role. Workers are paid through the site, and typically pay a flat fee or percentage of their earnings to stay on the job. From fractional CFOs and consultants to graphic designers, work of all types is being gigified. Freelancers are projected to outnumber full-time employees by 2027 (Upwork 2017).

Another type of contingent worker is the contractor, or independent contractor. These work directly for a company, either as needed, on call, or for specific projects. The work they perform can be remote or in-house and they run the gamut of skill sets. Contingent workers aren't just ride-share contractors. They can be entry-level workers through highly skilled scientific, technical, and executive staff—and are typically sourced directly via word of mouth, referral, and social networks.

Temporary workers, or "temps," are also a type of contingent worker. Temps are typically provided by third-party staffing agencies to augment existing staff. Often, they're used for a temporary surge in demand, such as seasonal work for the holidays or to support a new product launch or expansion.

This movement to a fluid workforce opens up the door for virtual globalization, or boundary-less hiring. Finding the right person with the right skills at the best cost—regardless of where they are. With contingent workers, you don't have to deal with the same complexities of full-time employees. Think about work visas, payroll taxes, health insurance, or office perks. No kombucha, no problem! You can also release them whenever you want, no "performance improvement plan," severance, or awkward conversation.

Although there are a ton of benefits to tapping this new workforce model, it comes with new responsibilities, too. It requires a culture that embraces the fluid workforce—including open communication, inclusiveness, and transparency. Businesses must embed technology to connect, track, and empower these dynamic teams. It requires proper documentation (don't screw this up!), flexible time and payment systems, unique benefit offerings, and open collaboration tools for everyone. We'll go into more details throughout the book. We'll use the terms "employees" and "workers" interchangeably for continuity purposes, but in all cases we are referring to a fluid workforce consisting of various classifications of workers. It's important to keep in mind how the ideas presented apply to various types of contingent workers. (see Table 1.2.)

TABLE 1.2 Static workforce versus fluid workforce.

THEN	NOW
Static Workforce	**Fluid Workforce**
Process and structure	Speed and agility
Permanent employee (full-time employees only)	Employees (full-time, part-time), contingent workers of all types
Locations, departments, hierarchy	Flat, team-based collaboration
Job for life	Projects and gigs
Physical locations	Digital workplace

Source: Zenefits, 2021.

The Office is Dying . . . Kind Of

There's a lot of debate about the role of the office in a postpandemic world.

One thing is certain, it's changing. People used to move to work. Now, increasingly, work moves to people. As more companies shift to the fluid workforce, work is moving people out of cities, offices, and even desks. Studies show that approximately 80 percent of work is now deskless (Emergence Equity Management 2018). Today's work is happening in the field, on the fly, from home, and on the go. People are working wherever and whenever they want. Or, as their family, schedule, and circumstances allow.

This is just the beginning. The gig economy and modern work technology have created "digital nomads." Not tied down to any particular location, these digital nomads travel from spot to spot while working remotely. They may work from a cafe, a cool hotel, or a beach in Costa Rica. Countries such as Barbados, Bermuda, and Antigua are even offering tax incentives and work visas to attract digital nomads. It's less about work/life balance and more about work/life integration and harmony. Vacation, errr, work trip, anyone?

Work was already going virtual. The COVID-19 pandemic just fast-forwarded it a decade. Businesses responded to the need for social distancing by transitioning their teams online. Jobs once considered onsite or office work only, were forced to transition. Through this process, there were a few interesting discoveries. First, more work is successfully being done virtually than we previously imagined. Much of this is technology-driven. Second, productivity for virtual work materially increases for most jobs. Eight out of 10 workers say their productivity increases, and most executives agree. And, 9 out of 10 employees say more flexible work arrangements increase morale (Curry 2020b). Not having to commute and less office distractions are major factors. And finally, the obvious cost savings. There's less overhead for office space, property taxes, building supplies, security, and office perks.

This is no fad. Following the pandemic, three out of four CFOs say they intend to continue to shift some employees to remote work permanently (Gartner 2020). But, before we write the office eulogy, let's get real. The office isn't really going to become completely extinct. However, its purpose and format are forever changing. Businesses are shifting the purpose of the office from permanent working space to flexible collaboration and meeting space. It's there for those who need it, when they need it—more for "hoteling" and meetups now. This will place an important role in the new world of virtual work. People crave social interaction and connection. And of course, in some businesses, it's imperative for production, operations, and customer interaction. In some of the same ways WeWork disrupted office space, the new world of work is following suit. Businesses in every industry are reducing their real estate footprints and lease terms in favor of flexibility. (see Table 1.3.)

TABLE 1.3 From physical office work to digital remote work, 2021.

Then	Now
Physical	**Digital**
People move to work	Work moves to people
Office (by default)	Home (by default)
9 to 5	Anytime
Desk	Deskless
Computer	Phone
Office as required, permanent workplace	Office as optional workspace, culture and collaboration hub

Source: Zenefits, 2021.

This shift in workplace dynamics ushers in new challenges. How do you manage communication and ensure everyone is in the loop? How do you prioritize and oversee work across a distributed team? How do you avoid employee burnout? How do you coordinate schedules and workflow across different time zones? Managed effectively, a distributed, fully engaged workforce is an advantage. But left to traditional workplace methods, things can fall apart. Today's most successful people leaders have made this leap. So can you.

Your Employees Don't Work for You

The work*force* has changed. The work*place* has changed. You know what else has changed? Work *style*.

Traditionally for most people, a job was . . . well, a job. The accompanying approach to oversee the work was a military type top-down management style. Direction was set by company leadership and passed down through the ranks. Orders given, no questions asked. "Sir, yes sir!"

That's all changing. People no longer are content to be treated like an order taker, or replaceable cog on the assembly line.

Today's workforce is unique in its generational diversity. There are five distinct generations in the workplace, each with their own experiences, motivations, and expectations. There is some common ground. All generations value fair pay and benefits. Beyond that, things get tricky.

Traditionalists, Boomers, and Gen Xers tend to be more deferential to authority. They respect firm direction from management. However, a command-and-control approach will likely backfire with younger generations. Millennials and Gen Zers put more value on workplace flexibility, culture, and purpose. They really care about the employee experience. And then, there's technology. Think about it. Boomers like phone calls—"hey, let's chat." Millennials prefer text and instant messaging—"just ping me." Gen Z? They want in-app notifications with emojis. Oh yeah, we almost forgot the traditionalists . . . we're going to need to meet up and "talk about it"—in person. (see Figure 1.4.)

All of this is in a state of flux. Younger generations grew up with technology. It's an integral part of how they operate. But it's catching on with traditional generations—"digital immigrants" are rapidly adopting consumer technology as parents and grandparents flock to apps like Facebook and TikTok too. According to research by Workfront, this is creating some common ground when it comes to technology in the workplace:

- 88 percent of workers say technology is an important part of the employee experience.
- 91 percent of workers say they crave modern technology solutions.
- 84 percent of workers say businesses today are missing opportunities by not moving to more modern solutions.
- 86 percent of workers say this year's respondents say next-generation employees expect workplace technology that looks more like Amazon and Instagram.
- 94 percent of workers say searching at work should match the ease of Googling (Workfront 2020).

Some things are becoming pervasive. Today's workers want to have a voice and make a difference. They want mutual trust and respect. They want collaboration, community, and flexibility. They want to learn and grow. And, they want to have a little fun along the way. But, importantly, today's workers—in every generation—have more choice than ever before. From gig and independent contractor work, to working from home for companies in other countries, they have options. If you don't provide a workplace environment that fulfills these needs, someone else will. At the end of the day, as an employer, you work for your employees, just as

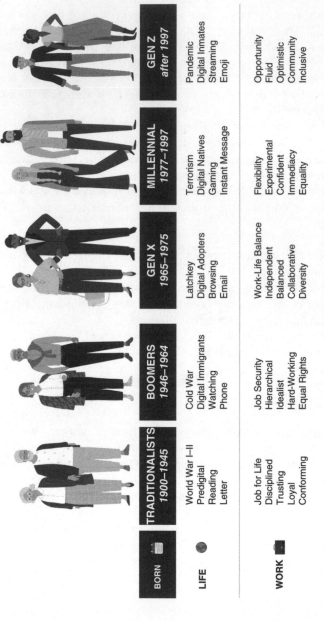

	TRADITIONALISTS 1900–1945	BOOMERS 1946–1964	GEN X 1965–1975	MILLENNIAL 1977–1997	GEN Z after 1997
LIFE	World War I–II Predigital Reading Letter	Cold War Digital Immigrants Watching Phone	Latchkey Digital Adopters Browsing Email	Terrorism Digital Natives Gaming Instant Message	Pandemic Digital Inmates Streaming Emoji
WORK	Job for Life Disciplined Trusting Loyal Conforming	Job Security Hierarchical Idealist Hard-Working Equal Rights	Work-Life Balance Independent Balanced Collaborative Diversity	Flexibility Experimental Confident Immediacy Equality	Opportunity Fluid Optimistic Community Inclusive

FIGURE 1.4 Explanation and comparison of all five generations working side by side in 2021.

Source: Zenefits, 2021.

TABLE 1.4 Top-down environment versus bottom-up environment.

Then	Now
Top Down	**Bottom Up**
Employees shut up and do as told	Employees have a voice, and choice
Company-imposed goals and processes	Team-driven initiatives and workflow
Worker receives specific task with limited interaction	Team members collaborate and share ideas
Information on a need-to-know basis ("classified")	Transparent and open communication ("on demand")
Lack of motivation and purpose	People find purpose and passion
Technology is a nice-to-have	Technology is a must-have

Source: Zenefits, 2021.

much as they work for you! Your job is to create a company and culture that's better than competitors and alternatives. To create a workplace that attracts and retains the best people for the jobs. One that allows them to learn, grow, and do their best work—for themselves and your company. (see Table 1.4.)

CHAPTER 2

So Long, HR

A lmost everything about work has changed radically, from the relationship between a company and its employees, to the importance of culture and the employee experience, to the technology revolution. We're living in a new world.

But most business leaders and human resource professionals acknowledge that the traditional approaches and practices for managing the organization's most vital asset haven't kept up. Most agree that the function of HR itself needs, not just to evolve, but to radically change in order to meet the needs of the twenty-first century.

This has put the role of HR in hot debate. Many ask, why do we still call the department responsible for its people human resources? How often do we refer to people as *humans* or *resources* anyway?

Before we fly forward, let's take a quick step back.

Quick History of a Controversial Topic

Where did HR even come from? What's its purpose?

The "personnel" department was a product of the industrial revolution in the early 1900s. Initially dubbed "industrial and labor relations," HR was created as an intermediary between management, workers, and labor unions. It helped companies oversee work conditions, hours, and activities in accordance with emerging regulations.

From the get go, there was a fair share of contention. Factory supervisors and owners didn't understand the connection between working conditions and improved productivity. But personnel professionals did. They tried to get managers to follow procedures without having any direct power over them. Hard-driving supervisors—and even many employees desperate for work—saw labor relations as a hindrance to productivity and looked for workarounds. Introducing . . . the policy police.

Over the next several decades, there was an influx in regulations for employees and employers. This created a new era of record keeping and documentation to keep up—more forms, filings, and paperwork. Someone needed to enforce adherence to these guidelines and keep up with all the tracking and reporting, so personnel departments took on the burden. Introducing . . . the paper pushers.

By the 1980s, personnel teams became known as human resources (HR). In some circles, human relations. Even their largest membership association, the American Society for Personnel Administration (ASPA) renamed itself the Society for Human Resource Management (SHRM) in 1984. Human resource teams grew in size to manage the organization's growing workforce regulation and documentation needs. They also handled transactional tasks such as time tracking, payroll, and benefits processing. This resulted in an "administrative age" for HR.

By the twenty-first century, HR was taking on more strategic responsibilities, at least, in some organizations. Progressive HR teams led initiatives like recruiting, hiring, and onboarding, which was relabeled talent acquisition. They rolled out performance management, learning and development, and succession planning initiatives—also known as talent management. Although the role and importance of HR grew in many companies, it was still unable to shake the stigma of the early era administrative, policing, and policy side of its reputation.

Why Everyone Loves to Hate HR

In 2005, *Fast Company* said what a lot of people were thinking when they dropped the scathing—at least, to those of us in HR(!)—cover story, "Why We Hate HR" (Hammond 2005). The authors attended a SHRM conference and followed with an exposé, stating, "The human-resources trade long ago proved itself, at best, a necessary evil—and at worst, a dark bureaucratic force that blindly enforces nonsensical rules, resists creativity, and impedes constructive change." It went on to highlight the potential, "HR is the corporate function with the greatest potential—the key driver, in theory, of business performance—and also the one that most consistently under delivers."

Despite the rhetoric, not a lot changed. Ten years later, *Harvard Business Review* followed with the title on its cover, "It's Time to Blow Up HR and Build Something New," representing a mandate to rethink the approach to HR. What's all the fuss about? Do people really hate HR?

Not exactly. They really just hate the *idea* of HR and think it's time for something new. Let's take a look at the key constituents and how they really think and feel about the role of HR.

What CEOs Think of HR

For business owners and CEOs, HR administrative work is considered a chore. After all, you got into your business for a reason. It was to *do* something: to build an amazing product, or service, or customer experience. It's something you're passionate about. You didn't get into business to "do HR." At an early stage, this generally comes down to paperwork and administration.

How bad is it? Small business owners spend up to 35 percent of their time on HR-related tasks and paperwork (SCORE 2014). That's more than a full week every month! Moreover, 40 percent of small business owners say bookkeeping and taxes are the worst part of owning a small business. Another chore is compliance. And according to a study by Babson College, more than 60 percent of business owners say they struggle keeping up with compliance and regulations. With over a hundred new regulations passed every year, it's no wonder. And the stakes are high. The average citation cost exceeds $30,000. This is one of many things that keeps small business owners up at night. The bottom line: CEOs don't hate HR, they hate the busywork and sleepless nights that come with it. Especially when they have to do it all alone.

What Employees Think of HR

Today's workers want a voice and an advocate they can trust. They need someone who can reconcile their interests with those of the company. They want a work environment and culture that empowers them to do their best work. Here's the problem. In some organizations the role of HR is still the company police department. You can only get in trouble. HR is seen as political and only exists to protect the company. Historically, their policies introduced rules and bureaucracy that slowed employees down. Employees were reprimanded by HR. Employees didn't trust HR. Actually, they feared anyone who worked there.

Of course, not all employees feel this way. Things have gotten a little better in recent years. But there's still a long way to go. Employees need someone who helps them do their best work while also looking out for the mutual best interests of the company.

What HR Thinks of HR

Guess what? Even HR hates HR. Wait, what!? Well, let's clarify that. Even HR loathes the stigma that accompanies the label. Human resource leaders have spent years trying to dispel the myth that an HR person is someone who just prints paychecks, enforces rules, and fires people. This has been a topic at HR conferences for decades. Unfortunately, it's an uphill battle. It's difficult to break a perception so many years in the making.

Here are a few confessions directly from HR leaders:

People often have a negative reaction or bias to HR.
—Jennifer, HR leader

Human resources is just so dry. Which is why people are creating more fun titles to get away from the bias when we hear HR.
—Sarah, HR leader

HR has a branding problem, and language matters.
Humans are not "resources."
—Amy, HR leader

But, HR Matters . . . a Lot

Despite the hate, stigma, and rhetoric, of course HR matters. If people are a company's greatest asset and source of value, having a caretaker of that investment—a function to foster the growth and development of the workforce—is an imperative. There's never been a greater need for a deliberate discipline to focus on helping the company navigate major workplace shifts and turn the workforce into a competitive advantage. Here are a few reasons why:

- **Knowledge workers are the fastest-growing sector of the workforce.** Today's economy runs on knowledge. Even once-routine jobs require a new level of judgment and critical thinking. Think HVAC, solar installations, electric cars. Learning matters more to knowledge workers and is becoming an employment currency for the best companies. Businesses need help institutionalizing these growth opportunities.

- **Corporate brands and employment brands are converging.** Workers are choosing to work at companies whose purpose they identify with. They're choosing to work at companies with a compelling employee-value proposition or places known for great learning opportunities. And, companies are realizing that brand equity comes from people. The worlds of marketing and HR are converging with the employee experience becoming as important as the customer experience.
- **Leadership styles are evolving for the modern workforce.** Yesteryear's top-down authoritarian management styles backfire today. Servant leadership ("you work for your employees") inverts this traditional model, placing the needs of team members front and center. Today's leaders need to provide meaningful work, coaching, and growth opportunities. This is a shift companies and managers are trying to figure out.
- **Digital transformation is disrupting the DNA of companies, inside and out.** Going digital increases market competitiveness. It provides a better customer and employee experience while boosting profitability. It's no wonder companies are scrambling to transform their business models, processes, and experiences. There's a race to the cloud, mobile, and AI that is fundamentally shifting how companies operate. This is shifting the requisite workforce skills and all aspects of the employee experience.
- **The new world of work is here . . . now.** The changes outlined in Chapter 1 are significant and ongoing. Workplace, workforce and work style shifts introduce a new set of problems for leaders, managers, and employees. Those that are quick to adjust and turn adversity into advantage will win. Others will be left behind.

These are major systemic changes that impact work. These shifts are too big for individual employees, front-line managers, or even busy business owners and CEOs to navigate alone. They need help. The question is: will HR shift too? Will they stand up to the calling?

An Identity Crisis

Most HR pros will be the first to admit they're facing an identity crisis. Human resources teams continue the good fight for strategic significance and a "seat at the table." One of the biggest challenges is what marketers refer to as *brand perception:* the perceived feeling a consumer has about a brand. In the case of HR (the brand), these perceived feelings come from employees, managers, and peers inside the organization (the consumers). Often, people have a negative feeling about the HR department.

Marketers call this negative brand equity. Don't worry, HR isn't the only department to stare down this challenge. Let's take a look at a few other examples and how they've tackled similar situations:

- **From Snake Oil to Sales Executives.** In the nineteenth and early twentieth century, the sales profession developed a stereotype as swindlers. "Sell the sizzle, not the steak!" "You sound like a used car salesman." Fortunately, more empathetic, scientific, and consultative approaches evolved. Today, sales is seen as a more admirable and skilled profession.
- **From Mad Men to Modern Marketing.** The Mad Men advertising era certainly had its moment in the creative age of the 1960s. It also had its backlash—namely, evil advertisers brainwashing society with cigarettes, sexism, and dangerous food. Marketers were little more than the arts and crafts team. Decades later, advertising became more empathetic, scientific, and sophisticated. Advertising broadened into modern marketing with more responsibilities including communications, PR, brand marketing, digital marketing, and more. It became a strategic business function. (Yes, there's still some bad marketing out there.)
- **From Accounting to Finance.** Accounting was once a very tactical business function: counting money, paying vendors, and reconciling budgets. Technology automated basic bookkeeping responsibilities, thereby freeing up finance teams to focus on more important work, elevating the entire discipline. Today, finance teams build strategic plans and manage fundraising, investors, facilities, legal, and operational controls. It's one of the most important business functions.

Stockbrokers became wealth managers. Customer care became customer success. The list goes on. HR isn't alone in its fight for being a driving force for change and progress. Other functions have shrugged off their own stigmas and reinvented themselves. It's time for HR to do the same.

CHAPTER 3

The Rise of People Ops

Amajor shift is upon us. The most successful businesses are leaving the human resources (HR) stigma, perception, and halo behind. But, it's more than just a renaming. They're doing something new entirely. They're taking a completely new approach to HR called people operations. They're embracing technology and data, and they're redefining the new world of work.

At this point, we've made it clear why we need a new approach. Now let's take a look at what it looks like. People operations is an idea whose time has come. A transformation. A movement.

Goodbye HR, hello people ops.

People Ops Defined

People Operations (People Ops, or POPS) is a people-centric business approach that emphasizes workforce empowerment to drive growth. With a focus on automating traditional HR processes, POPS shifts attention from tactical administrative work to people and productivity. Focused on designing a great employee experience and culture, people ops drives the pivotal moments that make work exciting, rewarding and engaging for your team. Positioning companies to achieve their goals while valuing people and helping them be their best, POPS focuses on streamlined operations, using data to drive decisions and support tangible business results. When you empower your people to do their best every day, you build a culture that becomes a sustainable competitive advantage. People ops is the future of work.

Let's break this down. People ops is simply a combination of two key elements:

- **People** /'pēpəl / (n.) are beings that have certain capacities or attributes such as reason, morality, consciousness, or self-consciousness, and being a part of a culturally established form of social relations such as kinship, ownership of property, or legal responsibility.

- **Operations** /ˌäpəˈrāSH(ə)ns / *(n.)* is everything that happens collectively within a company to keep it running and earning money. It incorporates the systems, methodologies, people, processes, and technologies needed to make the organization function.

These are the two most critical components of any business. *People* are the most valuable asset, opportunity, and expense. *Operations* are how the company delivers on its very purpose and reason for being. Combined, "people operations" is one of the most important and impactful business disciplines.

For the duration of the book, we'll use the term *people operations* for three distinct but related concepts:

1. A philosophy: a point of view on a way of doing things, including the study of knowledge, best practices, and academic disciplines; this is really the focus of this book.
2. A discipline: a craft dedicated to strategies and execution of the philosophy; we'll highlight examples of the discipline in action throughout the book. We call them "POPS Stars."
3. A function: a department or role within an organization with a defined set of responsibilities focused on implementing the philosophy, manifesting the discipline, and ultimately responsible for the "people experience" inside an organization. At an early stage of a company's lifecycle, there might not be a dedicated people ops team; often the CEO or other business leader owns this function. (This is actually one of the benefits of the people ops approach: fewer resources are needed. We see examples all the time of companies going from zero to over a hundred employees by leaning on technology instead of a dedicated HR or people function.) In larger organizations, the people ops function/organization can take a variety of labels including "people operations," "people experience," "people and culture," "people and talent," simply "people"—or just "POPS."

We'll use the term to refer to all three of these concepts interchangeably as they're all the focus of this book. And, we'll use the synonymous terms:

- People operations—formal
- People ops—abbreviated
- POPS—casual and fun (and because the world needs another acronym)

Oh, and, at least, POPS is . . . well, kinda catchy and marketable.

We'll continue to use the term human resources (HR) in the book as well, typically denoting the old way, and concepts that many of best companies are moving away or graduating from.

Work That Really Matters

One of the ideas behind people ops is focusing time and energy on things that matter most to the business, and automating what doesn't. The Pareto Principle, more commonly known as the 80/20 rule, states that 80 percent of an outcome can be driven by 20 percent of the effort. And cautiously, the other 80 percent only gets you 20 percent of the outcome.

The Pareto Principle is about being extremely deliberate about where and how you focus your efforts. This is particularly challenging for small businesses with so much opportunity and such finite resources. The same goes for HR teams tasked with all types of random tasks. Many of the to-dos—think recordkeeping, compliance, and reporting—are lower-value, but high risk. An oversight can be costly, but there's really little business upside. Doing something unimportant well does not make it important.

This is a classic trap of traditional HR. This is where technology is critical. It's necessary to automate the 80 percent of lower-value, high-risk busywork so you can focus on the 20 percent of efforts that will result in the 80 percent of the results (see Figure 3.1). Technology will do the repetitive menial work better, faster, and with less human errors. And humans will

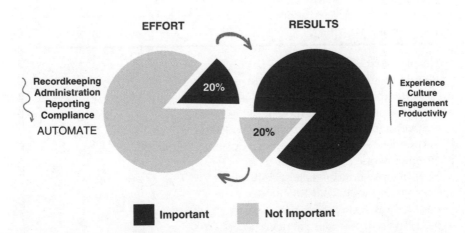

FIGURE 3.1 Smart companies are looking to automate the tasks that take 80 percent of their time, but aren't important, and instead refocus that time on work that matters, like experience, culture, engagement, and productivity.

Source: Zenefits, 2021.

do a better job at things like designing a great employee experience and productive workplace culture.

What People Ops is *Not*

Now that we've defined what people ops is, let's be equally clear on what it is not.

- *It's not a fancy new name for traditional human resources.* As mentioned above, people ops is more than a new title, it's a new philosophy, a new discipline, and a new function that displaces the need for traditional HR.
- *It's not a Silicon Valley fad.* Like a lot of innovations, high-growth technology companies have been some of the earlier adopters of people ops principles. And it makes sense; people and culture are critical and fiercely competitive. But it's not about kale smoothies and ping pong. Companies in every industry are embracing people operations methods.
- *It's not just a fancy new technology.* Automating mundane and repetitive tasks is key to unlocking time and focus for more important work. It's also key to capturing data, which is imperative to measuring your progress and delivering meaningful business insights. But people ops is much bigger than technology. It's a new approach.

People Ops Manifesto

No paper. No forms. No filings.
People Ops lives in a digital-must world.
No spreadsheets. No manual tasks.
People Ops embraces automation.
No authoritarianism. No politics. No hassle.
People Ops empowers people to do their best work.
No guesswork. No anecdotes.
People Ops surfaces data and insight.
No fluff. No waste. No BS.
People Ops is driven by outcomes.
No busywork. No inefficiency.
People Ops drives productivity.
Less paperwork, more people work.
This is People Ops.

TABLE 3.1 The differences between human resources and people Operations.

THEN: HR	NOW: POPS
HR Administration	**People Operations**
Process	People
Administration	Operations
Activities	Outcomes
Tracking	Experience
Instinct	Data
HRIS (Human Resource Information System)	POPS Platform

Source: Zenefits, 2021.

The Shift to People Ops

Traditional HR was focused on tracking employees, enforcing rules, and ensuring compliance. People ops is focused on maximizing business results and optimizing workforce productivity by making work exciting, rewarding, and engaging. See Table 3.1 for a comparison.

Like the best business functions, people ops is operationally forward. It's focused on helping achieve business priorities through people, data, and insights. People ops favors outcomes over activities, "points, not yards."

Here are the key factors in this shift from HR to POPS:

- *Shifting from manual to automation*—using technology instead of humans for repetitive tasks such as data entry, processing, and reporting.
- *Shifting from guesswork to data*—capturing, analyzing, and sharing data-driven insights about the workforce instead of relying on gut instinct and anecdotes.
- *Shifting from cost center to profit center*—optimizing for workforce productivity and results (e.g., revenue and profits) instead of expense and efficiency (e.g., time and costs).
- *Shifting from management to experience*—treating the employee experience like the customer experience, optimizing it to create an advantage.

The People Ops Methodology

The people ops methodology is the recipe to automate HR, design a great employee experience, and unleash the full potential of the workforce. When your people are at their best, your business is too. It's the ultimate force multiplier.

The POPS methodology includes four steps, which we call "the ABC's of POPS":

Step A: Automate administration and compliance. *Make the stuff you have to do easy.* Easy for you, your managers, and your employees. Use technology to declutter and eliminate as much busywork as possible. This means going completely digital. Ditch the spreadsheets, filings, and forms. Everything should be in the cloud for speed and mobility. Things like data entry, manual data processing, reporting, and compliance should all be automated.

Step B: Build a great employee experience. *Put your people first.* The employee lifecycle should be treated like your customer lifecycle, with people's experience front and center. After all, who delivers your customer experience? So, start from within with pivotal people moments that matter. Employee listening, open communication, and transparency are foundational. Consider flexibility, learning, recognition, and well-being in order to build a strong organizational culture.

Step C: Create workforce productivity. *Make every moment count.* Build a high-performance, high-energy culture that motivates the entire workforce to achieve new heights. Help your people do their best work by eliminating friction and inspiring performance. Embed clearly defined goals, feedback loops, and motivators into daily workflows. Improve workplace collaboration, engagement, and mobility.

Step D: Drive growth and profitability. *Impact business performance.* People ops leaders work closely with the CEO and other business leaders to define key strategies and goals for the company and workforce. The goals of the people team should align directly with the goals and key priorities of the business. Further, POPS teams surface workplace data and insights across the employee lifecycle to diagnose problems, identify opportunities, and prescribe actions. Being data-driven is foundational to the people ops movement and how to demonstrate value to the rest of the business.

The Benefits of People Ops

What type of companies is people ops for?

- *All industries:* Companies in every industry are turning to people ops. Although highly professional and technical workforces were early adopters, businesses in every category are realizing that people are their ultimate differentiating factor. In addition to business-to-business (B2B) industries such as high-tech, business services, and manufacturing, an increasing number of business-to-consumer (B2C) industries such as healthcare, retail, and education are using it to create a competitive advantage.

- *All company sizes:* Although a lot of the specific examples in the book are focused on small and midsized businesses, the concepts of POPS apply to large companies too. With a larger employee population, enterprise organizations are often forced to evolve their people strategies early to deal with the large worker-to-HR person ratio. For small and midsized businesses, there's an equally, if not greater, opportunity to embrace people ops. Why? Small businesses can't afford to focus precious resources, time, and money on anything that isn't mission critical. Automating administrative work unlocks time and energy to focus on building a great culture, boosting productivity, and growing the business. It's easier to do this at an earlier stage than trying to turn the Titanic. But again, the concepts apply to companies of *all* sizes.

Who is responsible for people ops?

- *Small business owners, operators, and CEOs:* People ops is a smarter way to run and scale your business. Instead of investing in traditional HR data entry, tracking, and enforcement—or outsourcing it—focus on automating HR administration using technology. This frees up valuable time and resources for things of higher value such as investing in your company's products, growth, and customers. By applying the people ops principles, business leaders are improving operational excellence. They're creating a better people experience that helps with recruiting and retaining talent. This provides a more scalable foundation for sustainable growth.
- *Human resources and people leaders:* People ops is an invigorating new way of thinking. Today's most progressive leaders are moving from HR to POPS. It incorporates some traditional HR concepts but with a newfound focus on business strategy and operations, the people experience, and data-driven insights. By using a more modern, tech-forward approach to the fundamentals, people leaders can focus more time and effort on driving workforce effectiveness. This is achieved by programs that center on the employee experience, culture, and productivity. People ops is run like any other key business operation, driving meaningful and measurable outcomes.

Your World with People Ops

If you want to build a great company, start with your own people. The people ops approach is a win-win-win. It's a win for your business. It's a win for your employees. And, it's a win for your people leaders and teams.

Good for business: People ops helps accelerate growth, cut costs, and reduce risk exposure.

Good for employees: People ops provides a better people experience. It helps make work more exciting and rewarding. It offers improved benefits, flexibility, and well-being.

Good for people leaders and teams: People ops helps elevate people leaders and their teams to do more important and rewarding work. By becoming more data-driven, and focusing more on key business goals and the employee experience, people ops leaders build value for their own careers and teams.

Companies moving to people ops report:

- Up to 90 percent time savings on administrative work
- Up to 80 percent time savings on reporting
- Up to 67 percent faster new hire onboarding
- Up to 75 percent fewer benefits errors
- Up to 90 percent fewer payroll errors
- Up to 75 percent less compliance time and costs
- Improved employee experience

Source: Nucleus Research, 2018.

Why Is People Operations Such a Hot Topic Now?

The term *people operations* started being used in books and manuscripts around the turn of this century, and its use has accelerated significantly over the past decade (see Figure 3.2). Simultaneously, the popularity of the term *human resources*—based on appearances in books, manuscripts and online searches over the same respective time periods—is down substantially (see Figure 3.3). This is despite the growing importance of HR concepts due to increasing workplace regulations, complexity, and talent shortages, as well as substantial growth in trade associations, online communities, academic programs, and technology solutions.

What ignited this rapid shift? There are several key trends that make people ops an idea whose time has come. One of the catalysts was Google. They added fuel to the people ops movement when they rebooted their entire HR function and adopted the "people operations" moniker internally within the company.

In his *New York Times* bestseller *Work Rules!*, author and former Google SVP People Operations Laszlo Bock said it well: "Let's face it, the HR profession is not held in the highest regard." Data shows he was spot on.

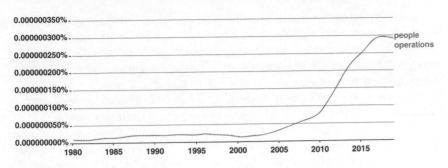

FIGURE 3.2 Google Trends data for "people operations" 1980–2020.

Source: Google Books Ngram Viewer (http://books.google.com/ngrams).

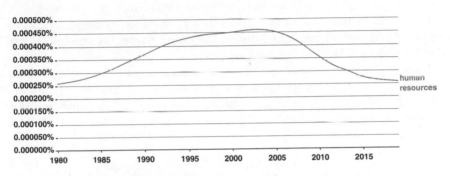

FIGURE 3.3 Google Trends data for "human resources" 1980–2020.

Source: Google Books Ngram Viewer (http://books.google.com/ngrams).

Bock continued, "At Google, conventional business language wasn't well-regarded. 'HR' would be viewed as administrative and bureaucratic. In contrast, 'operations' was viewed by engineers as a credible title, connoting some actual ability to get things done" (Bock 2015, pp. 349–350).

The book goes on to offer valuable lessons from inside Google on how they challenged the status quo of HR with their own people operations. Although some of the ideas are more applicable for large enterprises with thousands of people, it's well worth the read for inspiration. In addition to being both technology and data-driven, a lot of Google's programs focus on employee empowerment, motivation, and learning. This has paid dividends with Google being recognized over 100 times as an exceptional employer, including #1 Best Company to Work For in the US (*Fortune*) and the #1 Top Diversity Employer (*Forbes*).

But companies in every industry and location, not just Silicon Valley start-ups, are quickly adopting similar thinking and transforming the way they work too. According to LinkedIn, people operations-related job titles have grown almost six times faster than human resources-related job titles over the past five years (see Figure 3.4). The fastest-growing title? Director of people operations. Specifically, "chief people officer" grew 2.4 times faster than that of "chief human resources officer" (LinkedIn 2020).

It's an exciting time for people ops. Not only is it a great way to build a company, it's also a great way to build a career. Between 2014 and 2019, the chief people officer (CPO) was the #2 "fastest-hiring C-suite job" on LinkedIn out of all C-suite titles. It was even more popular than the chief revenue officer (CRO) and chief customer officer (CCO). In 2020, three of the top 12 "fastest growing C-suite titles" were the chief people officer, chief talent officer, and chief diversity officer. CHRO—chief human resources officer—didn't make the list. There's clearly a movement taking place. More on this trend and related career opportunities in Chapter 18, The Rise of the CPO: Building a Modern People Ops Team.

The takeaway? People operations is the future. It's a paradigm shift. It's a new way of thinking. It's a new approach for companies of all sizes and industries. The benefits are significant and real. It's a better way for business leaders, employees, and people teams to empower their greatest advantage—their people.

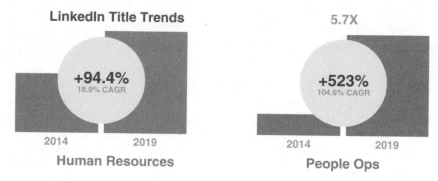

FIGURE 3.4 The number of job titles for people ops increased 5.7 times faster than job titles for human resources from 2014 to 2019.

Source: LinkedIn, 2020.

CHAPTER 4

People Ops in Action

In this chapter, we'll show you what people ops looks like in action. We'll introduce a framework, called a maturity model, that helps evaluate your own progress in moving from human resources administration to people operations. And, we'll share some specific examples of companies who have successfully made the move.

You'll learn what each stage looks like, including the key strategies, key performance indicators (KPIs), opportunities, and risks. We'll step through each stage at a high level now. We'll carry this framework throughout the rest of the book as we go into more detail in Parts II and III. In the meantime, let's go!

Introducing the People Ops Maturity Model

The *People Ops Maturity Model* (see Figure 4.1) measures the extent to which an organization's people operations is driven by established and documented best practices, processes, standards, and metrics proven to drive business outcomes. Based on our work with more than 30,000 small and midsize businesses, The People Ops Maturity Model helps a company assess, develop, and refine their people programs. In short, it helps you look at yourself now and also assess how and where to improve your people operations.

Use the model to:

- Create strategies proven to drive business alignment and success
- Enable companies to self-diagnose and assess their current state
- Assess the gaps between current and desired future states
- Provide a roadmap for achieving world-class people operations
- Develop and refine people operations priorities over time.

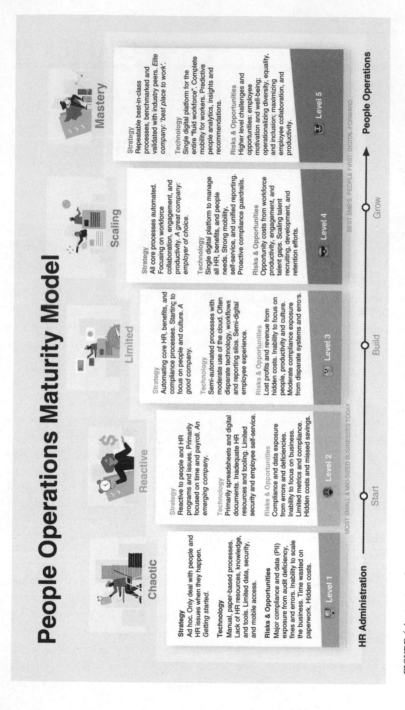

FIGURE 4.1 A visual representation of the five stages within The People Operations Maturity Model.

Source: Zenefits, 2021.

What Does People Ops Maturity Mean and How Does It Work?

People ops maturity is about the state of your people processes and employee experience, the level of digital automation, and level of risk associated with all your people programs. This includes everything from time tracking and payroll to employee benefits, engagement, and well-being. It impacts business productivity and profitability.

If your people operations are ad-hoc, just getting started, or in a state of chaos, then you're not mature. And that's okay. If your people operations are firing on all cylinders, driving best-in-class business results, and a great employee experience, you're more mature. That's how it works.

As you advance up the maturity scale, your people priorities are more aligned to key business drivers. Decisions are more purposeful and data-driven. The employee experience improves. So does company culture. Productivity goes up. Unnecessary people-related costs, errors, and risks go down.

Consider your answers to the following questions:

- "How well are we doing with our people operations?"
- "How do our benefits compare to those of similar businesses?"
- "What is our level of employee engagement, and is it good or bad?"
- "What is our people ops roadmap?"

If you don't have good answers, the People Ops Maturity Model can help. While we introduce the maturity model and its core components here, it will become a common theme. We'll step through each stage at a high level now, and reiterate key concepts throughout the book.

Don't mistake company size, tenure, or budgets for maturity. Just because a company is small or new, doesn't mean it's low in maturity. It could be. We see it all the time. But we also see sophisticated, forward-thinking start-ups come out of the gates in the middle of the maturity model. And just because a company has been around for decades or has hundreds of employees, doesn't mean it's mature. We talk to businesses every week with hundreds, even thousands, of employees that are flying by the seat of their pants in level 1. These are the fun ones!

Also, not every business needs to aim for the highest tier, level 5. While we hope many do, it's not always necessary depending upon the state, aspirations, and specifics of the business. We see very few cases where staying at level 1 makes much sense. There's just too much exposure with cost and risk. The most successful companies skew to the right and we hope you aim to, too.

Level 1: Chaotic

At this level, you're probably wearing multiple hats—CEO, operations, office manager, administration—or just getting started as the first HR or people person. You're a multitasking, one-person powerhouse. If you're wearing multiple hats, you typically get to the administrative stuff only when you have to. Often just in time to hit a deadline. You know, make a pay run, submit that IRS filing, or respond to a nagging employee question. "Hey, what's my paid time off balance for the rest of the year?" You only deal with people and HR issues when they happen. If there's one word to summarize this stage, it's probably ad-hoc. (see Table 4.1.)

Processes are not very clearly defined. Things are pretty manual. Employee and HR records are mostly documented on paper-using forms, filings, and time sheets, or in basic digital documents. Accessing them often requires being in a particular location or on a specific computer. It's worked okay up to this point and there isn't really time to spend building processes and structure. This is typically accompanied by a lack of dedicated HR expertise. You don't know what you don't know, but, you're getting by.

The risks at this stage include a variety of compliance risks such as missing employment and tax documents, inaccurate worker classifications, Fair Labor Standards Act (FLSA) issues, policy gaps, and various audit deficiencies. There is often data privacy and security exposure from personally identifiable information (PII) being stored in nonsecure places. One citation or fine can cost tens of thousands of dollars in direct costs, plus legal fees.

Errors often result in overpayment of payroll and benefits costs. But one of the biggest hidden costs is wasted time. Data shows that companies

TABLE 4.1 Description of a "Level 1: Chaotic" in the People Operations Maturity Model.

LEVEL 1 SNAPSHOT

Process Consistency: Ad-hoc, no or poorly defined processes
Digital Automation: No or very limited, technology; a lot of repetitive manual tasks
Data & KPIs: Manually tracking things like headcount, payruns, tax accruals
Employee Experience: Employee experience is largely inconsistent
Mobile: Little to no mobility (people data and tasks need to be done from a specific location) rather than on-the-go
Risks: Flying blind with data and compliance; risk for errors, citations, fines, and data privacy

Source: Zenefits, 2021.

in this stage are spending eight to nine times more time than necessary on administrative work. If you're the CEO or wearing multiple hats in the business, this can take valuable time away from more meaningful priorities, like taking care of your customers and growing the business.

The first stage of people operations is about fixing these problems. Your goal is simple. Start to put a basic people ops foundation in place. Digitize your records so they're safe and secure in a single location. More on this in Part 2. Define and implement some basic processes for things like time tracking, payroll, and record keeping. Reduce the need for manual data entry and reporting. Move these basic processes to the cloud so that you can access information anytime, anywhere. And begin to free yourself from arduous busywork.

How to know you're at level 1:

- You're spending more than 20 percent of your time on data entry, record keeping, and administration.
- You don't have a defined process, checklist, or workflow for basic tasks like hiring a new employee.
- You're storing employment records (new hire agreements, time-off balances and accruals, payroll history) on paper, in filing cabinets, or in something like Google Docs.
- You're not up to speed on state and federal employment regulations.

Objectives in level 1:

- Reduce the time spent on data entry, record keeping, and compliance.
- Establish some basic, consistent processes for managing time, pay, and compliance.
- Digitize your back office, including HR, payroll, and time records.
- Reduce risk from audit and data security deficiencies.

Level 2: Reactive

Companies at this stage often have an operations or finance person doing HR as a side hustle. Or maybe you're the single HR manager. Perhaps you even came into the job from an operations or generalist role. You're a champion of the health of the business with a lot on your plate and no time to waste. You want to do the right thing for your customers and your employees. Although you know that employee experience and company culture matter, so do compliance and cash flow. Therefore, in response to people's issues, you're acting in response to situations rather than proactively creating or controlling them. Like many companies at this stage, you're in reactive mode. (see Table 4.2.)

TABLE 4.2 Description of a "Level 2: Reactive" in the People
Operations Maturity Model.

LEVEL 2 SNAPSHOT

Process Consistency: Core time, pay, tax processes defined; others still ad-hoc
Digital Automation: Some technology; but still some repetitive manual tasks
Data & KPIs: Digitally tracking employee records, time, and payroll, but lack
  broader aggregated trends
Employee Experience: Average employee experience; people can view some
  of their own HR information online, but not everything
Mobile: Minimal mobility; most tasks need to be done from a computer rather
  than on-the-go
Risks: Decent pulse on state and federal workplace compliance; risk for ongoing
  regulations updates; and hidden costs from errors and oversights

---

Source: Zenefits, 2021.

Some basic processes like time tracking, payroll, and taxes are defined. And there's a way to keep a pulse on compliance essentials. Some of this is reliant on vendors and partners including accountants, brokers, and technology providers. But many things are still done manually. A lot of processes are still "TBD," "kind of," or "it depends." Employees can access some information on their own but still have to come to you for basic information like schedule details, time off, and benefit inquiries. When it comes to employee records and workforce data, some of it is stored in spreadsheets and online systems. Other things are still handled manually or through email. You're tiptoeing into the twenty-first century but *everything* isn't quite at your fingertips like other aspects of your life.

Challenges at level 2 include an inability to get ahead of things—like putting together a thorough review of your processes, systems, and evolving compliance requirements. If you're in an operations or finance role, it's difficult to focus on the business too. If you're the sole "people person," it's difficult to focus on the employee experience and building culture, because you're bogged down in busywork. You can access basic workforce data pretty quickly without too much hassle—things like headcount, turnover, and PTO liability. But more sophisticated insights or "people analytics" like compensation, turnover, and diversity trends are foreign concepts, or simply take time to track down. You do your best with documentation and hitting compliance deadlines but it's not perfect.

There are often hidden costs at this stage from errors related to manual data entry and reporting. This includes things like missed payroll deductions and prorations, as well as tax and benefit administration issues. In addition to lost profits, risks at this stage include compliance exposure from missed deadlines, overlooked regulations, and audit deficiencies.

The objective of level 2 is to build on your people ops foundation. Continue to define core people processes, and move them all online. Going digital is a key to competitiveness. Integrate related processes like time tracking, pay rates, payroll, and benefits deductions into a single workflow. You want to begin consolidating record keeping and files into a singular employee record. Begin providing access to employees so they can securely update and manage their own information. Finally, you want to begin putting some compliance guardrails in place with some automated reminders, updates, and alerts. It's time to go from reactive to proactive.

How to know you're at level 2:

- You're spending more than 10 percent of your time on administrative work.
- You have some processes defined, but they're largely separate workflows.
- Employee, time, payroll, and benefit records are stored in various places, both online and hard copies.
- Employees can access and update some of their own information online, but not all of it.
- You have a decent grasp of workplace regulations but you are not proactively keeping track of monthly or quarterly changes.

Objectives in level 2:

- Further reduce the time spent on data processing, reporting, and compliance
- Integrate workflows for things like managing time and payroll, and benefits deductions.
- Digitize more of your back office, including benefits administration.
- Allow employees to access and update their own information (pay stubs, time worked).
- Reduce risk from ongoing regulatory compliance changes.

Level 3: Moderate

At this level, you probably have a dedicated people leader—or, you're an operations superstar embracing technology to scale up and gain an edge. You're taking things to the next level. Your focus: designing a great employee experience and building a great culture. You know that the best companies make this a priority, and you can only do this with a solid foundation in place. You're establishing consistent, seamless, and reliable processes. You're leaning on automation and employee self-service. Because you're digitizing everything, you're capturing newfound data and able to surface insights to make better and faster business decisions. (see Table 4.3.)

Most of your core processes are completely digital. This includes scheduling and time tracking, time-off management, payroll and taxes, and benefits administration. Employees can access their own information and make appropriate adjustments on their own. This includes tasks like benefits selection and adjustments, time-off requests and approvals, accessing organizational charts, and co-worker contact information. Most of it is done from their phones, but some may still require a computer. You just tap to approve. Because you're digital, you have a predictable system down for dealing with reporting and compliance. Most of your data is online, but you still have a few systems and data floating around in some spreadsheets. But that's okay. You're eyeing higher-level priorities, things like aligning employees to the purpose, vision, and goals of the company; providing performance feedback; and increasing productivity.

Level 3 obstacles tend to center around consolidation of processes, systems, and data. By integrating and streamlining your workflows, it saves even more time. Studies show 40–50 percent of administrative time can be saved by consolidating systems. Most of this comes from reducing the need to import, export, and sync data and reports across systems. No need to reconcile time and pay data. No need to review benefits deductions and adjustments. Consolidating workflows also reduces human error and oversights caused by manual data manipulation and re-entry.

TABLE 4.3 Description of a "Level 3: Moderate" in the People Operations Maturity Model.

LEVEL 3 SNAPSHOT

Process Consistency: HR, payroll, benefits processes consolidated and streamlined

Digital Automation: All of the above are automated in the cloud

Data & KPIs: Line of sight to basic workforce metrics such as costs, turnover, and benefits utilization at your fingertips

Employee Experience: Modern, digital employee experience; people can find it easy to focus on their core job

Mobile: Most tasks can be done from a phone, anytime, anywhere

Risks: Good pulse on workplace regulations and changes as (or soon after) they happen

---

Source: Zenefits, 2021.

But most of the challenges at this stage are higher-level opportunities. Things that start to move the needle, and actually make a real impact on the business. Think of it as going from defense to offense—from paperwork to peoplework. Opportunities to better align and focus your workforce. Is the entire workforce crystal-clear on the organization's mission, vision, and purpose? Are company goals set and cascaded down to every employee? Is there a defined process for providing feedback to employees? What's the cadence? How is it documented? Is it secure and compliant? The opportunity for surfacing valuable workplace insights improves as you gain new data points.

The goals of level 3 center on consolidating and integrating core processes. This reduces time, costs, and risk while freeing up time to focus on your employees. Employees should be able to find their own answers and make their own updates as appropriate. Consolidating workflows and information sources simplifies reporting and improves compliance, with most data available in seconds. Answers at your fingertips. Now you can shift focus from process to people. Here you want to prioritize the employee experience, culture, and engagement. These will be foundational to strengthen your employment brand, employee retention, and workforce productivity. Although these initiatives should always be on your mind, here you can take real action on them. If you haven't already, you should be extending these processes and initiatives—in the appropriate form—to your entire fluid workforce including contractors, contingent workers, and part-time workers.

How to know you're at level 3:

- You're spending less than 10 percent of your time on administrative work such as data consolidation, reporting, and verifications.
- Most of your people processes are defined, and, for the most part, integrated—you only have to enter information once or twice.
- Most of your employee information is stored in a single, secure place; there are some minor exceptions for some ancillary systems and data archives.
- Employees can access and update most things on their own, they can answer many of their own questions (time-off balances, access performance feedback, W-2s).
- You have a good grasp on workplace regulations and changes when they happen.

Objectives in level 3:

- Consolidate workflows and put them on autopilot, saving even more time.

- Fully empower your employees to manage all aspects of benefits, payroll, and HR on their own.
- Move from reactive to "proactive compliance" with a system for being informed of changes as/before they happen.
- Shift from paper and process to people and culture, starting with the employee experience.

Level 4: Scaling

This is where people ops really starts to shine. You ideally have—or are—a dedicated people ops team at this point. Your focus: unleashing workforce productivity. Now that you've made the stuff you have to do easy, you can do the most rewarding work of all: the peoplework. Your company doesn't think of workers as replaceable resources that need to be managed. You know they're people that need to be invested in. They need to be developed and grown in order to reach their full potential—and your organization's too. You're leaning on technology to better align, connect, and engage the entire workforce. There's a common sense of purpose and values. Everyone is in it together. With loyalty and productivity on the rise, you're elevating the output of the entire organization.

Just as you used technology to automate back-office processes in the first stages, you continue to put technology to work. This time, it provides personalized, behavioral triggers proven to produce better outcomes. You send and receive nudges and reminders for things like setting goals, providing feedback, and setting meeting agendas. Your recruiting—or talent acquisition—efforts are becoming targeted and strategic. You use aggregate market compensation data to know if your offer letter will likely get rejected because the pay rate is too low for the job. You're capturing feedback and listening to your employees. More importantly, you're acting on it. Employees, given autonomy, become more engaged and results-oriented. They're doing their best work, and they love you for it. (see Table 4.4.)

The challenges at level 4 involve moving from tactical to higher-level, strategic work—things like recruiting and retaining the best talent, teaching managers how to be great leaders, and motivating and inspiring them to help their teams do their best work. We get more into this in Part 3. It requires an elevated mindset—for you, your leadership team, and your front-line people managers. This requires empowering and supporting managers, not doing their jobs for them. You move from managing and doing it all, to influencing others through systemic programs and change management. There will be blockers and naysayers. There will also be champions and supporters. And, they will need help. By engaging champions early and often as positive examples, you help accelerate change and progress.

TABLE 4.4 Description of a "Level 4: Scaling" in the People
Operations Maturity Model.

LEVEL 4 SNAPSHOT
Process Consistency: Goal setting, performance, and compensation management; employee listening, feedback, and engagement
Digital Automation: All the above are automated in the cloud, along with employee collaboration
Data & KPIs: People analytics related to key business priorities and outcomes (e.g., cost of turnover)
Employee Experience: People feel connected to their work and the company culture; strong employee sentiment
Mobile: People are autonomous to do their best work wherever it makes the most sense for them—and for the business
Risks: Losing out on good talent (recruiting or retention)

Source: Zenefits, 2021.

Balancing newfound opportunities can also be a challenge. From recruiting and onboarding to training and development, there's a lot to do; talent management, communication, and community building can be difficult on their own. Trying to prioritize all these evolving needs alongside day-job tasks can be overwhelming. Having defined priorities, a roadmap, and open communication are imperative.

The goals of level 4 center on galvanizing the entire workforce on your company's mission, purpose, and values. Instill these into your people operations programs in the form of rituals, programs, and tactics. They should be in your goals, surveys, and communications. Make sure everyone has goals and knows how their work contributes to the goals of their department and company. Ensure there are programs for ongoing feedback from managers, across teams and projects. How do you know if all of this is working? Measure it, of course. Employee feedback, engagement levels, job performance, goal achievement (read more in Chapters 14 & 15) should all be quantified and correlated. Graduating from administrative metrics to workforce productivity insights and business KPIs is part of this stage.

How to know you're at level 4:

- You're spending most of your time with people and leadership.
- You're designing programs to recruit, engage, and retain the best talent.
- You're defining processes for performance management, compensation, employee feedback, engagement, and collaboration.
- Employee sentiment is strong and improving.
- The initiatives you're working on tie directly to key business priorities and challenges.

Objectives in level 4:

- Help people understand the company vision and values and how their work contributes to the business.
- Implement programs to define and measure goals, and capture performance feedback—at individual, team, and company levels.
- Measure employee sentiment, feedback, and engagement.
- Measure recruiting, development, and retention effectiveness.

Level 5: Mastery

Congratulations, you're crushing it. You've turned your biggest expense into your greatest asset. Your entire workforce is firing on all cylinders. Your people's interests are aligned with those of the company and they're living the brand. Your employee experience is world-class. Engagement is through the roof. So is retention. Resumes are flying in. The best talent in town—or out of town—wants to work for your company. You're winning top-employer and best place to work awards. You've created a movement. Your competitors are scared and want to know how you do it.

Level 5 Mastery is about turning people operations into a sustainable competitive advantage. Your employee experience, culture, and people operations playbook is foundational to your company strategy. It's how you build and scale your company. It's how you differentiate in the market. Now, you're using this to drive business performance. People operations is an integral part of the company's strategy. You don't consider a new initiative, expansion, or product launch without people operations. Your people ops metrics and KPIs are tied directly to business priorities and outcomes. You've moved from running the workforce on anecdotes and instinct to data and KPIs—across the entire employee lifecycle. It's foundational to measuring progress and outcomes. You're also embracing predictive analytics and insights. These metrics and priorities are shared at the leadership and board level. (see Table 4.5.)

Level 5 challenges are higher-order opportunities. How do you sustain your advantage? How do you scale the business to the next level? How to ensure a continuously diverse, productive, and healthy workforce? New obstacles will emerge and you'll be in a better position to handle them. Common opportunities include: expanding internationally, integrating and engaging contingent and gig workers, and improving mental health and financial well-being. Optimizing diversity, equality, and inclusion programs are also front and center. Finally, parlaying your successes—what works and what doesn't—into learnings for your peers and others is a key part of level 5. Great satisfaction and success come from sharing with others.

TABLE 4.5 Description of a "Level 5: Mastery" in the People Operations Maturity Model.

LEVEL 5 SNAPSHOT
Process Consistency: Candidate and employee experience, employee well-being, business, and workforce planning, DEI
Digital Automation: All aspects of the people experience are automated in the cloud
Data & KPIs: Employee and team well-being, predictive people analytics, peer benchmarks
Employee Experience: A best place to work
Mobile: Virtual, agile workplace—anyone can be connected and engaged anytime, anywhere
Risks: Losing your people operations advantage

Source: Zenefits, 2021.

How to know you're at level 5:

- You're solving business problems instead of people problems.
- You're analyzing predictive insights, benchmarks, and trends.
- You're getting recognition for your workplace and employment brand.
- You're looking for innovative and disruptive tools, processes, and next practices.
- Colleagues and peers consistently come to you for perspective and recommendations.

Objectives in level 5:

- Help your company actualize its mission—and your people, theirs—through people operations.
- More deeply understand and empower your entire workforce.
- Build on and evangelize diversity, equality, and inclusion (DEI) progress.
- Make the world a better place. :)

In the following sections, we'll dive deeper into the maturity model for each topic.

What to Do With the People Ops Maturity Model

If you want to break away from traditional HR administration and move to people operations, you need a clear vision and plan. If you've already started, and envision more, you need a blueprint for progress. The People

Ops Maturity Model is designed to create an understanding of your current situation, desired future state, and a roadmap to get there. Use it to benchmark your own organization's level of sophistication and identify the best—and next—practices for you to improve. Start by evaluating what's important to you and your company. It's different for every business. You do you.

For a free people operations maturity model assessment, visit www. zenefits.com/pops-quiz

The People Ops Roadmap

As you go through the rest of the book, we recommend using the maturity model as a framework to develop your own people ops roadmap. In the software development world, product managers maintain a product roadmap that outlines the vision, priorities, and progress of a product over time. With an endless to-do list of ideas and requests (also known as a product backlog), the product roadmap helps inventory these ideas and prioritizes those that matter most. It acts as a blueprint and action plan to keep everyone on the same page. It helps align executives, board members, and employees on short- and long-term priorities, timelines, and deliverables. Product managers aren't the only ones who build stuff. People ops teams can, too.

Building a people ops roadmap starts with understanding where you are in terms of your current process, program, technology, and data maturity. Hopefully, you are beginning to get a sense of where you are now. The next step is identifying a desired future state. Parts II and III of the book should help with that. Once you understand the gap between your current and potential future state, you'll want to identify the challenges, opportunities, and risks that will have the biggest impact on your business. How will you measure incremental success? What are the metrics that matter, and what impact will progress have on the business? Socializing and capturing feedback on these potential initiatives will help prioritize them on your roadmap based on your business context. Once a draft is developed, you'll want to capture feedback from your leadership team and peers and employees. Then share, iterate, and communicate it often. This is your operational blueprint and a step in the right direction in going from HR administration to people operations.

For a free people operations roadmap template, visit www. zenefits.com/pops-extras

Automate HR: Kill Paperwork

CHAPTER 5

Make the Stuff You Have to Do Easy (Go Digital)

In Part I of this book, we laid out the foundation of people operations. We discussed how the HR landscape has changed in the last decade and the rise of the new workforce. We talked about why people hate HR and how piles of paperwork are the silent killer of your productivity.

Now it's time to get practical. It's time to spell out how to actually make these changes in your company. In this section of the book, we address the most common (and costly!) mistakes we see HR departments make, and how—by leveraging technology—you can free up your time to be more people-focused and profitable.

Think of Part II as your POPS playbook on how to automate your HR processes.

Automation: The Power Behind the People Team

Can you relate to these stories?

We are in healthcare, so have a ton of requirements to track. Before automation, I literally had a whole room of very expensive San Francisco area real estate dedicated to files on my team.
—Adryon Ketcham, CEO, GOALS for Autism

The limited technology we had in-house when I joined (the operations team) was not only disconnected, it looked like my Grandmother's old PC running on a DOS operating system. I knew that

> *our employees, who are mostly college students, needed some-*
> *thing as easy as an app on their phones.*
>
> *—Krystal King, director of operations, Lofty Coffee*

Even with all the digital solutions that surround us, how many of us are guilty of relying on sticky notes, spreadsheets, and overfilled filing cabinets to manage sensitive employee information.

And we know the response too many HR managers receive when they approach leadership about their limited resources:

> *Our company has been fine using manual tools for years. We don't*
> *need to spend the time or money upgrading our systems!*

Or . . .

> *It just simply costs too much to buy HR software for our small business.*

If you've made it through Part I, we both know the truth.

The role of HR has become increasingly complex in both large and small businesses. Not only are they responsible for a wide range of document and form-driven tasks, but HR's role continues to evolve into a multitude of responsibilities, from data analysis to crisis management, from mentoring to diversity specialization.

By doing things "the old HR way," you're prone to human error and opening yourself up to costly mistakes. Having your employees fill out forms by hand and relying on paperwork is bogging down your HR team with tedious desk work. Furthermore, these outdated approaches distract your organization from larger business goals. The time spent updating a W-4 form, tracking timecards, filing expense claims, or shifting schedules to accommodate a vacation request not only feels chaotic, it's a major productivity drain.

This is where **_HR automation_** comes into play. HR automation is the use of computers and technology to perform human resources work with minimal human assistance. Although self-driving cars may come to mind, the truth is automation is integrated into all facets of business. Yet HR professionals are only somewhat aware of this important trend. Only 37 percent of HR functions are automated, compared to IT services, which are 53 percent automated (Leinwand 2017).

Automation is not about having AI replace people or devalue the work they do. Rather, it's about replacing certain job activities to stop wasting time so that HR leaders can be more strategic. Forty percent of workers spend at least a quarter of their workweek on manual repetitive tasks and 70 percent say the biggest opportunity of automation is reducing time wasted on these repetitive tasks. If things like data collection, approvals, and updates were automated, workers would save six hours or more a week (Smartsheet 2017). That's practically an entire workday.

Automation doesn't apply to all tasks, but a 2018 report by KPMG International Cooperative found that most HR functions can be fully or somewhat automated. Of the 21 tasks that can be performed, only five would *not* be improved by automation. (see Figure 5.1)

As you can see, tasks that are low in complexity and low in value added are ripe for automation. What this chart doesn't show is that these types of tasks—data management, forms and workflows, and payroll services—are also some of the most time-consuming. The kind of stuff humans are terrible at, machines are flawless at. Computers can process large quantities of data quickly and it will be error-free. Humans labor over these types of tasks, stumbling with keystrokes and making typos. It's clearly time to hand over HR minutiae to computers.

Keys and Benefits to Automating HR

Companies that leverage technology to manage HR tasks see major gains both in operational efficiency and competitive advantage. But before we dive into the detailed processes of automating HR, let's introduce a few key concepts important to tech-enabled HR administration. A basic understanding of these terms will help you clarify the examples we talk through.

The Cloud

The cloud refers to any product or service delivered via the internet. When something is stored in the cloud, it can be accessed anywhere, anytime. These days, entire companies are stored and operated from the cloud, including inventory tracking and management, customer lists and internal documents, and processes. For HR specifically, cloud-based processes provide immediate and real-time access to specific data when users simply open a web browser or app. As a result, cloud-based businesses translate to fluid workforces (business processes can happen from anywhere there's an internet connection), reduced costs and complexity (the cloud eliminates the need for physical storage of information like time cards, forms, employee files), and improved information accessibility (you no longer are tied to on-premise hardware like time clocks or desktops).

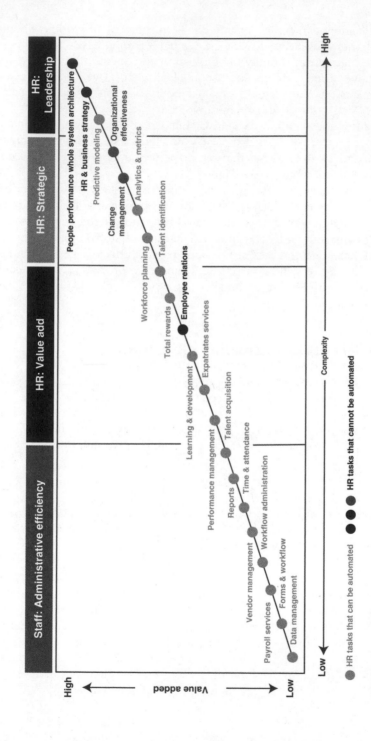

FIGURE 5.1 The HR service value chain.

Source: KPMG International, HR COE, 2010.

All-in-One HR

All-in-one HR refers to when all aspects of HR—including workforce management, payroll and benefits—are built into one natively built technology solution. The term **natively built software features** refers to when software features (in this case HR, payroll, benefits administration, performance management, time tracking, and more) are built within a company's primary code base. In other words, the features are not sold as integrations or after-market white-labeled solutions. This is important, because any time you have multiple software systems trying to talk to each other, which is the case with integrations, data must move from one system to the next, potentially compromising data integrity or risking technical lag time between systems. Even a two-minute delay can be problematic. You want your data systems to be as real-time as possible. A change to an employee's location, for example, impacts tax rates. Hours worked during a specific time period affect benefits eligibility (e.g., Affordable Care Act). Hours clocked in a day and week impact pay rates (e.g., overtime rules), which in turn impact payroll. These changes are happening every day. Due to the speed and frequency of changes, and automation of core business processes, the importance of having all data in a single system can't be stressed enough. It helps ensure all your workforce data is displayed with a reliable and consistent real-time view of the truth.

Workflow Automation

Workflow automation includes an orchestrated and repeatable set of activities. It's like an assembly line for discrete HR processes. Automating HR consists of a specific set of workflows that can be configured using basic rules (e.g., "if/then" logic), actions, and templates. For example, someone requesting a day off triggers an approval from their manager, then deducts time from the individual's available time-off balance, which then updates the individual's profile and company schedule to show the day off. Without smart workflow automation, all these tasks would need to be done manually, in sequence, without error.

Self-Service, or Self-Serve

With *self-service* software, users (or in this case employees) can access information and perform common tasks on their own, in-person, from their smartphone, or from any web browser. For example, employees can add or make changes to their own personal information (like changing their direct deposit information if they switched banks) or view common HR reports and data on their own. Human resource administrators can also access records and reports in a self-service model. Removing dependencies for access to information is important for speed and productivity, instant answers, and keeping costs down. BONUS: *HR leaders* don't carry the full burden of keeping information up to date! Employees can, and are expected to maintain the accuracy and integrity of their own data. This ensures your people data is always up to date, accurate, and keeps employees in need of administrative data out of your office and inbox.

Nudges

Nudges are gentle, digital reminders to take a specific action. You probably get one from your alarm clock (buzz) and from your email on your phone (push notifications). Nudges are a critical part of modernizing HR, too. Nudges can be sent in many directions. They can be sent from HR administrators to employees; from employees to HR administrators; from employees to managers; or they can be sent from the technology to anyone. For example, a manager might receive a nudge when an employee requests a week of PTO. The manager's nudge would remind them to approve or refuse the request. Or, if you flip it, an employee might get a nudge from their manager when it's time to complete their self-reported performance review. Nudges help businesses scale communications efforts and reduce the nagging-police burden from HR professionals.

Guardrails

Guardrails are intelligent interventions designed to prevent damaging actions or avoid unintended consequences. In real life, physical guardrails prevent kids from falling from bunk beds. In a software context, they can prevent self-harm as well. With hundreds of complex regulations, HR software guardrails are important for compliance. It's easy for people to skip a step, miscalculate numbers, or mis-classify something. Tiny errors can have big consequences. In addition to compliance, guardrails help avoid costly errors like overpaying for payroll, taxes, and benefits. For example, using data, software can prevent you from underpaying or overpaying an employee, or making an offer that is higher than the average market rate for a particular job. A guardrail can help prevent you from mis-classifying an employee as part time, exempt, or non-exempt. (see Figure 5.2)

Privacy and Security

The terms *privacy and security* refer to the safeguarding of data and users of data in a digital system. Storing *Personally Identifiable Information (PII)*, or any data that can be used to identify an individual, is serious

Are You Sure?

Erin is an hourly employee, which means **they are likely considered non-exempt** under the Fair Labor Standards Act (FLSA).

To qualify as exempt, an employee must meet all of the following conditions:
- Is paid on a salary basis
- Is paid at least $23,660 per year or $455 per week
- Performs exempt job duties

Keep in mind, it's your company's responsibility to correctly designate employees as exempt or non-exempt.

Change Back to Non-Exempt   **Yes, I'm Sure**

FIGURE 5.2 An example of a software guardrail.

Source: Zenefits, 2021.

business protected by many federal, state, and international laws. Failure to comply with privacy and security measures can result in fines, penalties, and jail time. Regardless of whether you're storing sensitive data in physical locations (like paper forms or filing cabinets) or online (in emails, the cloud, or spreadsheets), you need to protect your employees' personal data. Human resource technology can help keep sensitive data like PII, financial data, and healthcare information secure. User permissions limit access to certain information, and self-service options allow people to manage their own sensitive information independently without needing to print it, email it, or even share it with an HR representative. Geo-location, biometrics, and other techniques (see Chapter 8) further verify user access. Technology-enabled processes provide an accurate digital record of any changes and audit logs.

Data Insights and Analytics

Data Insights and Analytics are knowledge that a company gains from analyzing an aggregated set of data points. People and workplace insights help make more informed decisions and reduce the risks associated with relying on gut instinct. By digitizing all aspects of HR (including payroll, benefits, performance management, time tracking, etc.) business leaders capture more workforce data. This additional data is used to surface insights, analyze trends, and make more informed decisions about your workplace. For example, you can see trends in headcount, turnover, and diversity rates over time by location and department. You can see trends in your overtime pay, PTO liability, and benefits costs. You can see how team engagement and performance are trending across the workforce.

Where to Begin

While you're considering the value HR automation could have on your business, it's helpful to have some guidance on how to get started. Again, consider Part II of this book as exactly that. Now that we've gong over some key terms, in the next few chapters, we will go over how to automate most (if not all) of your HR tasks that are better suited for machines, not people. From recruiting and hiring, to payroll and benefits, we walk you through which low-value, low-complexity HR processes to delegate to technology, and how to do it.

Feel free to flip to a particular section you want to learn more about, or read Part II chapter by chapter. The goal is to guide you through the digital implementation of HR technology so that you can focus on the more strategic components of people operations (which we get into in Part III).

CHAPTER 6

Step 1: Create Digital Employee Records

O kay, now that you've got an understanding of what we mean by the term *going digital* let's dive in with some specific examples.

Whereas traditional HR focused on discrete processes and administration, people ops is about the *people*. The entire approach is built ground-up with your people in mind. So, what better place to start than with the employee profile?

Create an HR System of Record

The first step to automating HR is creating an *HR system of record*. An HR system of record is the complete digital warehouse that stores the *employee record* for every employee in your organization, including all full-time, part-time, contractor, and contingent employees. An employee record includes important details about each employee including their social security number (SSN), employment eligibility, home address, employment documents, and more (see Table 6.1). In a POPS world, this information is stored securely in the cloud, protected by appropriate user permissions. Sensitive information, such as banking and health information, is entered and managed by each employee (more details in Chapter 7) and never transfers hands. The company or HR administrator manages company information, such as work locations and compensation details. Your HR system of record becomes your single go-to source of truth for everything about your workforce, and it's the backbone to automating the rest of your HR administrivia.

TABLE 6.1 Aspects that are included in an employee record. This information can be digitized in an HR platform, reducing the needs for duplicate data entry.

Employee Profile
The following information should be stored in your HR system of record:

Basic Information
- Legal name
- Preferred name
- Legal gender
- Preferred pronoun
- Date of birth
- Social security number
- Electronic signature record

Contact Information
- Personal email *see why this matters in the Tips section
- Work email
- Addresses (multiple)
- Emergency contact

Experiential Information
- Work preferences
- Travel preferences
- Dietary restrictions
- Special needs
- Shirt size

Employment Information
- Start date
- Title
- Departments and work groups
- Work location (tax impact)
- Employment type (FT, PT, contractor type)
- Compensation type (salaried, hourly)
- FLSA status
- EEO information

Financial Information
- Bank accounts
- Payment preference (paper check, direct deposit)
- Paycheck distribution (per account)

Tax Preferences
- Federal (filing status, allowances, additional withholdings, signature)
- State (withholding %, additional withholdings, signature)

Work Eligibility
- I-9 employment verification
- Employment eligibility documentation (passport, license, visa)

Training and Certifications
- Harassment training
- Job training
- Certifications
- Licenses

Equipment
- Devices
- Software
- Services

Documents
- Employment docs (offer letter, I-9, compensation agreements)
- Company docs (handbooks, policy guides, confidentiality agreements)
- Background checks (consent, results)
- Tax docs (Federal W-4, State W-4)
- Healthcare docs (ACA 1095-C, insurance agreements)
- Training and certification docs

Applications (setup, provision, connect required accounts)
- Work email
- Productivity applications (chat, project management, etc.)
- Expense management
- CRM
- Retirement
- Single Sign On
- Other

Source: Zenefits, 2021.

Figure 6.1 shows an example of the data that should be stored on a single digital employee profile. With a digitized employee profile, it shouldn't take more than a few seconds (or clicks) to access or enter any of this information for you or your employees.

In addition to a subset of the information shown in Table 6.1, contractors require specific documentation for payments, taxes, and proper classification as shown in Table 6.2.

Change happens! It's important that any changes to the information shown in Table 6.2 are tracked, logged, and time-stamped. There should be an audit trail of changes to any of the data shown in Table 6.3, capturing the information before and after the change, date of change, and who made the change (e.g., employee, manager, HR).

Beyond the basic profile information, the information shown in Table 6.4 and Figure 6.2 should be available in the same system, on the same employee record, providing a true 360-degree view of your people.

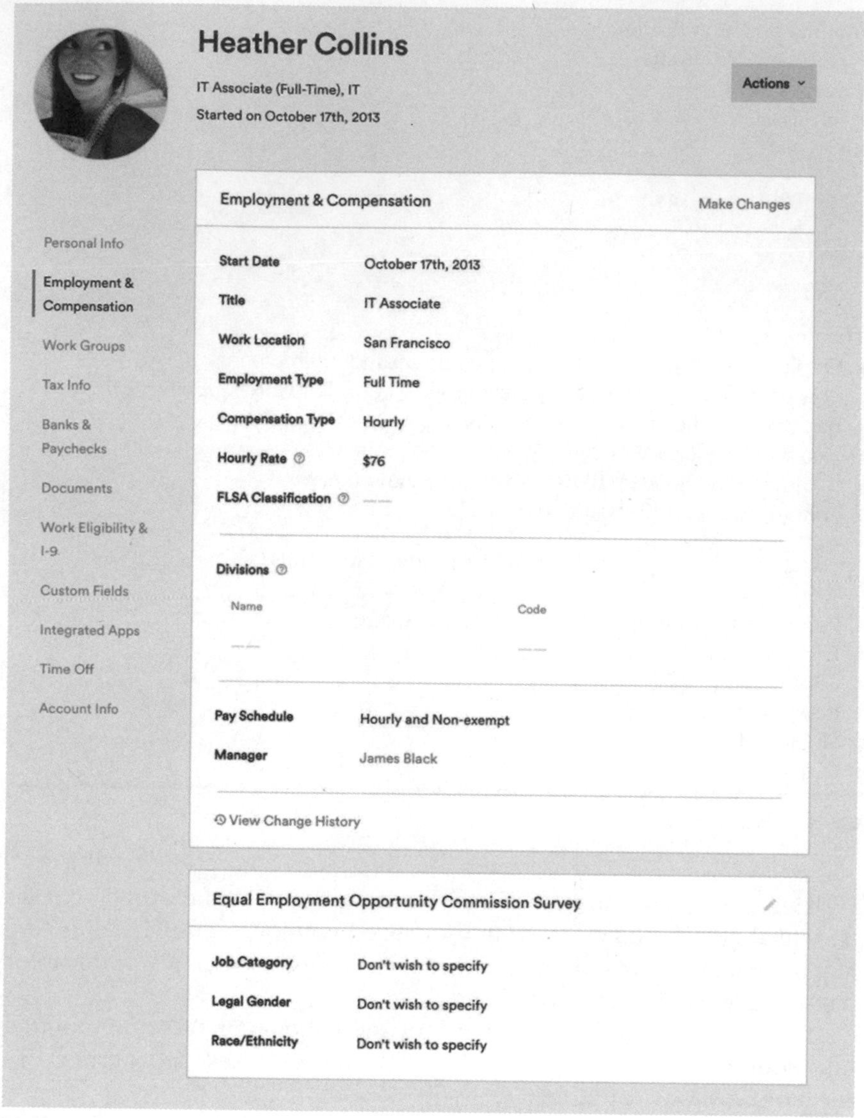

Heather Collins

IT Associate (Full-Time), IT
Started on October 17th, 2013

Actions ∨

Personal Info

Employment & Compensation

Work Groups

Tax Info

Banks & Paychecks

Documents

Work Eligibility & I-9

Custom Fields

Integrated Apps

Time Off

Account Info

Employment & Compensation   Make Changes

Start Date	October 17th, 2013
Title	IT Associate
Work Location	San Francisco
Employment Type	Full Time
Compensation Type	Hourly
Hourly Rate ⑦	$76
FLSA Classification ⑦	-----

Divisions ⑦

Name	Code
---- ----	----

Pay Schedule	Hourly and Non-exempt
Manager	James Black

⟳ View Change History

Equal Employment Opportunity Commission Survey

Job Category	Don't wish to specify
Legal Gender	Don't wish to specify
Race/Ethnicity	Don't wish to specify

FIGURE 6.1 An example of a digital employee record in Zenefits. All employee data is kept and managed within an HR platform in a clean and easy-to-use digital environment.

Source: Zenefits, 2021.

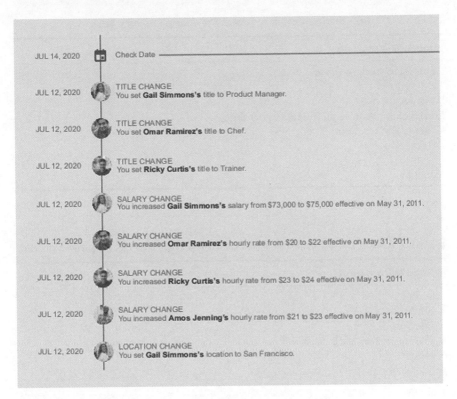

FIGURE 6.2 Digital HR platforms automatically track changes to employee data throughout their work history. This makes a digital history that can be audited or referenced at any time.

Source: Zenefits, 2021.

TABLE 6.2 Contract workers require a different subset of information on their digital record, as shown in Table 6.1.

Contractor Profile
Classification (e.g., independent contractor, agency temp, volunteer, vendor)
Business name
Business type (e.g., individual, LLC, partnership, corporation)
EIN
Tax class
Exemption type
W-9 form
Payment preferences
Visibility and permissions
Agreements (consulting, contractor, IP assignment)

Source: Zenefits, 2021.

TABLE 6.3 HR information that is required for change history logs.

Change History Log
Dates (start and end date)
Title
Work location
Employment type (e.g., full time, part time)
Worker type (exempt)
Compensation
Bonus
Manager

Source: Zenefits, 2021.

TABLE 6.4 Additional information that is supplementary to the employee profile.

Related Information

Schedule
- Shifts (by day, week, and pay period)
- Position
- Day, time, recurring
- Hours
- Conflicts

Time Off
- Out of office
- Pending requests (approval status, reasons, dates, hours, etc.)
- Upcoming time off (dates and calendar)
- Calendar
- Time off policies
- Balances (by type, current/scheduled/available, liability)
- Time off timeline (event log of all requests, balance resets, rollovers)

Time Clock
- Timesheet by day and pay period (time in/out, breaks, jobs, rates, OT, PTO, etc.)
- Reporting type (self-reporting, mobile device)
- Approver
- Meal break settings (nudges, guardrails, paid/unpaid, penalties)
- Overtime rules and settings
- Work groups (projects, divisions, positions)
- Pay rates

Payroll
- Earnings types
- Deductions
- Garnishments
- Reimbursements
- Employer contributions

- Pay stubs
- Payroll timeline (event log of all payments, changes and updates)

Benefits
- Eligibility status (by line of coverage)
- Enrollment status
- Dependents
- Benefit types
- Benefit plan details (insurance cards, group info)
- Benefit claim information
- Summary of benefits and coverage
- Benefits timeline (event log of all history, changes and updates)

Performance
- Goals (progress, status, details, alignment)
- Reviews (scores, status, self-reviews, peer feedback, manager feedback)
- Check-Ins (progress, feedback, notes)
- One-on-Ones (meetings, topics with status, to-do's, notes)

Source: Zenefits, 2021.

Digitize Your Org Chart

Once you have all your employee records entered digitally into your cloud-based HR system of record, you can start organizing your workforce in some neat ways.

For one, you can create a dynamic org chart (see Figure 6.3) with real-time directories. Because your employee records are digital and actively maintained by each person decentrally, your org chart will push up-to-date contact information across your organization in real time such as personal email addresses, phone numbers, and job titles. This helps employees gain quick access to contact information in case they need to reach out to their peers or team leaders.

A digital org chart also helps employees understand organizational relationships between teams, departments, managers, and direct reports and peers. This is great for new hires getting up to speed on who's who.

Keep All Employee Documents in the Cloud with E-Signatures

With digital HR, your employee documents can be managed easily from the cloud. Upload important documents such as confidentiality agreements, sales compensation plans, incentive plans, equity agreements, employee handbooks, or policy updates into your HR system. Select which employees

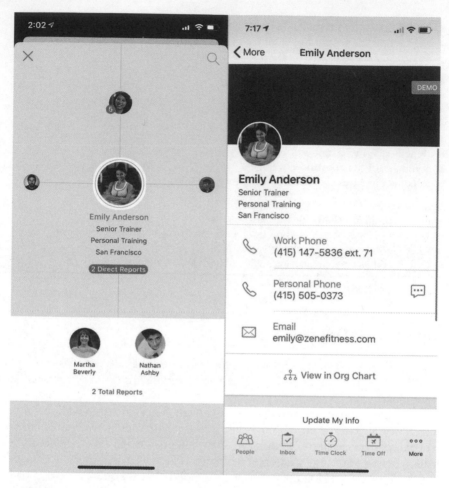

FIGURE 6.3 A digital org chart can show team structures and relationships between people, as well as contact information displays.
Source: Zenefits, 2021.

need to receive the information, and your HR system will send it automatically. The system prompts and captures (digital) e-signatures directly in-platform, meaning you never miss a beat or lose an employee signature on a policy or important document. This can help keep you and your company out of legal trouble. But more importantly, it keeps your employees in the know about policies, expectations, and processes, thus preventing litigation.

Define User Permissions for Your HR and Employee Data

If security is not already a top priority, it should be. One of the most important aspects of HR is keeping employee information private and secure. To keep a tight watch on sensitive data, set up *user permissions* in your chosen HR platform. User permissions define who in your organization can access what information in your software.

To set up permissions, consider who in your organization needs access to which information, and only provide as much access as people need. Batch the levels of access into groups, such as: Administrators (can edit and access all information, including accessing and changing the relationship with the software provider); Editors (can edit and access certain information, but cannot access relationship with service provider); Users (can access read-only information in the software and cannot make changes). This might be a good general rule to follow:

- **Administrators:** HR leaders, C-level executives, board members, accounting professionals, auditors
- **Editors:** managers
- **Users:** employees

With user permissions defined, you'll keep data both secure and accessible at once, all without concern of data breaches or lack of data integrity.

Important Tips When Building Out Your HR System of Record

There are a few very important things to remember when building out your HR system of record, which we can't stress enough.

The first is to keep data secure. HR technology enables employees to handle their own sensitive information instead of emailing it or sending you hard copies, with protects their information. Set clear expectations that employees are to manage their own information as soon as they sign their offer letters. This includes social security numbers, banking information, and insurance information. Avoid paper, forms, and spreadsheets for security and unification (a single record) any time they are available.

Recommend that your employees set up their employee records with personal email addresses, not work ones. This is important because employees may need to access work-related documents before, or well after they end, their working relationship with your company. A personal email address is better for things like benefit elections, posthire documentation and disbursements, and COBRA. Of course, your HR system will document the work email too, but the personal email and phone number should be your primary forms of critical communication.

There are also a few common mistakes to avoid.

The first is the use of spreadsheets. Some folks think *going digital* means scanning a document or loading it in a spreadsheet so that you can access it online. Spreadsheets are really good for a lot of things, but in terms of workplace management, they really only make the problem worse. People data is dynamic, private, and needs to remain safe and protected. Spreadsheets—or even email, Box files, or Google Drive—do not have the security enablements to keep your business or its employees safe. Instead, all information should be stored securely in a single, cloud-based application with appropriate roles and user permissions provided.

The other mistake to avoid is setting up *too many* cloud-based HR systems. Choose one! Why? Multiple systems mean multiple work processes, and multiple points of entry for data breaches. It becomes someone's day job just keeping everything in sync, from manually copying and pasting information from one system to the next, to reconciling data across systems. We want to create less work, not more. Get one digital HR system of record, or platform, that integrates as many of your HR functions as possible.

Hey, Congrats . . . Step 1 Is Now Complete!

With a digital HR system of record in place and information from all employees entered into your HR system of record, you've digitized the backbone of your HR operations.

In the next chapter, we go over Step 2: how to automate your hiring and onboarding process. This will help you decentralize HR data management and ensure a fluid first 90 days for your new hires.

The Old HR Way: Employee records were a mix of paper archives, online emails, spreadsheets, and files. Rudimentary systems tracked basic information like pay history but didn't provide a "360 degree view" of the employee and their work history. Contractors where overlooked. Accessing information took minutes, not seconds.

The POPS Way: Technology provides a single, cloud-based version of the truth for the entire workforce. Employee data is digital, managed by individuals, and can be used to build other workplace features like digital org charts and employee directories. Data is private and secure.

CHAPTER 7

Step 2: Automate Hiring and Onboarding

Let's say you've just found the perfect person to fill your open job. Congratulations! We know you've already invested a lot to get this far.

- The average job opening attracts 250 resumes (Glassdoor 2020).
- It takes 28 days to fill an open position (Jobvite.com 2019).
- 60 percent of recruiters say they regularly lose candidates before they're able to schedule an interview (Yello 2020).
- The interview process takes an average of 23 days (Chamberlain 2015).

Hiring and onboarding is a complex process with many repetitive, moving parts. But it also plays a pivotal role for your business success. A strong process lays the foundation for business stability (less turnover), growth (fast hiring-to-onboarding turnaround), and profitability (hiring the right team to make it happen).

So, you don't want to risk finding that perfect person. You've got to move fast to ensure that top talent doesn't take another offer; and then you need to ensure you set them up for success for their first couple of weeks with your business.

If you're running hiring and onboarding manually, you may not be getting the competitive edge you need. For one, you might not be demonstrating a level of professionalism you're looking to achieve in those very important first few impressions, losing the candidate to another company. If you do sign them, a manual onboarding process puts you at risk of being out of compliance. According to the U.S. Immigration and Customs Enforcement website (2019), if your new hire fills out an I-9 employment eligibility form incorrectly, and you are audited, the fine could range from $230 to nearly $2,300 per violation.

Here's the good news: if you've set up an HR system of record, almost every part of your hiring and onboarding process can be automated, too. This ensures the quickest and most professional new hire process for everyone you bring on board. Plus, it outsources the process of gathering important new employee information for each new hire, reducing the burden on HR.

In a people operations methodology, your goal is to power your business by engaging your people from the very beginning, while offloading many of the tedious but crucial tasks to HR technology. In the hiring and onboarding process, there are dizzying amounts of such tasks including executing a legally approved offer and employment contract, checking all the regulatory boxes with correctly completed forms, ensuring provisioning of everything from computer equipment to tools, confirming the review of your handbook and operating practices, and setting short- to mid-term goals. Much of this process can be automated. (see Table 7.1.)

Intrigued? Great. Let's put it in context so you can see exactly where HR technology helps automate your hiring and onboarding process so that you give each new hire an empowering first impression.

TABLE 7.1 What can be managed by computers in most hiring and onboarding flows, and what must be managed by humans.

What you can automate (best for computers)	What you can't automate (best for humans)
Hiring	Hiring
■ Templates to populate and send offer letters and agreements, then track acceptance	■ Your actual selection
■ Background checks	■ Determination of the best (competitive and fair) compensation and benefits package
■ Electronic signatures	
Onboarding	Onboarding
■ Guardrails for accurately completing onboarding documents (HR compliance regulatory forms: employee forms W-4s, W-2s, NDAs, etc.)	■ Company policies, missions, and values for your employee handbook
■ Storage, delivery, and acceptance of employee handbooks	
■ Employee record data capture for all of the aforementioned in one place, one time!	

Source: Zenefits, 2021.

POPS STAR

"Compliance mistakes could be the difference between keeping a small business afloat or sinking it," says Jodie Heal, president of Heal Accounting and former auditor. "I love that with the right technology and digital forms, people can't fill out the forms incorrectly! You can't progress to the next step or leave a section in a W-4 blank."

Jodie's unique tech-forward workplace management approach helps ensure better business continuity for her 300 small business clients. And, it helps her differentiate her own business. Jodie was cited as one of three CPA "top women to watch" in the state of Maine.

POPS STARS are Zenefits customers or small businesses featured on our podcast, who've embraced technology and/or built employee experiences that help advance their POPS maturity and their business success.

How to Automate Hiring

When we talk about automating hiring, we don't mean employers should take human consideration out of the recruiting and hiring process. Rather, we mean you should automate all nitty-gritty tasks associated with hiring—the tedious and repetitive ones—that are frankly better handled through computer automation. Let's look at which tasks are easily automated in further detail.

Offer Letters

Whether you're hiring one person, 10, or 100, it's smart to find ways to scale your hiring process. This means finding tasks that repeat and automating them. A good place to start is with offer letters. Offer letter templates can be templatized, built once, but used time and again. Smart templates contain a mix of noneditable text fields for legal language that's consistent between all candidates, and editable text fields for personalization for each candidate.

Templatizable language could include welcoming language, your company address, your company contact info, and people/team contact information.

Personalized fields could include things like the candidate's name, job title, compensation details, start date, employment contingencies, role responsibilities, reporting structure, typical working hours, additional benefits (health insurance, bonus, retirement planning, paid time off, etc.), and the date that the offer expires. A personalized field will also include the signatory.

Build a template for each employment type you might hire: full-time, part-time, contractor, contingent worker, intern, and any other employee type you may have.

A template could look something like Figure 7.1.

Templates smooth out the process for administrators and make the job offer process more beautiful and consistent for new hires. New hires can review and accept your letter from any device. Meanwhile, your HR platform automatically attaches completed offers to your new hire's employee record. As soon as new hires accept your offer, the automated process alerts you of your new employee! Congratulations.

For a free sample agreement, visit `www.zenefits.com/pops-extras`

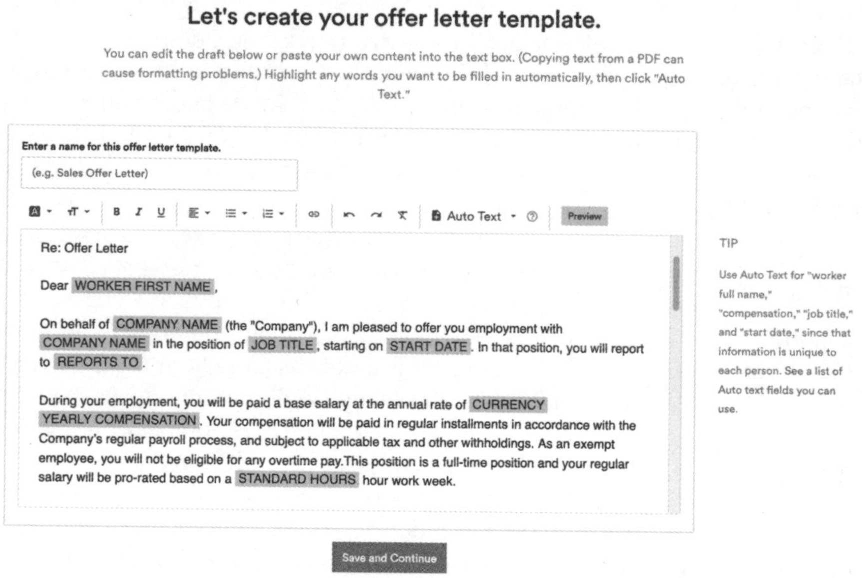

Let's create your offer letter template.

You can edit the draft below or paste your own content into the text box. (Copying text from a PDF can cause formatting problems.) Highlight any words you want to be filled in automatically, then click "Auto Text."

Enter a name for this offer letter template.

(e.g. Sales Offer Letter)

Re: Offer Letter

Dear WORKER FIRST NAME ,

On behalf of COMPANY NAME (the "Company"), I am pleased to offer you employment with COMPANY NAME in the position of JOB TITLE , starting on START DATE . In that position, you will report to REPORTS TO .

During your employment, you will be paid a base salary at the annual rate of CURRENCY YEARLY COMPENSATION . Your compensation will be paid in regular installments in accordance with the Company's regular payroll process, and subject to applicable tax and other withholdings. As an exempt employee, you will not be eligible for any overtime pay. This position is a full-time position and your regular salary will be pro-rated based on a STANDARD HOURS hour work week.

TIP

Use Auto Text for "worker full name," "compensation," "job title," and "start date," since that information is unique to each person. See a list of Auto text fields you can use.

Save and Continue

FIGURE 7.1 An example of an offer letter template. The highlighted sections are where HR admins will need to personalize offer letters. The rest of the text can remain similar.

Source: Zenefits, 2021.

Hiring Agreements

As part of your onboarding you may want to include additional hiring agreements such as intellectual property (IP) agreements for members of your development or marketing teams, or nondisclosure agreements (NDA) for anyone with privileged access to your key business strategies and data. You can personalize any of these agreements for your business once, and then, by using the auto text editor, use them again and again. Set up hiring agreements for each relevant employee and then automate the process. Make sure to add your company's signatory and send for your new employee's digital signature to add to their profile records.

Hiring Documents for E-signature

Make the document process easy by sending offer letters, and any other important documents, through your HR system of record. New hires and signatories can both sign documents in seconds via their HR app, wherever they are and from whatever device they use. This makes document signing easier and ensures all documents are stored and secured in your secure cloud-based platform.

Background Checks

A background check may include employment, education, criminal records, credit history, motor vehicle, or license record checks. Activate background checks to run automatically for any jobs that require them. Consider the right types of background checks for each job and attach those to your flow. For example, for any role in your business that requires driving or delivery, you might also include motor vehicle reports.

You'll also need to determine who in your company will have access to the background check information, for example, the hiring manager and/or the administrator of the automation tool.

How to Automate Onboarding

Okay, we've gone through how to automate the hiring process, but what about the all important onboarding phase of each new hire? *Employee onboarding* is the process of getting a new hire in compliance with new hire paperwork and ensuring they have the tools, training, and resources needed to do their jobs well. Although individual roles will differ from job to job, many onboarding processes are consistent and routine, like completing federal forms and setting up direct deposits for pay. These repeated processes shouldn't be taking up your time. Here's how you can use technology to automate your new hire onboarding.

Build an Onboarding Flow

With digital technology at your fingertips, you can build a repeatable onboarding flow for each of your worker types. This is essentially a flow chart of steps that each employee must complete. Your HR system will walk employees through the necessary steps, one by one, making your onboarding process consistent, well-paced, and entirely out the hair of your HR administrators.

Different companies will have different lengths of onboarding flows, but almost all will have the following steps:

- Completing all new hire paperwork
- Signing any employee documents (see the section "Keep All Employee Documents in the Cloud with E-Signatures" in Chapter 6)
- Completing the personal details of their digital employee record
- Familiarizing themselves with various aspects of the business
- Socialization of employees to the team and company culture

Empower New Hires to Self-Serve the Onboarding Process

As referenced in Chapter 5, this is where your digital onboarding system will collect, in a secure online environment, all the key personal data that will be the cornerstone of employee records.

As an employer, you have a legal duty to protect the personal information and data of your employees, and you have a significant financial and reputational incentive to take reasonable steps to maintain the privacy and security of the information.

An HR platform allows your employees to access the same HR portal that your admins manage, and input their own information directly. They can do this from an HR app directly from their personal phone or computer. This eliminates any need for emails, paperwork, or secure document exchanges.

Automate your digital onboarding process to prompt employees step-by-step for their:

- Personal email and a password for their access

- Signature of all onboarding documents, offer letter, attachments, and handbook
- Personal information: legal name, date of birth and social security number, plus legal gender are all default options to meet federal and state employment requirements. But you should also consider adding additional, inclusive optional fields, such as gender identity, preferred personal pronouns, and more
- Phone number, work phone number, and alternate email
- Emergency contact information
- Federal and state tax details, such as preferred withholdings and filing status to generate a W-4 report
- Bank account details for direct deposit banking option
- Employment eligibility, including I-9 forms and documents

Use nudges to remind employees to complete their records, or better yet, automatically generate nudges that send out, based on certain times, triggers of incompletion.

When your employees self-serve data in your HR system, you ensure the protection of their data, greater engagement with your workers, and you provide a complete and unified onboarding experience for all your employees.

Welcome New Hires with a Great First Impression

Employees will feel confident in their new role if you welcome them warmly and get them quickly up to speed. Although managers have a lot to do with the success of a new hire's initial few weeks, you can help welcome new employees from day one. One great way to do this is to automatically send a welcome letter as soon as your new hire completes the onboarding process. This is one of many key opportunities to reconfirm to your new employee that you're committed to their success. (see Figure 7.2.)

As before, use a digital template to streamline this step with editable and noneditable text fields. Include information on work hours, location, maybe even a seating chart and parking or commuter options. This letter can also include attachments to request tools like computer systems, as well as keycard access to the building.

For a free sample welcome letter, visit www.zenefits.com/pops-extras

POPS STAR

At the start of the 2020 pandemic, the Denver-based company Sondermind had just proved its business model for delivering accessible mental health therapy to the public, securing $27 million in funding. The burst in demand for mental health care during the pandemic meant Sondermind had to grow its employee base quickly, and they decided to prioritize getting to know new hires better. So, the three-year-old company launched its first in-house people operations team, put in place HR software, and focused on supporting its new hires, versus just tracking them.

"With technology, we can effectively engage our employees even before they start. We've cut out unnecessary first-day paperwork, enabled managers to have greater ownership of employee information, and integrated calendars to track birthdays, new hires, and SonderVersaries to ensure all employee milestones are celebrated," says Director of People Operations Tori Soler.

"We recognize the role that a bad job experience can contribute to mental health challenges. So we want to lead by example, modeling great engagement practices from the very first interaction and even using our own tools to ensure more holistic well-being for our people."

Sondermind streamlined its onboarding from hours per employee to 30 minutes. "With 56 new hires in the first four months of 2020, we've saved 110 man hours and vastly improved the new employee experience."

Keep Your Onboarding Game Strong with Triggered Nudges and Custom Emails

Ensuring employee success is an ongoing endeavor that should extend beyond week one with both role- and company-level goals for mastery and involvement in your business. Help managers keep a pulse on their new hires by sending automated nudges from your HR system. These nudges can be triggered at key milestones, like:

- Day -7 Nudge:
  - Remember! Send a welcome gift the week before their start date.
- Day 1 Nudge:
  - Did you remember to invite your new hire to a welcome lunch (or virtual lunch), align on their first 90 days, and connect them with a peer mentor?

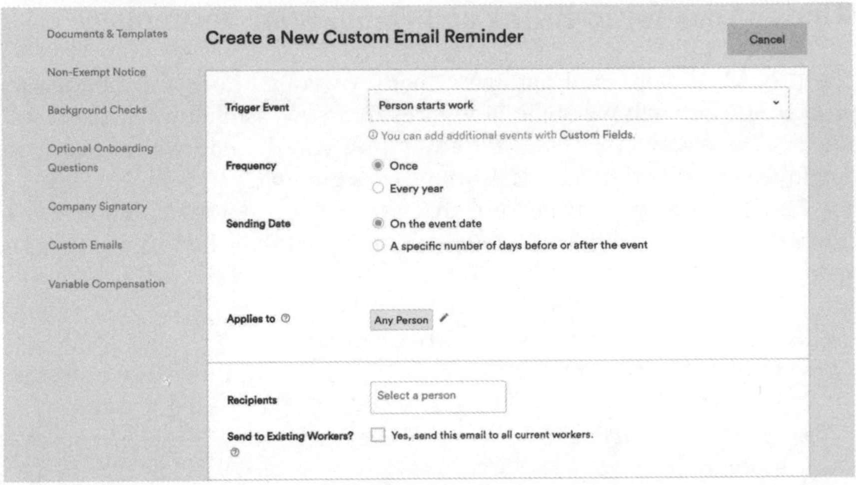

FIGURE 7.2 An example of creating an automated email based on an employee-based trigger. In this case, an email should be sent "once" when an "employee starts work" and "on the event date" meaning the employee's start date.

Source: Zenefits, 2021.

- Day 7 Nudge:
  - Reminder! Set up weekly 1:1 meetings with your new hire.
- Day 14 Nudge:
  - Reminder! Send a new hire survey to your new employee.
- Day 90 Nudge:
  - Reminder! Send manager note for 90-day performance check-in.

You can do the same thing for custom emails, which can be sent to employees or managers based on certain triggering events set up in your system.

Best-in-class companies automate all of the above in a single workflow with a single people operations platform.

For a free onboarding checklist, visit www.zenefits.com/pops-extras

What to Look for in Hiring and Onboarding Technology

The preceding steps will automate many of your hiring and onboarding processes. They will welcome new hires in a professional way, create scalable and repeatable processes for any hiring you do, and will engage your employees to self-serve HR data from the beginning.

But how can you make sure that the HR technology solution you're considering purchasing and implementing can do all this? Here are some features to look for:

- Integration with other systems. For example:
  - Applicant Tracking Software (ATS) to streamline your recruiting process
  - Learning Management System (LMS) to help guide required employee training
  - Background check technology for one-click background checks
  - Productivity tools like Google's G-Suite or Slack
- Configurable templates, to make building your own documents a breeze
- Event-triggered custom emails for manager nudges, employee engagement, and a smoother ramp to success

And Just Like That, Step 2 is Complete!

You've now created repeatable, scalable processes for hiring and onboarding that allow for both personalization and automation. This improves your professionalism, compliance, and the initial employee experience at your company.

In the next chapter, we dive into automating time tracking and payroll. This will help you manage payroll taxes and ensure accurate pay. Let's dive in.

The Old HR Way: HR hiring and onboarding processes were tactical and manual. New hire and onboarding paperwork was made one-off and manually with each new hire.

The POPS Way: Uses templates and digital workflow to automate a consistent, professional hiring and onboarding experience. New hires are walked through HR requirements step-by-step through their HR mobile app and self-enter sensitive personal data, while nudges remind admins of key steps.

CHAPTER 8

Step 3: Automate Time and Pay

There's more to payroll than just issuing checks.

You've got to wrangle time sheets, validate the accuracy of time worked, ensure the proper withholdings from each person's paycheck, and deliver checks to employees . . . all while staying in compliance with federal, state, and local tax codes and employer regulations.

What's more, time and pay are the basis of your employee contract with your workers. When you consider how much payday means to your employees, it makes sense that it's one of the most critical touch points between a company and its people. Get pay wrong once and you'll tarnish your trustworthiness as an employer. Get pay wrong twice, and your employees will start looking for another job (Bolden-Barrett 2017).

Employers have a legal responsibility to the federal and local governments to withhold and pay taxes from employee wages, too. These employment taxes include federal income tax, Social Security, and Medicare taxes. Too often, businesses fail to pay accurate taxes, which has resulted in the IRS's Tax Division naming criminal tax enforcement one of its "highest priorities" seeking "money judgments, permanent injunctions, and criminal convictions that often carry substantial prison sentences, restitution, and financial penalties" for those found in violation (US Department of Justice 2018).

There are also hundreds of compliance requirements to know and follow—the number of which quickly balloon when you employ people in multiple states. In addition to handling all major federal, state, and local taxes, small businesses are also responsible for staying current on:

- Reciprocal state tax agreements
- Courtesy withholding
- Subject wage limits
- Tax credits
- Exemptions and exceptions

- Supplemental wage taxes
- Employee type
- Business type
- Business ownership
- Proration
- Changing laws related to paid family and paid sick leave
- Changing forms (such as the changes to Form W-4 due to the Tax Cuts and Jobs Act of 2017)

But, despite most people's best intentions, mistakes happen. And it costs you—big time. It costs you time, money, penalties, brand reputation, productivity, and potentially even jail time. The Wage and Hour Division of the US Department of Labor reported in 2020 that more than $322 million in back wages were owed to workers in fiscal year 2019—a number that has grown each year for the past five years—with an average of $1,025 for each employee due back wages.

Maryland Business Owner: 24 Months in Prison

In January 2013, Alphonso Tillman was sentenced to 24 months in prison and three years of supervised release for failing to account for and pay employment taxes. Tillman was also ordered to pay restitution of $2,205,991. According to his plea agreement, Tillman was the president and sole owner of two companies that provided security guards to protect commercial and residential properties. Both companies withheld taxes from their employees' paychecks, but Tillman failed to file the required forms or pay the payroll taxes due, with the exception of payments from IRS collection efforts. The total amount of taxes lost from Tillman's failure to pay these taxes was $2,205,991 (Murthy 2014).

Source: Journal of Accountancy (Murthy 2014).

So, the question is, do businesses really need to pay someone to manage timekeeping and payroll week in and week out? Or could this task be delegated to technology, freeing the HR and accounting department to be more strategic?

Although it's true time and pay are one of the higher-value and more-complex tasks that HR departments typically manage, research *consistently shows* technology is better qualified for this task. Technology is more accurate, frees up time for HR leaders to spend on more strategic tasks, helps the business stay in better compliance, and positions the business for tomorrow's future of work.

- **Accuracy and reliability:** the American Payroll Association (APA) estimates automation cuts payroll processing costs by 80 percent and reduces errors in invoices and paychecks (Duval 2018).
- **More strategic focus:** organizations with integrated timekeeping and payroll overachieve their revenue targets by seven percent (DeRosiers 2018).
- **Greater compliance:** automating payroll sets you up to meet thousands of compliance standards, such as with the ACA, FLSA, and the Sarbanes-Oxley Act, a federal law that ensures accuracy of financial statements.
- **Positions companies for tomorrow's future of work:** concepts like on-demand pay, or wage frequency are payroll theories that are starting to make some noise. Employees want to be paid when they need to be paid. But this level of payroll agility won't be possible without digital, and fully integrated, payroll systems to your core HR system.

In this chapter, we look at best practices in automating employee time, scheduling, and pay. You'll see exactly what we mean in a minute, but for now, check out Table 8.1's quick cheat sheet of what can be automated in time and pay, and then let's walk through the steps it will take to set up automation for time and pay in your business.

How to Automate Time and Attendance and Pay

Automating employee time tracking and pay can be one of the most lucrative HR automation steps you can make, in terms of earning you time back. It takes 7.1 hours, on average, to manage time, pay, and taxes according to a 2021 study of 510 HR professionals. This same process takes companies leveraging Zenefits an average of 23 minutes and 12 seconds. Additionally, calculating, withholding, and remitting taxes happens automatically. Ready to save some time?

Set Up Your Company's Legal Information In Your People Platform

When you automate payroll, your software is doing business on your behalf. You'll need to give it information to correctly represent your company.

To do this, you'll first want to plug in all your company details into the software, much like each employee did while setting up their individual employee records.

Company information will include your:

- Legal company name
- DBA (Doing Business As) company name

- NAICS Code
- Company address
- Business entity type
- Business tax status
- Ownership information
- Company signatory (person responsible for signing and approving documents for the company)
- Company bank information

TABLE 8.1 What can be managed by computers in most time tracking and payroll processing workflows, and what must be managed by humans.

What you can automate (best for computers)	What you can't automate (best for humans)
- Time tracking - Verification of employee locations for location-specific work - Overtime calculations - Meal break reminders and penalties - State and local income tax withholdings - Pay type drop-down menus - Earnings types drop-down menus - Payrun schedules - PTO requests/approval process - Changes to HR info updating payroll - Payroll records - Payroll transparency - Voluntary and involuntary employee withholdings and submitting them to the appropriate governmental entity - Quarterly and year-end payroll taxes - Eligibility for tax credits and minimizing amounts owed - Employee benefits eligibility - FICA, Social Security, and Medicare deductions and payments - Federal, state, and local tax guidelines and adjusting payroll figures as needed to maintain compliance - Federal, state, and local tax filings	- Definitions of pay types - Definitions of earnings types - Definitions of deduction types - Establishing your payroll schedule - Establishing your PTO policy - Swap shift schedules - Approving of hours worked - Signing important documents for banking, tax, or legal information

Source: Zenefits, 2021.

You'll also need to configure who at your company is receiving payroll. To do this, attach payroll details such as employment type, compensation type, and wages or salary information to each employee's digital record. Setting this up once allows the software to run autonomously thereafter. Figure 8.1 shows an example of how this might look.

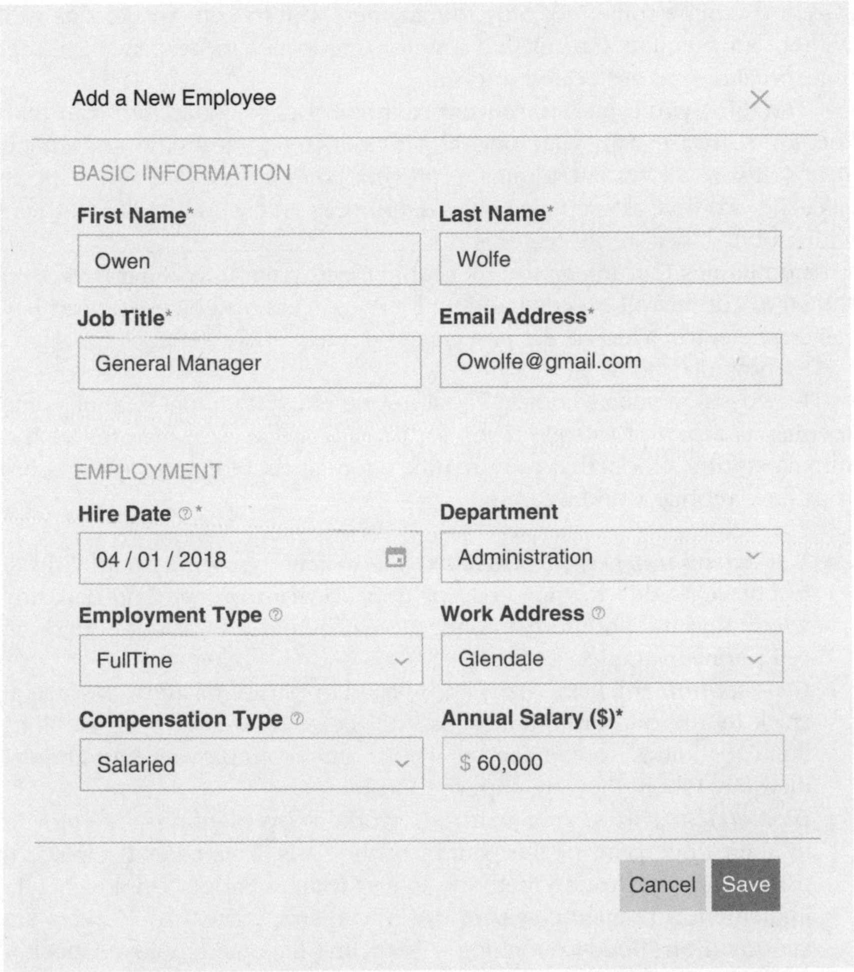

Add a New Employee ✕

BASIC INFORMATION

First Name*

Owen

Last Name*

Wolfe

Job Title*

General Manager

Email Address*

Owolfe@gmail.com

EMPLOYMENT

Hire Date ⓘ*

04 / 01 / 2018

Department

Administration

Employment Type ⓘ

FullTime

Work Address ⓘ

Glendale

Compensation Type ⓘ

Salaried

Annual Salary ($)*

$ 60,000

Cancel Save

FIGURE 8.1 An example of assigning a hiring date, department, employment type, compensation type, and salary to a new hire. This information augments an employee record.

Source: **Zenefits, 2021.**

Configure Your Time and Pay Software to Run Autonomously

The APA found that 75 percent of businesses are affected by "time theft," costing up to seven percent of their gross annual payroll (Osterhaus 2015). That means if your business pays $1 million in payroll, you're probably losing $70,000 in stolen time.

But don't be quick to shift blame to employees. A manual timekeeping system is cumbersome, not only to managers, but to your workers as well. Without an accurate and reliable way for employees to keep track of their time, breakdowns are bound to occur.

The thing you can do to prevent payroll errors is to integrate your timekeeping software with your payroll provider. Integrated time and attendance software allows HR admins to prevent payroll theft and automatically calculate overtime rates. It also gives employees an easy way to track hours, with mobile clock in/out features.

Companies that integrate timekeeping and payroll systems have been shown to cut payroll-processing time by 90 percent and have reduced payroll errors by, on average, six percentage points.

So how do you do it?

Let's assume you've chosen an all-in-one HR system that includes timekeeping as a part of its suite. Look for providers that have features such as automated time clocks that capture time attendance, biometric systems, and apps for a mobile workforce.

- *Web-based timekeeping trackers:* These have grown in popularity in recent years due to their ease of use. You can access time data anywhere that has an internet connection, whether it's through a desktop, cell phone, or tablet.
- *Geo-location trackers:* Many web-based applications allow workers to clock in and out through a mobile device or app. They have geo-location capabilities, so you can see if your remote employees start and end their day where they are supposed to be.
- *Biometrics:* This system manages workers by identifying employees by their fingerprint or the pattern of their iris. This takes the place of using other verification methods, like swiping a badge. Employers who implement a biometric system use it to restrict access to workers and cut down on "buddy punching"—you can't have an employee clock in and out for a friend.

The first thing you'll need to do is review payroll information inside the software. Determine your start date (when you want to start paying employees) and configure your pay frequency (weekly, biweekly, semi-monthly, monthly) so your software can automatically run calculations.

You'll also need to set up how employees will track and record their hours. Choose a method that makes time tracking ridiculously easy for your employees, such as mobile clock in/out features of HR software phone apps. You'll also want to appoint someone in your organization to approve hours logged. This is a human step used to verify hours worked. Many all-in-one HR systems will automatically select an employee's manager as their timesheet approver.

Finally, you'll need to set up your HR system to understand where your employees are located (this should be inferred from your employee record) so that the software can accurately track minimum wage requirements, state income tax withholdings, and overtime rates associated with each state.

Once you configure your time tracking rules inside your HR system of record, the software will automatically calculate earnings, deductions, and withholdings for each pay period and alert HR admins only when payroll is ready to run.

This quick configuration workflow saves you hours of manual work, and prevents errors.

Integrate HR Directly into Your Payroll System

One of the biggest time sucks of HR is rectifying all the tiny changes that impact employee pay. Things like raises, bonuses, PTO, unpaid time off, new garnishments, unexpected withholdings, or changes to benefits elections all impact how much money an employee ultimately takes home. Any time a change is made, it needs to be reflected in people's paychecks, immediately. Otherwise you're forced to make costly changes and reruns of payroll.

With HR technology enabled, changes automatically push to your payroll provider, so that your HR records are updated uniformly.

With manual systems, or even if you run digital HR processes that don't *fully* integrate, you'll find changes to HR can be painstakingly laborious. You'll need to hunt down information from individual employees, ensuring changes are accurately translated into your payroll system. And you again increase your risk for errors as you manually transcribe information from one system to the other.

A single system for HR, time tracking, and payroll allows for simultaneous, and instantaneous updates across the board. This simplifies your job from doing the actual adjustments and risking errors, to real-time updates and a simple approval process.

Automate Your Federal and State Tax Filings

At this point your software has full records of your payroll information, so it only makes sense that it would be able to handle tax filings, too.

To set up automatic tax filings, all you'll need to do is input your federal and state tax information, such as your federal employer identification number (EIN), state tax ID numbers, and tax rates. Then your HR software will calculate, remit, and file your taxes for you.

Automate Your State Economic Security and State Department of Revenue Requirement

You can automate your state economic security requirements, such as unemployment insurance, in a similar manner. Upload your state unemployment compensation account number (UC), unemployment insurance rate (UI), and withholding account number.

Create Pay Type Templates

Once your user profiles are defined, and your employees are entered into a single system, the fun part begins: creating systems that scale. The first step is to create pay type templates (see Figure 8.2). *Pay types* are the recurring pay scenarios your company uses frequently. For example, you could have pay types for regular hours, overtime hours, holiday hours, vacation, bonuses, incentives, etc. *Pay type templates* are premade rules and definitions affixed to the various pay types inside your company.

Each time you onboard a new employee, designate their pay type inside the platform. Doing so ascribes certain policies carried within the definition of the templates, keeping payroll accurate.

Create Drop-Down Menus for Earnings, Deductions, Reimbursements, and Other Functions

It may sound simple (and we hope it is!) but creating drop-down menus for various aspects of pay makes your payroll process cleaner, easier, and less prone to error. (see Figure 8.3.)

Drop-down tabs allow you to configure the relevant earning types, pre-tax and after-tax deduction types, garnishment types, reimbursements, withholdings, and other key pay data (back taxes, reimbursements, employee/employer benefits contributions). If and when someone's paycheck needs

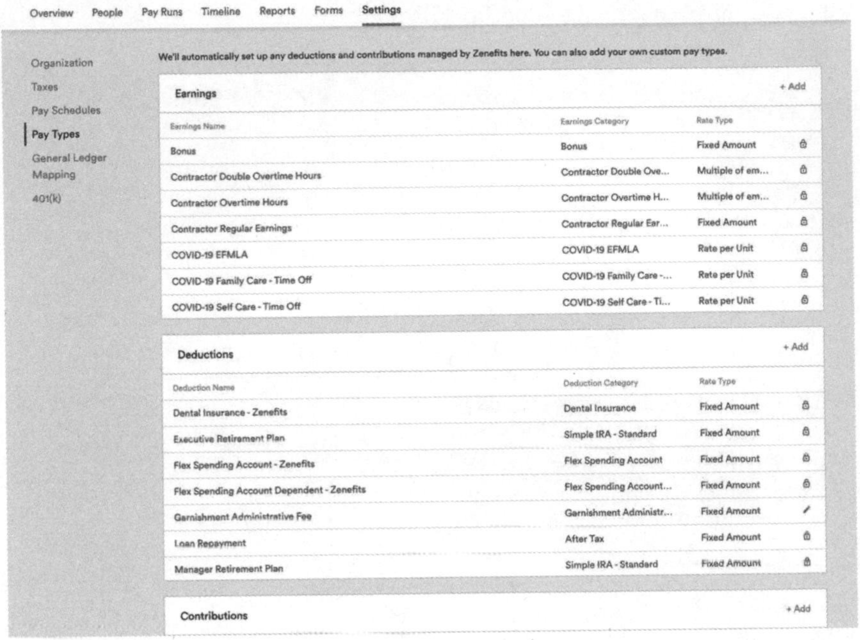

FIGURE 8.2 An example of predefining pay types into templates that can be used throughout your payroll process.

Source: **Zenefits, 2021.**

adjusting, payroll administrators can easily select an adjustment from a drop-down menu. Required adjustments automatically update your payroll for the impacted employee, and the organization's records. This saves you time and builds consistency in your recordkeeping.

Keep Complete Digital Payroll Records without Lifting a Finger or Opening a Filing Cabinet

This is one of those steps that isn't a step. Lucky you.

According to the US Department of Labor's FLSA (revised 2008), employers are required to keep track of payroll records for three years. If you're running payroll on paper or even on spreadsheets on your computer, this requires a fair amount of organization and file keeping. If you're already inputting employee data into a cloud-based HR platform, you'll automatically get digital copies of all transaction data. No effort needed.

FIGURE 8.3 An example of using drop-down menus for preloaded earnings types to keep pay more consistent across your organization.

Source: Zenefits, 2021.

You no longer need to worry that fire or vandalism will ruin your records. All your data is securely contained in the cloud.

Keep Payroll Data Accessible and Transparent for Both HR Admins and Employees

There are a host of reasons that people need access to their pay information. And they should be free to access that information without the help of HR. This is considered *democratized data*, meaning everyone has access to data without running into gatekeepers.

With automated, secure, cloud-based payroll data this is possible. Leveraging their user permissions, admins, managers, and employees can all access pay data from their mobile app or desktop. This gives immediate access to pay information, earnings, W-2 forms, and so forth without employees feeling like they have to "ask HR." It also keeps other data, such as other employees' personal information, safe and secure.

What to Look for in Time and Pay Technology

The preceding steps will automate many of your payroll processes. They will sync employee time and hours with payroll, automate HR changes through to paychecks, and keep your HR systems uniform and in compliance.

But how do you know if your current payroll provider can achieve this level of automation, and/or what are some qualifying questions you could ask other HR platform solutions to find good ones? Here are some questions to ask:

- Does your payroll product integrate with accounting and HR software?
- Does your payroll integrate with employee time and attendance?
- Could you run payroll in as few as three clicks of a button?
- Could you revert to different payroll drafts with saved digital records while running payroll?

Boom! You Just Finished Step 3!

If you follow the aforementioned suggestions, you will successfully integrate your HR, pay, and time tracking under one digital roof. This provides seamless employee data management. If and when your data updates anywhere, it updates everywhere, leading to a more positive employee experience and fewer fines and penalties. Oh—and very accurate payroll.

In the next chapter, we take a similar approach to the benefits side of the house. If your company offers benefits of any kind—health, commuter, 401(k)s, and so forth—you'll be glad to learn how these processes, too, can be automated.

The Old HR Way: Disparate systems for time tracking, accounting, and payroll. Changes were made manually.

The POPS Way: Single system for time tracking, scheduling, and payroll automatically pushes information to keep the whole system accurate and uniform.

CHAPTER 9

Step 4: Automate Health Insurance Benefits

Getting benefits right is a huge driver to your business's success. *Benefits* are any additional advantage an employer gives to its employees, including both monetary and nonmonetary perks such as health insurance, paid vacation, equity, flexible work arrangements, life insurance, commuter benefits, remote work stipends, and more.

Roughly 30 percent of total employee compensation is paid out through benefits, and businesses use them as a key way to attract new talent and retain top staff (Gonzalez 2020). Most benefits options are not required by law, but one is: *health insurance.* Health insurance benefits, aka healthcare, include a combination of medical, dental, and vision insurance. Employers with 50 (100 for California, Colorado, Vermont, and New York) full-time employees (FTEs) or full-time-equivalent employees are required by law to provide medical coverage to at least 95 percent of eligible staff. Offering health benefits at companies with fewer than 50 full-time employees is optional, but most employers recognize the need in order to compete with larger businesses in the war on talent.

Managing health benefits is a complicated process with many stakeholders, deadlines, approvals, and processes. It also happens to be the number-one benefit employees seek from their employers (Zenefits 2020). And 50 percent of small business employees say it's the primary reason they stay at their job (Curry 2020a). So, the stakes to get it right are high.

Truthfully, we could spend an entire book talking about how benefits impact your brand, its complexities, and compliance (and we have—check out *The Small Business Guide to Health Insurance* at zenefits.com/pops-extras). But we know you're not here to prove the value of benefits, it's to learn to *automate* this stuff. So let's cut to the chase.

TABLE 9.1 What can be managed by computers in most benefits administration workflows, and what must be managed by humans.

What you can automate (best for computers)	What you can't automate (best for humans)
▪ Benefits elections during the new hire onboarding process ▪ Open enrollment management and administration ▪ Plan comparisons ▪ Adjustments and deductions to payroll based on benefits elections ▪ Federal forms 1094-C and 1095-C filings ▪ Compliance with ACA regulations	▪ Choosing your insurance carrier ▪ Choosing your broker ▪ Choosing which plans to offer ▪ Choosing employer contribution rates ▪ Choosing employee eligibility

Source: Zenefits, 2021.

Health-benefits administration is far better suited for technology to manage than humans. As Riia O'Donnell, a human resource professional with over 15 years of hands-on experience says, "When it comes to benefits administration, third-party providers are the answer to a SMB's healthcare prayer" (O'Donnell 2020). (see Table 9.1.)

How to Automate Your Health Benefits Administration

So how do you automate something as important as benefits? It turns out, it's not too tough. Let's go over nine steps that will make benefits administration easy and automated in your business.

Choose an All-in-One HR Platform that Includes Benefits Administration

We'll assume you're using an all-in-one HR platform where information syncs automatically between your payroll, HR, and benefits systems. Make sure to choose an HR platform that *includes* benefits administration as a native (non-third-party) feature.

Beyond real-time data uniformity, you'll also want to configure your HR software to automatically trigger workflows based on certain events. For instance, while a new hire is completing their onboarding paperwork, tell your HR system to automatically trigger the benefits enrollment process once the core onboarding is complete—in the same app and workflow. Your employees will see one continuous process, and will appreciate when they don't have to *re-enter* personal information (such as legal name, address, SSN, etc.) because your HR system automatically pulled that info in from their recently completed onboarding process.

The same is true if existing employees *make changes* to their personal data. Imagine you have a tenured employee who gets married, or goes through another Qualifying Life Event (QLE). Your benefits system can immediately recognize that event and trigger a new open enrollment period for that employee. Remember when QLEs meant weeks of back and forth communications between your carrier, you, and your employee? Yeah, well you can forget that now.

When data flows seamlessly between your HR applications day-to-day benefits management, changes to deductions and annual renewals are all handled by your automated HR system.

Shop and Select the Right Benefits

Small businesses recognize the need to offer benefits to remain competitive in the war for talent, but the majority continues to struggle with affordability and the complexities of curating and managing a benefits strategy. Using a digital insurance marketplace (e.g. Zenefits), you can shop and compare plans and carriers without having to engage a broker or carrier. You can assess plan coverage, estimate total cost, and present information to leadership all before engaging another company. This empowers HR leaders to take plan costs into their own hands, eliminating gatekeepers of information, and making health coverage more affordable for small businesses.

Digitize Your Carrier and Plan Information

Third-party benefits administration technology provides digital displays of carrier information and plans. After shopping rates and getting quotes from different providers, you can choose and enable the plans you want by selecting them in your HR system. This provides a digital "menu" of sorts for employees to view and compare plan options to learn more about them. Digitizing plan options allows your employees to view their plans on their own time, from their personal devices, helping them make the right plan decisions for themselves and their families. No more emails, spreadsheets, PDFs, or printouts!

You can also preconfigure rules for situations like employees not selecting or defining coverage. This is called *plan mapping*, which helps ensure your company is staying within compliance and streamlines the entire enrollment process.

Manage Employee Eligibility with a Tap

With all of your employee data preloaded from your digital onboarding flow, you'll find it easy to manage employee eligibility for each line of coverage (medical, dental, vision, life, and so on). You can simply tap employee eligibility settings on the employee dashboard to toggle them on or off.

Set Up Company Contributions

Make employer contributions easy. Set up your chosen employer contribution rates for each line of coverage in your HR system of record and it will automatically calculate for each participating employee in each pay period. Flexible options should allow you to contribute specific percentages or flat amounts to the primary insurance holders, as well as dependents.

Automate Your Open Enrollment (OE) Workflow

Open Enrollment has typically been one of the least fun aspects of HR. It's a lot of coordinating and there are a lot of stakeholders. It always seems to end up with more than a few people being frustrated and confused. Not anymore. With an automated OE workflow, employees will be led through an enjoyable employee experience, led by your people platform. They will receive an automated email signaling the start of their OE period, and then can manage their enrollment at their own pace using their smartphone or personal computer. Your system will monitor the enrollment process and automatically send nudges to employees who need to take certain actions.

To configure this level of automation, first tell your people platform when your OE period starts and ends. This gives your computer the understanding of when your annual rates start and expire. You'll want to review employee eligibility in your employee dashboard to ensure that only employees who have benefits privileges receive the automated OE flow.

As soon as your annual health insurance renewal period begins, your people platform will automatically send an email signaling the start of the OE period. This email should include information on how employees can self-direct to the benefits application within your HR system to complete the process as well as any information regarding changes to plans, carriers, rates, or benefits options. Once an employee clicks into their benefits application, they will find easy-to-understand digital displays of carriers and plan information. Unlike in-person processes or paper forms, digital enrollment provides intuitive information architecture that allows employees to answer questions before they come to you. For instance, employees can click question mark icons to learn about certain key terms or click on hyperlinks for more information. Admins can track your group's enrollment progress easily with dashboard analytics, but generally have limited involvement once the automation process is set up.

And for employees, the automated OE process is clearer and more intuitive (see Figure 9.1). It takes as few as three minutes.

COMPARE MEDICAL PLANS

	EverydayHealth 2 . . . ⊗	Silver Portfolio 30 . . .
Carrier Name Plan Name Cost Per Month	**$56.25**	**$31.25**
FIND A DOCTOR	Search	Search
BENEFITS SUMMARY (SBC)	View SBC	View SBC
PLAN INFO		
Deductible ⑦	$2,500	$3,000
Copay ⑦	$50	20% ⑦
Plan Network ⑦	Contact carrier	Contact carrier
Specialist copay ⑦	$90	20% ⑦
Coinsurance ⑦	20%	20% ⑦
Out of Network Coinsurance ⑦	50%	50% ⑦
Emergency Service ⑦	20%	20% ⑦
Out of Pocket Maximum ⑦	$7,000	$5,000
Does OOP Max include Deduc . . .	No	No
Employer Account Contribution	-	$100 (into HSA)
PRESCRIPTION INFO		
Pharmacy Deductible ⑦	$250	See SBC ⑦
Supply Days ⑦	See SBC ⑦	See SBC ⑦
Tier 1 Drug Cost ⑦	$35	20% ⑦
Tier 2 Drug Cost ⑦	$90	20% ⑦
Tier 3 Drug Cost ⑦	$180	20% ⑦
	Select This Plan	Select This Plan

FIGURE 9.1 With benefit plans fully digital, employees can review, select, and compare plans before enrolling in one. Enriched data fields allow users to self-service answers to questions or learn more.

Source: Zenefits, 2021.

Easily Pull Reports

Query your HR system for required federal reports or to learn more about your workforce with a few clicks. For instance, you can gain complete access to enrollment completion reports, enrollment selection reports, cost breakdowns, and census information. This data can inform your annual renewal in the upcoming year and help you make smarter decisions around your benefits portfolio and what you'll be offering to your employees, as well as inform cost quotes curated by your broker.

Complete Carrier Enrollment All Digitally

Avoid managing multiple tech systems. In addition to seamless data integration for your workforce data, your HR system of record provides the capability to complete carrier enrollments. Automation with carriers around benefits enrollment means less burden for you, and greater alignment to ensure your employees have active coverage on your benefits effective date.

Automatically File Federal Forms

A people platform can analyze the entire contents of its *data lake,* or storage repository that holds a vast amount of raw data in its native format, to assess which compliance regulations your company is responsible for. The system not only automatically completes the forms for you, but it will also file them on your behalf. This lets you rest assured that you're on top of federal regulations. Forms 1094-B/C and 1095-B/C are great examples of this. Forms 1094-B/C and 1095-B/C are benefit report forms required by applicable large employers (ALEs) by the ACA. Essentially, if you have more than 50 full-time employees (100 in California, Colorado, Vermont, and New York) you must provide health insurance options for your workers, and prove that you did with Forms 1094-C and 1095-C. In a manual process, you'd be responsible for gathering all that necessary information and filing on time. In a POPS world, HR tech does it all for you.

What to Look for in Benefits Administration Technology

Complete the aforementioned steps, and your benefits administration will be a breeze. New hires will automatically enroll in benefits and self-serve the open enrollment process each year. Admins can manage enrollments, benefits shopping, plan choices, and defining key dates for benefits renewals. In the best-case scenario, this can all happen with a few taps of a screen, on any device.

To help ensure you get what you need in HR benefits automation software, here are a few good questions you should take with you when you're vetting a software subscription:

- Does the benefits system integrate natively with the HR system of record in a single workflow and app?
- Can employees make their OE selections from their mobile phones?
- Do changes in benefits selections automatically deduct from payroll?
- Can you use your own insurance broker?

Way to Go—You Just Finished Step 4!

Benefits administration is complicated and finicky. The healthcare system at large is complicated and finicky. Small businesses need ways to fast track their benefits systems so they can get back to the work they care about. Luckily, third-party benefits software provides exactly that. From automating paper forms with employee data, running automatic deductions from payroll, and keeping on top of day-to-day changes in the workforce we really can't see a better option for small companies.

Tie It All Together: Create and Upload Your Digital Employee Handbook!

If you've completed all the automation steps outlined in Part II of the book, congratulations, you've just moved your business, your role, and the impact for your people to level 3 on the People Operations Maturity Model (see Chapter 4). This means you're accelerating beyond the HR chaos and reactive modes that significantly slow down, disable, and suck the fun from many businesses without a scalable foundation in place to operate.

We're as excited as you are to dig into what's next in Part III, where you get to consider some amazing strategies to engage your people and measure how that impacts their careers and your business. But before you go, a great way to put a bow on the key processes you've automated and likely revised is to capture it all in your Employee Handbook along with your core company mission, values, and unique policies and procedures.

To use our interactive employee handbook builder tool, visit www.zenefits.com/pops-extras

If you have to create an employee handbook, we've got you covered too.

Just like the immense savings of tracking and storing job offers, additional hiring documents, benefits selections, and pay deductions all in one place, digitizing your employee handbook in a central documents file right in your system allows for seamless version control and acknowledgement management. Push a link to employees when they join or whenever you update your handbook, add a digital signature acknowledgement form at the end, and voilà! The system tracks all signatures, and can send automated nudges to anyone missing an acknowledgement signature until you have 100 percent acceptance.

If there are two words we hope you'll take away from Part II and what you've learned about building an automated foundation for your people operations, it's these: easy peasy.

Now let's get into the truly transformational stuff in Part III.

The Old HR Way: Benefits administration was a paperwork process that was often time consuming and confusing for employees and admins.

The POPS Way: Benefits administration is digital and automatically syncs with employee records. Employees can compare plans digitally and enroll in benefits on their smart devices.

Build an Incredible Employee Experience

CHAPTER 10

The Bones of a Successful People Operation

In today's world, *time* is the holy grail of resources. Everyone's searching for it, but no one can seem to find enough of it. We're busy, busy, busy. Busy doing our jobs, busy picking up the kids, busy managing our social media accounts. It's rarefied air when you even have one hour of one weekend to yourself. Luckily, by automating the bulk of HR administration to technology, through the tips in Part II, you've actually earned a huge pile of this elusive substance (at least in your professional life): Time! With HR administration fully automated, you're no longer bogged down by an unending pile of administrative crap. You're no longer tethered to drudgery. And you finally have the mind space to actually do the work you believed HR was all about: managing and operationalizing the development of your people.

This, my friend, marks one of the most monumental shifts in HR in a long time. It's a shift from *paper*work to *people*work.

People work. What is it exactly? In a nutshell, it's the work that seeks to empower people to do their best work. It aims to discover what authentically motivates people both professionally and personally to drive success. It explores how team dynamics foster individual successes. And it learns where business processes can be enhanced or tweaked to guarantee that human capital is the most powerful asset in a company. This is what it's all about.

The shift from paperwork to people work is such a tectonic plate adjustment to HR, that it justifies a new category of HR language. We would rather not call people work HR because it's not the policy police or the glorified office manager that people in your company thought HR was. Plus, why would we want to carry forth such tarnished reputations? We must call it what it is: people operations (POPS). Again, people operations is the department that operationalizes human-centered business design and carries out its execution.

In progressive companies, POPS has emerged as one of the most critical and strategic functions through creating work environments where people thrive, using data to inform key human-resourcing decisions, and is becoming a proactive (maybe even predictive) voice in the business process. Just as the CFO manages financial capital assets to maximize the impact of monetary investments, the chief people officer (CPO) manages *human capital assets* to maximize the impact of the people investments. Want your money to do something for you? Talk to the CFO. Want your people to do something for you? Talk to the CPO.

We know not every business is in the same place of transitioning from HR to people ops. And many may not see the value of doing so. But consider this. Companies that adopt a human-centered approach to business see a 32 percent lift in revenue, deliver outcomes to their market 2x faster, and outperform the S&P by 211 percent (IBM n.d.). If you *are* ready to make the transition to POPS, we're ready to help you get there.

Part III of this book is your practical guide to making the shift from running a traditional HR function, to building an employee-centric business with a people ops methodology. We go over how to sell POPS to leadership, how to ensure it drives key objectives forward, and how it actually plays out in the day-to-day. By the end of Part III, you'll have a list of strategic areas to focus on in support of a people operations shift, including compensation strategy, communication plans, performance alignment frameworks, and employee engagement. We'll also touch on some of the softer aspects of people management, such as how to drive and change company culture, how to embody a workforce that supports diverse and inclusive thinking, and how to make remote work, work for your business.

Oh, and one more thing. An important theme to people operations that we feel must be called out is *data*. As people teams shift to digital tools, they must simultaneously step up the challenge of becoming more data-savvy. They must be familiar with how HR data systems work and become proficient at using data to drive decisions. This is not dissimilar to what has happened in other areas of business over the last few decades. Quality control teams, for example, enabled with sophisticated Enterprise Resource Planning (ERP) software, had to learn how to predict quality assurance issues before they happened using data-enabled warnings. Or sales teams, enabled by Customer Relationship Management (CRM) software, had to learn how to predict closed/won revenue with remarkable accuracy. And customer success teams, too, had to learn how to model churn based on Employee Net Promoter Score (eNPS). Each of these areas underwent a major technological transformation in their specific lines of work, and each was forced to adopt an incredible rise in data sophistication in their roles. This will be the same for people ops practitioners. They'll need to advance their data skills to keep up with the changing times, particularly as more HR and employee data goes digital. We'll get into more specifics regarding how people teams can use data throughout Part III, but things such as being able to see which business decisions are making the biggest impact on employee well-being through data, or being able to A/B test various programs within the company (Chapter 12) to ascertain which tactics result in which outcomes will all become more important factors in the future.

But before we get too far into the specifics of what the future could look like, let's get back to today, and how *your business* can make the switch to people operations.

Aligning to Business Goals

The most important thing you need to keep in mind as you transition into a more people-centered business is aligning to bigger business initiatives. This is critical for two reasons.

First, it will be easier for you to get internal buy-in for a people operations initiative when it's taken seriously. Human resources hasn't always been seen as the most mission-critical function of the business. But you have the power to change that misconception. When you cement your departmental goals as closely to core business objectives as possible, you'll be able to prove your value much easier.

The second reason why aligning to bigger business objectives is key, is because your company needs to stay in business. People operations goals will only be as strong as your business is solvent. If the company starts losing money or gets in a tough spot, you could be out of a job, and so could your team. The more successful your company becomes, on the other hand, the more opportunities you'll have to demonstrate how people operations is inextricable to business success.

Set Goals That Display Impact

The best way for people ops to demonstrate support to the business is to set appropriate and *cascading goals*. Cascading goals work like concentric circles, or Russian dolls, where goals are purposefully linked to achieve something bigger. In other words, the work of the individual matters to the success of the team, which matters to the success of the department, which matters to ensure the success of the business. Or backward, the business can't achieve its mission without the department, which in turn can't achieve its goals without the team, and so on.

If HR is seen as a strategic function, you may have the direct opportunity to get in a room with your CEO, CFO, and other key stakeholders to stitch your goals directly into biggest priorities for the year or next couple of years. But if you're like most HR professionals, where HR is seen more as an administrative function that occasionally helps managers with workplace issues, you'll need to build credibility with the C-Suite first. Prepare to roll up your sleeves here. Meet with employees and managers in various departments around the company. Ask them about their key priorities. Learn how their functions work, and how they fit into the bigger picture of the business. You may even want to shadow key roles to get a deep awareness about how things work.

Once you understand the business direction (however you achieve that), then look to build objective, measurable goals that demonstrate how people operations supports each goal.

A simple three-column list is a great way to organize your thinking (see Table 10.1). First, list business goals (or departmental goals if you don't have C-level access). Then, work to develop how your POPS team will support them. Add key metrics that will be tracked for each goal (more on how to set really good goals in Chapter 14).

Here's an example. Let's imagine you have access to C-level goals as an example. Say your company is trying to grow its revenue base by 10 percent per year. Your POPS goal could be to reduce sales time to productivity by 15 percent per year. Or, if your company wants to increase quarterly profitability by 5 percent, your POPS goal could be to increase quarterly employee engagement scores by 10 percent.

Vet each goal for practicality, clarity, and alignment. Ask yourself:

1. Are my goals "SMART" (Specific, Measurable, Achievable, Relevant, Timely)?
2. Are the correlations between the business's goals and our departmental goals clear and obvious?

These quick screening questions ensure good goal setting and measurable metrics. When goals are met, you'll have demonstrable data that inextricably links the work of POPS to business achievements.

Keep in mind, goals can't be set once and done. You'll need to revisit your goals in lockstep with the company cadence. Does your company set goals annually? Monthly? Quarterly? Develop a departmental process

TABLE 10.1 A simple three-column list to align people operation goals to larger business objectives and establishing metrics to measuring success.

Business Goals	POPS Goals	Metric
Grow revenue base by 10 percent this year.	Reduce sales time to productivity by 15 percent this year	Time to hire (last FY vs. current FY)
Increase quarterly profitability by 15 percent	Increase quarterly employee engagement scores by 10 percent across the company	Employee Net Promoter Scores (eNPSs) (last FY vs. current FY)

Source: Zenefits, 2021.

that reflects this business rhythm. Frequency isn't the important factor. What's key is the direct alignment between company goal setting and the POPS function.

Communicate Goals with Stakeholders

With goals in hand, regroup with your business leaders and share your vision.

Detail each goal you've outlined, how you'll measure it, and the impact you predict each initiative will have on the company. It's not enough to simply state the goal. You'll need to explain how and why you believe each goal will move the needle. Use data here. The more objective, data-oriented you are, the easier breaking the shackles of HR stereotypes will be. You're not the soft HR department. You're the data-oriented people operations team and you're aiming to convince your team of the importance and impact of peoplework. Make the distinction clear. For example, using the example from Table 10.1, you could detail how employee engagement leads to better profitability by calculating the delta of expected revenue from an engaged vs. unengaged worker. Or you could quantify the amount of time saved through faster recruitment. Do this for each goal.

We recognize not every business or stakeholder will immediately grasp associations between human-centered work and the business's bottom line. Less than half of people trust HR (Sullivan 2018). The shift from HR to people ops will be a process. But the time you spend educating, the time you spend quantifying, will be worth it. Greater education will lead to greater buy-in of your vision. Learning the business inside and out, developing appropriate goals, educating key stakeholders on the value of POPS, and developing personal credibility within the business, will all greatly aid in positioning POPS as a leadership function.

Check In!

Let's take a moment to assess how well you're positioned to introduce people operations into your company:

- Do you have a clear understanding of your company goals?
- Do your departmental goals align to, and help deliver on these company goals?
- Are your goals realistic and measurable?
- Do you have a process to track and measure your goals?
- Have you articulated how your POPS goals help advance the business on its core objectives?
- Can you think about how every program you're developing impacts employee satisfaction and productivity?

Focus on Productivity

In addition to affixing your department to solid goals, you'll want to focus on strategic outcomes. Most business leaders own a number. A number represents a certain aspect of the business where the results can be measured. Sales leaders own the sales number. Security leaders own the number of breaches. Your number is productivity. Productivity is a measurable outcome, not a strategy. It's "what" you are ultimately trying to achieve. "How" you're going to do it refers more to the strategies and execution of your role. It's similar to how diet and exercise affect your health. Diet and exercise are ways (strategies) that you hope to increase your health (outcome). The same is true in people ops. Your POPS initiatives—be it communication plans, compensation philosophies, etc.—are ways (strategies) that affect your productivity (outcome).

While things like "employee engagement" are hot buzzwords in human resource management right now, we caution that employee engagement is not the ultimate goal of POPS, and should not be the ultimate metric that you track. The ultimate goal is productivity. If you get too carried away with optimizing for employee engagement (or any other POPS *strategy*) you risk tracking a metric that doesn't impact the business. For example, it's not enough to have a highly engaged workforce because a highly engaged workforce might be working on the wrong projects. Working on the wrong projects won't lead to business results. You need to have both an engaged worker (strategy), and good goal setting (strategy) to drive productivity at large (outcome).

Tracking productivity, on the other hand, necessarily keeps the business objectives in mind and is thus more powerful. Specific productivity metrics will vary from industry to industry, but the fundamentals are then same. Productivity metrics should be defined up front, consistent, and is easy to track.

Table 10.2 shows a few examples of productivity metrics that could work for different industries.

Tracking a single productivity metric is the easiest way to keep a pulse on the overall health of your company at a glance, too. When productivity scores slip, you'll know something is up. Maybe there is a team that's overworked and they are making mistakes. Or maybe there's a manager who's not equipped at running her team, leaving several employees with little work or purpose. As a POPS leader it's your job to monitor company-wide performance and suggest improvements to ensure each person and team is doing its best.

The trick is, you can't get good productivity if you're considered a crappy place to work. In the words of Jim Collins, author of *From Good to Great*, ". . . if you have the wrong people, it doesn't matter whether you discover the right direction; you still won't have a great company. Great vision without great people is irrelevant" (Collins n.d.).

So, once you've automated HR and established clear goals, your next step is creating a work design that truly motivates people to want to achieve. This is where you can start getting strategic, introducing activities that will result in productivity.

TABLE 10.2 Examples of productivity indicators for select industries.

Industry	High-level productivity indicator
Services	■ Number of positive vs. negative customer calls ■ Ratio of support tickets created and resolved ■ Employee retention
Healthcare	■ Number of cases handled in a month ■ Employee Net Promoter Score (eNPS)
Tech	■ Sales conversion ■ Customer churn ■ Employee retention
Education	■ Graduation rates ■ Test scores
Finance	■ Assets Under Management (AUM) ■ Number of errors ■ Portfolio growth (by number of customers or dollar value)

Source: Zenefits, 2021.

You may find it useful to first get a quick snapshot of where your business is *today*, setting benchmarks for questions like:

- Are my workers engaged? To what degree, exactly?
- Are they incentivized to do the right work?
- Is the business creating opportunities that develop our top performers to do more for the business?
- What is our turnover rate? Is that good or bad?
- Would ex-employees recommend our company as a place to work?

Then you can start thinking about how to drive/create/design an improved workplace:

- *How* will we motivate our staff?
- *How* will we incentivize our top performers?
- *How* will we keep people interested in their work and provide career opportunities for them to develop?
- *How* will we treat our employees?

These last "how" questions set the stage for creating employee engagement strategies, compensation strategies, employee development strategies, and more. These are the employee experience designs that will truly unleash your workforce. Just as you'll be healthy if you exercise and eat healthy food, your business will be productive when your workers feel engaged, incentivized, and treated like adults.

Now that we've gone over the bones of a successful people operation —namely aligning to key business objectives and focusing on employee productivity as an outcome—the next three chapters take a deep dive into how to build a great employee experience, which is foundational to unleashing your workforce. We realize each business is different, and some sections may not apply to your organization. That's okay. You're welcome to read these chapters in order, or flip to specific sections you want to learn more about.

The Old HR Way: HR was seen as policing and administrative. Day-to-day tasks were stuck in managing paperwork, leaving little to no time to invest in developing people as a strategic asset.

The POPS Way: Position POPS as a core strategic function of the business and is committed to being a people-centric company where the well-being of employees is understood to impact the success of the business. People ops leaders drive SMART goals that help the business achieve its objectives.

CHAPTER 11

Employee Motivation

Let me ask you this: what motivates you? I mean, what *really* motivates you? Not just what gets you up out of bed, but what makes you feel alive, bigger than yourself, ready to dive into something regardless of how hard it is because you believe in it? Do you know?

True motivation is the basis for all sorts of crazy achievements. It's how babies learn to walk, how Elon Musk managed to land rockets back on Earth, and how businesses go from good to great. When we feel motivated to do something, obstacles seem to diminish and dream-busting realists stand down. But often it's hard to articulate what motivates us. For instance, can you really tell me what motivates you . . . right now? It's even harder to articulate what motivates others.

But in people ops, understanding what motivates our workforce is our raison d'être. The extent to which we can extricate true motivators and adjust our places of business to nurture such motivations can be the difference between a company that gets by and a company that defines the next era.

That's because when a company brings together a group of people who are authentically motivated, amazing things happen. Synergies happen. When you're motivated, an eruption of potential that you didn't think humanly possible within you, happens. It's the snapshot in time people look back to in their careers where they say, "Wow, that was an amazing, once-in-a-lifetime team and company to work for." And if you've had the good fortune of working with such a team, you know exactly what we mean. You were motivated and it felt so good.

Motivation has a lot of definitions, but we prefer a simple, broad one: the general desire or willingness of someone to do something. *Employee motivation,* then, is the level of energy, commitment, and creativity that an employee brings to their job every day (Shahzadi et al. 2014).

When an employee feels motivated, their work magnifies business impact, significantly improving productivity and profits. They're found to be 43 percent more productive (Murlis and Schubert 2001), and drive 21 percent more profit to their employers (Smarp 2019).

When an employee feels unmotivated, the exact opposite happens. They cost the business money. A lack of motivation among workers leads to $300 billion lost each year, according to analysts, due to downtime, mistakes, and extra management (Gaille 2017).

But let's contextualize this a bit. What fiscal and behavioral impacts can you expect on your actual business from motivated or unmotivated workers? How can you formalize a focus on motivation within your organization? And how does that work to maximize productivity and drive business objectives?

Breaking Down the Fiscal Impact of Motivation

Ultimately, motivation's presence (or absence) leaves you with one of two types of employees. There's the *motivated employee*, the 20 percent of people often credited with doing 80 percent of the work. There's the *unmotivated employee,* the 20 percent of people who only show up to work because they're obligated to do so, achieving very little. And then there's everyone else in between.

The unmotivated group arrives at work and sulks at their desks, taking extra long lunch breaks, and gossiping with their peers. It's the people who drive to work each day simply because they did it the day before, and if you ever asked them, "What sparks your daily enthusiasm for your job?", they'd balk.

But that first group of individuals—the motivated people—would answer that same question with, "I love my job. I'm able to work independently/heal people/work with my hands/create innovative products"/or whatever, it doesn't matter! What matters is that these people arrive at the job feeling as though they've arrived at the temple of their purpose. At the place that nurtures their potential. And they arrive with gusto. They're grateful for the opportunity to be involved in something bigger, something that they feel illuminates them as people.

Ultimately, you want to create a workplace that cultivates these types of workers—the engaged, happy ones—because they will make a greater impact in everything they do. While some of this has to do with the skills and attitude of the employee, the employer has a huge responsibility here too. To create a workforce that has above-average rates of engaged workers requires employers to make strong hiring decisions, retain top talent, and pivot motivators to galvanize bottom or average performers. If you can bump the number of engaged employees up by even 10 percent, you won't be disappointed in the results, and neither will your P&L.

Speaking of P&L, let's take a look at the fiscal implications of motivation with a hypothetical example.

Employee A and Employee B have the same role and are paid the same base salary: $50,000 annually (or $4,166 monthly, pretax). Both employees have a monthly sales quota of $15,000 of new sales per month.

Employee A believes in the product she is selling, agrees with the vision of the company, and appreciates the flexibility the job affords her. She feels like she's truly making a positive impact on the world by selling your product, and tells her customers as much. You can count on Employee A meeting her $15,000 of quota each month. Not only does she more than cover her labor costs, but customers she signs on are a great fit and report having an enjoyable sales experience. The deals she inks have a low likelihood to churn.

Employee B, on the other hand, doubts the product promise, and therefore doubts the success trajectory of the entire business. In between sales calls, he's mapping his next career move and often responding to personal emails while on the clock instead of getting on the phones. A lack of initiative is leading to a weaker pipeline, and you're finding he's rushing sales calls at the end of the month; discounting heavily. Still, Employee B is only averaging a third of his sales quota—$5,000 monthly. Although that covers his base labor costs, it's putting the company in a bad position. What's more, Employee B is likely to pursue the next job offer he's given, and it's unlikely he'll give your brand a good review on Glassdoor, or other review sites, if he does.

With two productive workers you would expect quotas being met each month:

Expected Revenue:

$$\$15,000\,(\text{quota}) \times 12\,(\text{months}) \times 2\,(\text{people}) = \$360,000$$

Expected Profit (Revenue – Expenses):

$$\$360,000 - \$50,000 \times 2\,(\text{people}) = \$260,000$$

But with only one motivated employee (A) and one unmotivated employee (B) you're looking at this instead:

Actual Revenue:

$$(\$15,000 \times 12) + (\$5,000 \times 12) = \$240,000$$

Actual Profit (Revenue – Expenses):

$$\$240,000 - \$50,000 \times 2\,(\text{people}) = \$140,000$$

You're looking at a delta of $120,000.

If Employee B quits, you're also facing the additional costs of backfilling his role.

COST ASSUMPTIONS OF BACKFILLING

How let's look at the cost assumptions of losing workers.

- Average cost per hire: $4,129 (SHRM 2017)
- Average time it takes to fill a given position: 42 days (SHRM 2017)
- Average length of time to fully onboard and ramp a new hire: 30–100 days (this based on common HR knowledge, but can vary depending on role)

For this example, we'll say your company is better than average, but not great, at getting new employees up to speed. You're able to hire in 30 days and onboard in 60. That's three months of down time if you need to backfill. It's also three months of revenue opportunity being down a rep. Plus, you've sunk dozens of hours from your people team and hiring managers into your new hire.

The good news is that you can hire a new person who might have greater desire to achieve. But that's always a risk. If you can't motivate Employee B, what's the chances you'll keep your new hire motivated and performing? In the chart below, we assume you've made a good new hire who contributes quota each month but takes some time to ramp.

This gets complicated, so let's use Table 11.1 to illustrate it.

Annualized, even having an unmotivated worker for three months, your business lost 35.6 percent of its expected earnings or, in this case, $94,129.

This is where people operations must step in and ask hard questions in order to learn more about motivation. You've got money on the line.

Was there an opportunity to remotivate Employee B to help him feel more connected to his work and drive greater sales?

- Could he have served on a product committee where he could help steer the direction of the products?
- Was sales the right job for his skill set, or would he have been better served in a different role?
- Was his manager aware of his lack of engagement?
- What would have changed Employee B's mind about your product?

TABLE 11.1 The cost of losing an unengaged worker assuming a backfill in "month 5" and standard onboarding speeds of new hires. Using hypothetical numbers for salary and labor costs, this example shows that the company lost 35.63 percent of expected profit.

Cost of losing an unengaged worker (assuming a strong new hire)		Employee A	Employee B	New Hire
Month 1	Monthly Salary	$4,167	$4,167	
	Sales	$15,000	$5,000	
Month 2	Monthly Salary	$4,167	$4,167	
	Sales	$15,000	$5,000	
Month 3	Monthly Salary	$4,167	$4,167	
	Sales	$15,000	$5,000	
Month 4	Monthly Salary	$4,167		
	Sales	$15,000		
Month 5	Monthly Salary	$4,167		$4,167
	Sales	$15,000		$0
Month 6	Monthly Salary	$4,167		$4,167
	Sales	$15,000		$0
Month 7	Monthly Salary	$4,167		$4,167
	Sales	$15,000		$5,000
Month 8	Monthly Salary	$4,167		$4,167
	Sales	$15,000		$10,000
Month 9	Monthly Salary	$4,167		$4,167
	Sales	$15,000		$15,000
Month 10	Monthly Salary	$4,167		$4,167
	Sales	$15,000		$15,000
Month 11	Monthly Salary	$4,167		$4,167
	Sales	$15,000		$15,000
Month 12	Monthly Salary	$4,167		$4,167
	Sales	$15,000		$15,000

Totals

Expected Revenue	$360,000.00
Actual Revenue	$270,000.00
Labor Costs	$95,833.33
New Hire Costs	$4,129.00
Expected Profit	$264,167
Actual Profit	$170,038
Delta	$94,129
% of Expected Profit Lost	35.63%

Source: Zenefits, 2021.

You'll note these types of questions aren't rooted in classic performance improvement plans, or PIPs. They aren't geared toward documenting misperformance to avoid potential employment lawsuits. They're rooted in key questions that help identify *why there's a lack of motivation* to address problems before they lead to bigger issues or costly termination. This is a key difference between a traditional approach to HR and a POPS approach. Classic HR tactics would be quick to document misperformance, including correctional paths to help fend off any litigation in the case of employee termination. A POPS approach is more inquisitive in nature. It leans into tough situations to learn about human behavior, using each employee's experience as a means to become a smarter, more effective company. If Employee B chooses to quit, a POPS approach would seek to understand where the business failed to motivate the worker, how (and to what extent) they could do better, and would take these learnings to inform future decisions.

Figuring out people's independent motivators and how to build a company culture around them is going to be some of the hardest work you do—but probably the most impactful. Each person is different, and very few people are motivated in the same ways. There are generational gaps, preferential gaps, life situation differences, mental and physical health differences. Again, this is *people* work. It's dynamic, varied, and full of baggage. Just like we all are. But it's important to be aware of your workforce's motivators, because it drives everything we do.

Luckily, work system researchers have developed a few employee motivation "models" that can serve as frameworks.

Employee Motivation Models

There *isn't* a one-size-fits-all approach to motivating people. Activating motivation involves an active (and nonprescriptive) combination of clear communications, expectation setting, understanding people's value systems, and appealing to people's emotions. But looking at select research can help you narrow your focus about how to achieve greater motivation across your company. Let's review a few of our favorites.

Doshi and McGregor: Play, Purpose, Potential

Neel Doshi and Lindsay McGregor (2015), a team of social and behavioral scientists who study and design high-performance work cultures, suggest there are three factors that lead to higher employee performance (play, purpose, and potential) and three factors that lead to lower performance (emotional pressure, economic pressure, inertia). Together, the three high performance factors make up "motivation." (see Table 11.2)

TABLE 11.2 Chart of Doshi and McGregor's Model of Motivation.

Doshi and McGregor's Model of Motivation	
High performance reasons to work	**Low performance reasons to work**
Play	Emotional pressure
Purpose	Economic pressure
Potential	Inertia

Source: Neel Doshi and Lindsay McGregor, *Primed to Perform: How to Build the Highest Performing Cultures through the Science of Total Motivation* (New York: HarperCollins, 2015).

According to Doshi and McGregor, an employee will feel motivated if their work contributes to something bigger (purpose), or is in some way fun or exciting (play), or if it's serving a larger purpose such as their education or experience (potential).

On the other hand, if people feel like they *have* to work to pay bills (economic pressure), or that they have to work to appease parents or spouses (emotional pressure), or that they're working just because that's what they've always done (inertia), there's a high chance they'll be unmotivated.

How this would look at your company? In a Doshi and McGregor model of motivation, POPS leaders would build work systems that felt fun and reiterated the greater purpose of the business's vision to society. POPS leaders would make sure each job role is clearly connected to the larger vision of the company, perhaps through cascading goals.

Pink: Autonomy, Mastery, Purpose

Daniel Pink, author of six books about business and human behavior, offers another perspective on how motivation works. According to Pink (2011), feelings of autonomy, mastery, and purpose are key (see Table 11.3). Things like being able to do work in your own way (autonomy), having avenues to deepen individual skill sets (mastery), and understanding how your work impacts a larger goal (purpose) are central to unleashing motivation.

TABLE 11.3 Daniel Pink's explanation of how autonomy, mastery, and purpose relate to motivation.

Daniel Pink's Model of Motivation
Autonomy—the desire to be self-directed
Mastery—the desire to continuously improve
Purpose—the desire to make an impact toward the company's overall mission

How this would look at your company: In a Pink model, POPS leaders would create a workplace that focused on building trust between managers and employees and setting high standards of achievement. Trust could be developed by establishing flexible work policies or committing to asynchronous work hours. This would allow individual contributors to build their own work situations (work from home, asynchronous work hours, etc.). High standards could include ambitious goal setting and support for continued education opportunities, like education reimbursements, continued education stipends, or mentorship.

Rynes, Gerhart, Minette: Money

Money is controversial when it comes to motivation. A large majority of modern research says pay isn't unconnected to real feelings of drive or purpose (Hasan 2014). But others say it's the single most important thing.

In a novel 2004 study, Sara Rynes, Barry Gerhart, and Kathleen Minette determined pay is the most universal employee motivator and that, in fact, most HR professionals undervalue its importance. The research suggests this is because people tend to downplay the importance of money when they self-report what motivates them. But when looking at meta-analyses of the data it becomes clear that money is one of—if not *the biggest*—employee motivators. Without money employees don't have a reason to show up to work. They quickly become disgruntled. And start looking for other employers to fit the bill(s).

Again, this is up for debate. Alfie Kohn (1999), another motivation researcher, would tell you money creates systems that are problematic in his book *Punished by Rewards*.

How this would look at your company: In a strictly money-based motivation model, leaders would focus on compensation, benefits, and fiscal incentives as your number-one concern. To drive motivation, they'd offer monetary merit-based rewards almost exclusively, including raises, bonuses, and performance incentives to continually drive motivation.

Building the Motivation Muscle in Your Company

You might agree with one of the motivation models presented earlier, or you may agree with another theory all together. Either way is fine. Your unique interpretation of employee motivation—and the way that plays out through your business culture—is a part of your unique brand identity. What's critical is that your model works for *your people,* the *talent you want to hire,* and *the business objectives* you're looking to achieve.

Now that we've reviewed the definition of motivation, illustrated the financial impact of its presence, and gone over some employee motivation philosophies, it's time to get practical. What are ways that you can turn motivation theory into action?

Again, there are many ways to answer this question. But if you're looking for a tried-and-true approach to bringing motivation into your place of work, try this easy four-step process: Ask, Analyze, Formalize, Revise. Let's learn a little more about each one.

Step 1: Ask

The first step is to ask questions. Ask people at your company what motivates them and what demotivates them. Ask Employee B why he was *unmotivated*, and Employee A why she *was*. Your curiosity doesn't need to be limited to internal teams. Get inquisitive about motivation at large. Are there other people managers at different companies who could share their experience about what makes *their* employees tick? Have they seen success using certain techniques? What about managers? Can they offer some insights?

Here are a few questions you could ask to get started . . .

Ask employees:

- Do you feel motivated in your work?
- What makes you feel motivated?
- What demotivates you?
- Are there things that would motivate you more?
- What do you notice about your co-workers? How are they motivated?
- What do you notice about your boss? How is he/she motivated?

Ask managers:

- What motivates your direct reports?
- Do you notice any similarities between motivators and types of employees?
- What motivational framework is working best for you?

Ask peers in people operations:

- What are some of your more successful ways to motivate your staff?
- What are some of the less successful ways you've tried to motivate your staff?
- Have you noticed any patterns in motivation among different generations/locations/demographics/teams?

Track answers to your questions (particularly from your internal teams) in a digital database that you can later query, analyze, and derive insights from. Start with basic information that you can consistently gather (see Table 11.4). This helps keep data clean and organized, so that you can easily query it for patterns or insights at any time (see Step 2: Analyze).

Invoking your inner curiosity, and committing to continually learning about motivation will enhance your connection with employees and improve productivity.

Step 2: Analyze

Your next step is analyzing the responses for actionable insights that work across the company. You're not trying to build Enrique's experience, Wendy's experience, and Luka's experience. You're looking to build *an* employee experience that works for Enrique, Wendy, and Luka. Analyze your datasets for patterns that maximize motivation across your current workforce. Here are a few examples of ways to look at your data:

- Look for similar motivators between certain subgroups or workers (calculate the "mode" average)
  - Teams
  - Departments
  - Age groups/generations
  - Geographies
  - Employee type (managers, individual contributors)
- Look for similar motivation rates (on a numeric scale) between groups of teams (calculate the "mean" average)

Once you have data-informed analysis, synthesize your findings in the form of insights. Here are fictional examples of what your data could tell you:

- Most sales managers (67 percent) are motivated by money
- No Gen Zers (0 percent) want to work from an office
- All workers (100 percent) are motivated by autonomy
- A majority of people in the customer support team are *not* meeting their monthly goals (53 percent)

TABLE 11.4 An example of how POPS leaders can start to gather simple, consistent metrics around employee motivation.

Employee Name	Team/ Department	Location	Self-reported employee motivation	How motivated is the employee (1–5 scale, 1 being low)	Is the employee meeting his/her goals monthly? (yes, no)	What is the manager doing to motivate the team?
Shanice H.	Customer Service	Chicago	"Doing work that matters"	2	No	Allowing Shanice to work from home, building independent projects

Source: Zenefits, 2021.

Pro Tip

If you have high levels of data sophistication, you can use more advanced people analytics. For instance, you could use a regression analysis (a mathematical way of sorting out which variables among a set of variables has an impact on an outcome) to assess how independent variables impact one another, such as looking at the impact of job locations, certain managers, and certain management styles on productivity. Or you could use a Spearman Correlation Analysis, a specific test that assesses the strength of a relationship between two ordinal sets of data, to measure the relationship between responses to "How challenging do you find your job?" with turnover rates. You can use this on a seven-point Likert scale, ranging from "extremely challenging" to "not challenging at all." This would show you the extent to which challenging work was related to retention/turnover.

Step 3: Formalize

You've asked people about their motivators, analyzed your datasets, and derived insights. It's time to synthesize your insights into business processes that will stitch motivation into the day-to-day fabric of your business. There are three great ways to formalize motivation into your business:

1. **Build a *motivation matrix*.** A motivation matrix (see Table 11.5) is essentially a grid that documents the best motivators for groups of people. It's flexible enough to accommodate multiple motivational factors, but structured enough to provide guidance for internal conduct. This is best for companies with 30+ employees.
2. **Integrate motivators into core values.** Reflecting your workforces' motivators into your core values is a bottom-up approach to building your company foundation (see Table 11.6). For example, if your workforce values autonomy, and your leadership supports that, perhaps you develop the core value "act like an owner." Here are a few other examples of how to translate motivators into core values:
3. **Teach the teacher.** Although it's a people ops practitioner's job to identify and formalize motivation in the business, it's up to managers to execute it on the day-to-day. Share your motivation findings with managers in your company, and then work them one-on-one to define action plans that will establish connections between work and larger motivations.

TABLE 11.5 A motivation matrix can help POPS leaders personalize motivators using cross sections of the business. Be careful to not discriminate against any groups of people in your matrix.

Motivation Matrix

	Sales	Marketing	Service
Gen Z	Autonomy + Play	Autonomy + Play	Play + Potential
Millennials	Purpose + Potential	Purpose	Autonomy + Play
Boomers	Autonomy + Purpose	Mastery	Mastery

Source: Zenefits, 2021.

TABLE 11.6 Examples of how employee motivators can translate into core values of a company.

Employee Motivator	Company Core Value
Autonomy	Act like an owner
Mastery	Raise the bar
Helping solve social injustice	Treat everyone as they want to be treated
Doing good for the world	Do well by doing good

Source: Zenefits, 2021.

Step 4: Revise

No strategy in business is ever really "done." Review and revise your motivation frameworks any time you have new information. Set a regular cadence to re-evaluate employee motivators and business objectives. A fast moving company, or a business with high rates of turnover, may want to revisit quarterly. A slower more stable company might be fine with annual reviews. Most companies are probably in between, on a six-month cadence.

Try It Out!

Think about an employee at your business who seems closer to Employee B in terms of motivation. What can you do to motivate them better? What questions can you ask them to learn about motivation in general? Does this employee seem to be more in line with a Doshi and McGregor model, a Pink model, or a Rynes et al. model of motivation?

Motivation is hard to articulate and it's subject to change in people's lives. But increasing your general knowledge on the subject, using data-based research models to inform your process, and getting in the weeds with your employees and their specific motivators is likely the best you can do. And by the way, it's fundamental to driving authentic productivity and meeting business goals.

In the next chapter, we look at compensation strategy. Regardless of whether pay is a part of your motivation framework, it's the most basic requirement between an employee and employer, and it is still important to get right.

The Old HR Way: Didn't care to listen to employees' dreams, ambitions, drives, concerns, or motivations. It was limited in realizing employees' full potentials because the business established itself as the power.

The POPS Way: Believes understanding what makes people tick is one of the most powerful ways to get them to do something willingly. Allocates time to researching motivational theory, developing motivation frameworks for business processes, and encourages managers to continually connect with employees to extract changing needs to inform the business all up. By doing so, these organizations have greater employee engagement, greater innovation, are remembered as better places to work, with great leadership. These businesses, on average, are more profitable.

CHAPTER 12

Fair Pay

Compensation strategy is one of the biggest and most obvious functions of an employment contract. It's also one of the most strategic parts of people ops.

However, it's one of the trickiest and most important to get right, especially in smaller companies.

Why? Well first, smaller businesses don't often have the same cash troves that big businesses have. The big guys can buy recruiters and better ad positions in job listing forums, and they can afford better salary and benefit packages. And second, someone's pay ends up being an explicit value contract between the employee and employer, one that employees are reminded of each time they see their paycheck. Because smaller companies often offer smaller wages relative to big companies, they risk being seen as underpaying their staff. Underpaying employees risks making them feel underappreciated, which can be disastrous.

To compete with big firms, and to avoid underpaying employees, small companies must "think beyond the paycheck." This means getting more clever about what's included in a total compensation package. They must think about the obvious benefits like health benefits, flex benefits, and equity. But they must also come up with benefits of perks unique to their business that keeps their company competitive in talent pools. Coming up with perks that meet talent market needs is hard, even before formalizing the program. First you have to come up with the solution (can you offer a local bus pass or access to a certain network of people)? And then you must complete the necessary paperwork to formalize it. But even though it's tricky and causes disproportionately more work for smaller firms, getting pay right is key to happy employees.

In this chapter, we look at how to get compensation *right* so you can grow your business the way you want to. Specifically, we'll look at:

- The components of a strong compensation strategy
- How to establish equity and fairness

123

- How to develop incentive structures that truly motivate employees
- How to analyze pay data to drive insights

You'll see throughout the chapter that these core concepts all work hand in hand with the others to create a comprehensive approach that leads to a great employee experience.

The Three Components of a Strong Compensation Strategy

A strong compensation structure starts with defining answers to three key questions:

1. **What is our underlying compensation philosophy?** This explains your company's position on pay. It also provides a framework for competitive total compensation packages and equal pay for employees.
2. **What are we looking to achieve?** This helps determine which kind of skills you need to have on staff, and how to prioritize various hires. And it also helps inform incentive strategies to drive intended outcomes among current employees.
3. **What is our budget?** Your budget gives you a sense of how many people and what level of experience you can afford to hire. It also helps inform raises, promotions, and compensation adjustments among current employees.

Let's take a look at each question a bit more closely.

"What's Our Philosophy?"

A *compensation philosophy* is a formal statement that explains your moral position on pay, and provides a framework for pay consistency. It helps guide your principles about how you dole money out, and what pay stands for at your company.

Your pay philosophy will be unique to your company. But we strongly recommend adopting a Fair Pay philosophy.

Fair Pay believes one's pay should match their merits, tenure, and skill sets. It remains unbiased by age, gender, race, religion, or other protected categories and prior relationships and stays competitive with other similar roles in similar geographic areas.

In other words, it's paying people the appropriate rate for the work that they're doing and the experience they bring. Note: equitable pay isn't the same as equal pay. *Pay equality* means similar pay among different groups. That would be like paying an entry level worker the same as the CEO.

Pay equity means fairness of one's pay proportional to their job, taking into consideration any monetary disbursements: salary, incentives, bonuses, and so forth. That would be like paying a mechanic with 10 years of experience more than you'd pay a mechanic with six months of experience.

Studies show employees feel happiest in their roles when they are paid equitably.

If you underpay workers, on the other hand, you're liable to create bad consequences. People who feel underpaid are more likely to shirk work, sabotage situations, or quit (Akerlof and Yellen 1990). In fact, employees could lash out in direct proportion to how unfairly they feel their pay is in relation to their efforts. Things like stealing business supplies, bad-mouthing the business to colleagues, or leaving nasty reviews on public forums about your company would all feel fair game.

"In simple English, if people do not get what they think they deserve, they get angry," the researchers said (Akerlof and Yellen 1990).

Paying people fairly puts people at ease, minimizes peer-to-peer gossip, and ensures the business remains just when hiring and compensating teams. In short, it's structurally required for a good employee experience. When combined with leveraging appropriate motivation factors, you're looking at a simple decision matrix of what to expect from your workforce.

Employers must remember, employees will only be inspired to do their best work in an environment of both fair pay and motivational factors.

"What Are We Looking to Achieve?"

The next question in formalizing a compensation strategy is what are you looking to achieve? Again, this question helps you understand what kind of

Check In!

Is your company paying fairly? Ask yourself these questions:

- Where do your workers live?
- What is the cost of living in those locations?
- Are you working to eliminate unconscious bias?
- Are you working within your stated salary ranges?
- Do people with the same job in your company roughly make the same amount of money?

skills you need to have on staff, how to prioritize various hires, and which incentives to use to drive the outcomes you're looking for.

Business needs change frequently. A big part of your job is making sure you have the right people to do the work required to make the company successful. For example, if you were a travel mug company looking to design mug packaging, you'd need the help of a packaging designer early on. But after your packaging needs were met, perhaps you no longer needed that skill. Your job (in combination with working with managers) is to anticipate those needs, identify workforce gaps, and find the budget to ensure the business can achieve its desired results. This is easy if you have a very small team, but as your company grows this task becomes increasingly complex.

It may help to think about talent needs step by step as they relate to business goals:

Step 1: Write out each business goal. What are your core business objectives? Again, direct alignment to overarching business goals should be the first point of guiding all POPS decisions.

Step 2: Rank the goals based on priority. Which objectives you *must* achieve rather than which would be nice to achieve. Sort your goals based on priority to the business to help inform the urgency behind each role, and how much you might be willing to pay.

Step 3: Define what's/who's needed to achieve those goals. Who are the people and what is the experience you need to achieve the goal? What skills or technical knowhow do you need? Do you already have existing employees internally who can manage the work? Or do you need to hire someone new?

Step 4: Document your "people gaps." Wherever you're missing talent, document the gap. It's extremely important that you write out where your business is missing key hires. This demonstrates your ability to anticipate human capital needs, and also buffers the people ops team from finger pointing when key business goals are missed.

Step 5: Come up with a compensation strategy for each gap. Look at compensation benchmarking tools to inform your people costs. You may want to pay more for roles that are more urgent. For example, if you are that travel mug company whose packaging designers are a critical need, you might want to pay that person in the 90th percentile, versus the 50th percentile for other less critical hires.

Step 6: Share your results with your leadership team. Once you've defined your labor gaps and estimated the costs to fill them, the final step is to make strategic recommendations on how to fill the roles. This could be a change to roles and responsibilities internally, or a plan to attract, recruit, and hire new people.

"What's Our Budget?"

You can't talk about payroll without talking about the budget. Your budget defines how much money you have for your people including their base wages, but also accounting for incentives, salary increases, and more.

Your budget helps define:

- The total number of people you can afford to put on payroll
- The extent of and types of incentive strategies you can use
- Salary ranges for various positions you're looking to fill
- The mix of total compensation (salary, benefits, and flexible benefits) you can provide to each worker
- The mix of worker types that are best to keep (contract, full time, part time, etc.)

HOW DO YOU KNOW WHAT TO PAY EACH WORKER? First, you'll need to get an understanding of going rates for the roles you're looking to fill or keep. Try reaching out to your personal network: friends, colleagues, mentors, and so forth. What have they been seeing as going rates for certain roles? What can their experience share? This is the quickest way to get ballpark numbers. But we caution it may also be subject to bias.

A more reliable solution, which we already alluded to, is assessing compensation benchmarking tools like Indeed, Glassdoor, Salary.com, LinkedIn Salary, or Zenefits. *Salary benchmarking tools* (see Table 12.1) offer real— and real-time—salary data for specific jobs in specific geographic regions. They can provide median salaries and salary ranges based on quartile, and they can also estimate salary changes projecting whether demand for that role will increase or decrease. For instance, you could query a compensation benchmarking tool to give you the average salary for a packaging designer with senior-level experience in San Diego. The tool would kick-back a certain figure that would represent the aggregate salary for that job.

TABLE 12.1 Example of how salary benchmarking tools work with hypothetical inputs and output.

Example of how salary benchmarking tools work:

Inputs	Job Title	Level of Experience	Geography
	Packaging designer	*Senior-Level*	*San Diego*
Output	**Median Salary**	$76,800	

Source: Zenefits, 2021.

Compensation benchmarking tools give you data that can help you make strategic decisions such as whether to hire someone full time, part time, or as a consultant. And if it makes more sense to hire locally or in another market.

WHAT IF YOU DON'T HAVE ENOUGH MONEY? If you can't afford top dollar (or even median rates) for key positions, don't panic. This doesn't necessarily mean you won't be able to hire top talent or keep star employees. It just means your job needs to get more creative.

Smaller businesses, while not having big pockets, have the strategic advantage of being more nimble than big corporations. They can be more flexible in the ways they incentivize work including both monetary and nonmonetary perks. *Monetary perks* (like earning equity in the company, performance-based bonuses, or profit sharing) and *nonmonetary perks* (such as flexible work hours, additional PTO, career opportunities) can be real value-adds for employees.

Lean into that flexibility and develop a total compensation package that has a lot of value to your ideal workers. You can even allocate a dollar amount to each nonmonetary perk to define its value.

Remember, too, pay negotiations are conversations. Both parties have the right to walk away. So come to the table with honesty and respect. If you can meet market rates, that's great. If not, explain the situation to the candidate. If you can only afford to pay a candidate $70,000 and you know they're worth $100,000, you can say, "Listen, I know you could go get more money somewhere else. But here's what I'm going to do instead: I'm going to be flexible with your time off, and I'm going to let you pick up your kids at 3 p.m. every day."

TABLE 12.2 A list of examples of monetary compensation and nonmonetary compensation.

Monetary compensation	Nonmonetary compensation
■ Incentives	■ Company culture
■ Bonuses	■ Snacks or discounts on food
■ Perks	■ Access to gyms/memberships
■ Stock units	■ Career growth opportunities
■ Profit sharing	■ Vacation/PTO
■ Tip income	■ Flexible work weeks
■ Commission	■ Mentorship
■ Overtime wages	■ __(anything else you can come up with)__

Source: Zenefits, 2021.

Or give them an extra week or two for vacation. Or explain to them that in their role, they'll have the opportunity to have a much bigger role than they would at another company, the opportunity to lead a team, or get some kind of experience they wouldn't get elsewhere.

Or whatever else your adroit mind comes up with!

The point is there are trade-offs. You can't always afford to pay market rates, certainly not top dollar. So you'll have to make it enticing in some other way. There has to be something in it for your staff so they agree to the compensation agreement, and agree that it's fair.

Oh, and by the way, a job isn't getting married. It's a job. Employees are here to do good work, and hopefully the employment agreement makes each party better via a mutual occupational experience. If it doesn't work out in the end, that's okay, and you can mention that from the outset. You can say, "Look, I can't pay you market rate but if you commit to staying 18 months, or 24 months, I'm going to give you an amazing experience and you will be able to earn top dollar in your next job. And I will help you find it."

In this way small companies can punch above their weight class in talent wars.

WHAT ABOUT INCENTIVES? Yep, your budget should inform incentive strategies, too.

Incentives are the perks (typically monetary, but not always) that are used to motivate existing employees. They should tie as closely to performance as possible.

They are the vehicle with which your business rewards the behaviors you're trying to drive. If you recall, earlier we mentioned how a goal of "employee engagement" could be misleading for your people team because engaged employees could be working on the wrong tasks. Incentives are a way to keep your people focused on the *right tasks* by providing strategic positive feedback loops that provide rewards for work done that makes a clear positive impact on business objectives.

Companies that leverage strong incentives see an increase in revenue, profit, productivity, and employee retention (see Figure 12.1). Poor incentives fail to motivate staff and put your company at risk of turnover.

Unfortunately, outside of research specifically studying the impact of incentives on business results, most businesses aren't sure whether incentives are effective. According to one study of more than 5,000 US businesses, the vast majority of businesses (92 percent) use incentive planning, but only 21 percent of executives feel confident they are working. This is in large part because companies don't track or measure the impact of their incentives, or the company lacks a formal process altogether, instead awarding incentives discretionally.

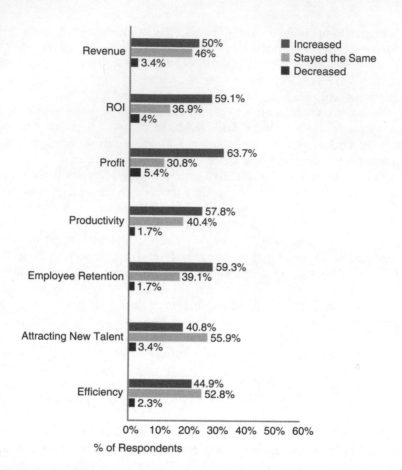

FIGURE 12.1 The impact of incentive compensation on desired outcomes in a business.

Source: FMI Net, 2013.

Don't leave impact open to interpretation. Start with a strong documented plan that includes the teams that are incentivized, the requirements of earning an incentive, the reward the employee should expect, and the timing for such rewards. Table 12.3 shows an example.

Your incentive plan should:

- Support efforts that move the business closer to its goals
- Be clear and achievable by all, and *not* favor any particular subgroup
- Make sense fiscally and infrastructurally

TABLE 12.3 Example of clearly defined incentives structures.

Team	How to earn more	What you'll earn	Accelerated earnings potential
Marketing	Obtain 50 net new leads in a month	$100 bonus	For each 20 new leads you bring in, on top of the 50, you'll earn an additional $100.
Sales	Meeting quota 3 months in a row	Earn an additional $100 bonus on top of your compensation plan	For each contiguous month of obtaining quota after your first three, you'll earn an additional $100.
Sales	Closing $50,000 in one month	Earn an additional $1,000 bonus on top of your compensation plan	For each additional $20,000 closed in the same month, you'll earn an additional $1,000.
Company wide	Being named for a "core value award" through peer nominations	Earn $1,000 VISA gift card	

Source: Zenefits, 2021.

It may seem at this point that incentives are easy enough to get right. Find a reward, find a goal, match them up. But we caution, incentive planning is actually much harder to get right in practice. Let's look at a few common pitfalls and ways to avoid them to illuminate common mistakes.

1. **Pitfall 1: Not encouraging true motivation.** Often, incentives are constructed at a team- or company-wide level, which risks missing the needs of the individuals.

   Get it right: Be as personalized as you can when building incentive plans. Use your motivation matrix or give people a voice in what rewards they want.

2. **Pitfall 2: Incentivizing the wrong behaviors.** It's easy to accidentally get incentives wrong, like in this real world example: A colleague's company was looking for ways to weather the initial COVID-19 economic shutdown. Marketing decided to run a promotion to drum up business. Everyone inside the company was excited. Especially when the promotion caught on. A record-breaking number of prospective customers

signed up to get the deal. Unfortunately, the promotion (which offered 30 percent off the product) never considered the compensation structure for the sales team, or adjusted for it. For each closed/won deal associated with the promotion, a sales rep missed out on 30 percent of their expected commission. The sales team quickly learned to avoid leads associated with the promotion in favor of full pay-out leads. The result? Frustrated potential customers (who were ignored by sales, in favor of full-paying leads) and less total revenue closed for the business (the company would likely have closed more total business if both full-paying customers and promotional leads were closed). The problem was that marketing leaders failed to consider the downstream impact of their promotion. And the wrong actions were motivated.

Get it right: When thinking about incentives at any level, take on the mindset of an algorithm. What are all the possible inputs and outcomes? For instance, how are the various ways employees could interpret the incentive plans? Can the incentive be written in a different way to more precisely drive the right behaviors?

3. **Pitfall 3: Failing to engage your top performers.** Star employees need carrots too, and if your incentive plans fail to meet the needs of these individuals, you're at a greater risk of losing them. Losing top performers means losing a lot (see Table 12.4). Much more than losing an unmotivated employee. Just how much? Let's look back at our sales employees example from Chapter 11 to see the financial implications of losing top performers. If you remember, Employee A was meeting quota, bringing in $15,000 per month, whereas Employee B was bringing in only $5,000 per month. If both employees met quota, you could expect $360,000 of new business in a year. When you lost Employee B you still managed $270,000. But losing Employee A, a top performer, and you're down to only $135,000 in new business for the year, *even assuming you bring in another top performer.* Losing your top performer was twice as bad for your bottom line.

Get it right: Provide fair pay and appropriate incentives. Treat your employees like adults, and ask them if the incentive structure meets their needs, or how they would adjust it to work better. Get the right criteria, and watch your business soar.

4. **Pitfall 4: Failing to communicate incentives.** Employees that either don't know how to earn an incentive, or don't know that an incentive exists, won't work to achieve one.

Get it right: Ensure your incentive structure is clearly communicated to employees. Employees who feel like they have role clarity are found to be 53 percent more efficient, and role clarity at large increases

TABLE 12.4 The cost of losing a top employee assuming a backfill in "month 4" and standard onboarding speeds of new hires. Using hypothetical numbers for salary and labor costs, this example shows that the company lost 75.95 percent of expected profit.

Cost of losing a top performer (assuming a strong new hire)

		Employee A	Employee B	New Hire
Month 1	Monthly Salary	$4,167	$4,167	
	Sales	$15,000	$5,000	
Month 2	Monthly Salary	$4,167	$4,167	
	Sales	$15,000	$5,000	
Month 3	Monthly Salary	$4,167	$4,166	
	Sales	$15,000	$5,000	
Month 4	Monthly Salary		$4,167	
	Sales		$5,000	
Month 5	Monthly Salary		$4,167	$4,167
	Sales		$5,000	$0
Month 6	Monthly Salary		$4,167	$4,167
	Sales		$5,000	$0
Month 7	Monthly Salary		$4,167	$4,167
	Sales		$5,000	$5,000
Month 8	Monthly Salary		$4,167	$4,167
	Sales		$5,000	$10,000
Month 9	Monthly Salary		$4,167	$4,167
	Sales		$5,000	$15,000
Month 10	Monthly Salary		$4,167	$4,167
	Sales		$5,000	$15,000
Month 11	Monthly Salary		$4,167	$4,167
	Sales		$5,000	$15,000
Month 12	Monthly Salary		$4,167	$4,167
	Sales		$5,000	$15,000

Totals

Expected Revenue	$360,000.00
Actual Revenue	$135,000.00
Labor Costs	$58,332.67
New Hire Costs	$4,129.00
Expected Profit	$301,667
Actual Profit	$72,538
Delta	$229,129
% of Expected Profit Lost	**75.95%**

Source: Zenefits, 2021.

Check In!

Questions to ask while creating a compensation strategy/policy:

- What is our compensation philosophy?
- What do we need to do in our business? (And how are we going to hire for that?)
- What is our budget?
- What are market rates for the roles we anticipate hiring?
- What are our salary ranges?
- Are our compensation strategies fair and in compliance with state and federal laws as well as our moral code of ethics?
- What are our incentive plans?
- Do our incentive plans drive the right outcomes?

---

overall work performance by 25 percent (Pijnacker 2019). So make sure each worker knows what incentives are available and how to earn them. Document your strategy and post it in a digital location where employees can refer to program details at any time.

Taking Compensation to Mastery Level: Using Pay Data to Inform the Business

We've mentioned data intelligence is becoming more and more important to people operations. And how it plays out in compensation strategy is a good example.

With digital employee data (demographics, performance management, employee engagement surveys, and more), you can start to slice and dice datasets to reveal various patterns and insights.

For instance, if you were interested in whether pay rates had an impact on employee happiness, you could look at the correlation between pay and employee happiness using Employee Net Promoter Scores (eNPSs) to measure happiness and salary rates for pay. A correlation analysis would reveal the strength of the relationship between pay rates and eNPSs.

The cleaner and more consistent the data you have, the more interesting your analyses can become.

For example, if you had the data, you could model the extent to which *any* of the following variables—manager, department, geographic location of employee, tenure status, salary band, benefits package—impact eNPSs, which would tell you which variable had the greatest impact on happiness. This is calculated using a ***regression analysis***, a mathematical way of sorting out which of variables among a set of variables has impact on an outcome.

You could also use pay data to ***A/B test*** pay structures. An A/B test helps you compare two variables. You might wonder, for example, which incentive strategy achieves greater profitability: annual bonuses or project-based bonuses? To test this, randomize a team into two groups. One group (test group A) would receive an annual bonus based on performance criteria, while another group (test group B) could receive project-based bonuses paid out at the completion of each project. Measure how well each group meets their goals to determine the effectiveness of the compensation strategy.

These are just some examples of how people ops practitioners can start crunching digital employee data. As people ops continues to evolve, we anticipate best practices in data analysis will emerge.

The Old HR Way: Lacks a documented compensation strategy. Uses discretionary incentive spending to motivate employees. Fails to measure impact of pay on performance.

The POPS Way: Maintains a fair-pay philosophy to pay employees equitably. Uses business objectives and a deep understanding of individual motivators to build incentive frameworks. Uses data analysis to further inform processes.

CHAPTER 13

Rethink Communication

Communication is a part of the soul of your company and will have a big impact on your employee experience. No matter how big or small you are, it's the means by which you're able to motivate, inform, connect, and engage your people. And given how much the world of work has changed, revisiting your communication strategies may be a priority.

The COVID-19 pandemic forced many American employers to rethink how they communicate. More employees were remote. Rules around customer engagement changed. But this provided an opportunity to review and refine how to communicate to be more successful.

Let's consider subpar communication practices first. If employees don't know what's going on, they're not set up for success and as a result, business results suffer. Quantified Communications found that businesses as small as 100 employees spend, on average, 17 hours per week clarifying unclear communications (Zandan, n.d). That's roughly $525,000 of annual costs lost to emails and phone calls that simply sound like, "I'm sorry, what do you mean? Can you please clarify ____?" And if customers don't know what's going on, add to that cost a loss of transactions and revenue.

Good communication practices, on the other hand, have an immediate and positive impact on workplace productivity, including a 25 percent lift in employee productivity and 47 percent higher returns to shareholders over a five-year period when a company has strong communication skills (Baldoni 2009).

Good communication is not just about what you say, but how you say it. The style, tone, and tenor of how communication is handled in a company says a lot about its culture. As a leader in people operations, you will work with other internal leaders to clarify your company's approach to communications, infusing the right components into various forms of company messaging to support your culture. Bigger companies often have an internal communications specialist whose entire job is to focus on this. In smaller companies, it often falls to the people ops team, because it's so closely tied to engagement. How often and in what format will your leaders disseminate information? Is your company's best channel email, text, video, posters, or some combination of these?

In this chapter, we look at the foundations of successful communication practices for companies of all types. Ready-built for any type of workforce (remote, in-office, telecommuting, or a hybrid of any of those) we'll talk about keys to good communication that can be used internally or externally, including:

- What is a communications strategy?
- Positioning a communications plan as a critical value add to the business
- Attributes of an effective communicator
- What you say, and how and where you say it
- Communication tech tips
- Measuring success

What Is a Communications Strategy?

A company or departmental *communications strategy* is an explicit plan that outlines the process of communications inside a company, and can encompass internal, external, or both.

It can include specifics on:

- How and when the leaders or teams share information with the workforce
- Who is included in company communications (do contractors, interns, vendors receive updates?)
- The company's position on style, tone, and content (are you formal or informal?)
- Which channels of communication will be used (Zoom, Slack, email, text, digital signage, etc.)
- Guidelines regarding key moments in the business such as promotions, hiring, exiting employees, key fiscal moments, benefit programs, product or customer wins, and so forth

It can also serve as another way to reinforce your values, by setting an example and including written guidance on how your people should communicate with one another, such as:

- We value openness, honesty, a solution-mindset, and kindness
- We use language that is inclusive
- We respond within 24 hours
- We listen and don't jump to conclusions
- We bring up concerns early, to stay ahead of issues

- We embrace diversity and inclusion by challenging preconceived notions and asking questions

Communication norms can be included in your employee handbook where existing workers or new hires have easy access to reference it; you can talk about it in orientation; and you can lead by example. Keep in mind that how your executives and the people team communicate with employees sets the tone for the entire company. This is a big responsibility—and a fun one.

Positioning a Communications Plan as a Critical Value-Add to the Business

Once you've established that having a plan for communications is a critical component of your company's success, it's time to demonstrate how your strategy helps the company meet its larger goals.

To do this, get granular. Just as you gathered data to show the connection between people ops objectives and larger business goals, gather data that demonstrates the connections between good communication and employee engagement, productivity, collaboration, turnover/retention, and recruiting. Demonstrate, too, what's at stake when companies *don't* communicate well (e.g., losing top performers, net loss of productive work hours, too much time wasted on clarifying poor communications, etc.). Then share what can be gained if a communication strategy is in place (e.g., better collaboration, fewer silos, greater trust, more alignment to the brand's mission or purpose, more idea generation, etc.). Show the impact of great communications to business success by using quantifiable data that makes clear connections between communications and the bottom line.

Once you get alignment from the top, you can use the same talking points about the value of a strong communications plan with employees and managers.

Attributes of an Effective Communicator

After working with your leaders to define an approach and strategy for the company, it's time to think about your own skills in this area personally and as a representative of the POPS team.

First, you'll need to think about what information is shared and when. This is important for expectation setting, and building a rhythm for your team. Set a calendar, consider the appropriate cadence, and make sure you know what channels you will use and when (see Figure 13.1).

	Daily	Weekly	Bi-monthly	Monthly	Quarterly	As Needed
Strategy/Goals					X	X
Small Team Meetings			X			X
Entire Team All Hands					X	X
Executive Team Meeting Updates				X		X
Blog or Team Intranet			X			X
Employee Engagement		X				X
Recognition	X					X

FIGURE 13.1 A general guideline regarding the recommended cadence of communication.

Source: Zenefits, 2021.

Having a plan for who communicates what and when is important for consistency and to ensure you don't miss anything and that you don't have too many communications coming out at the same time; people in general are overwhelmed with too much information. By setting the stage thoughtfully, you are helping your employees understand what they need to pay attention to—and giving them the space to do that.

On a personal level, as any good communicator knows, the most important aspect to good communication is not just a good plan of what and when you're going to say some stuff. Think about which person is best suited to deliver each message; as the POPS person, should your team be associated with rolling out the harassment training? Or is this a compliance-related training better owned by the CEO or company lawyer? If there is cake in the kitchen, who should send that information out? Really take a moment to think about what you choose to own in terms of messages that define you and your department.

On a personal level, you will also need to think about *how* you deliver your message. Get comfortable with owning it and finding your own style. The best communicators are authentic to who they are and knowing their audience. Good communicators treat people like adults, caring not only about what they say, but also how they say it. They are direct and able to land their points without damaging relationships. They own their message, and don't do a manager's job for them. Better to coach the manager to have a difficult conversation rather than do it for them.

The POPS role is to be a facilitator, a connector, the glue. Not the police, not the company mom. Not the person your grandpa told you HR was like. Just being normal and being yourself in terms of communication will go a long way toward erasing that HR stigma and helping elevate the employee experience. Here are a few ways to help you be a great communicator:

Be authentic, show genuine interest in both your verbal and nonverbal communication.

Be confident, know your stuff. Bring a strong, open-minded demeanor.

Be credible, tell the truth. This includes knowing what you don't know and sharing as much when people ask you questions that go beyond your knowledge base.

Be engaging, care about your audience. Ask them questions and don't make the dialog all about you.

Be curious, ask questions and listen to answers. Maintain a beginner's mentality, which means allowing yourself to be influenced and changed.

Be trustworthy, honor people's requests for confidence, be good to your word, and apologize when you mess up.

If you're in POPS, work to embody the attributes of good communication, and then help coach your workplace to be good communicators, too.

What You Say and How and Where You Say It

What you're trying to say is the content of your message, and the root of all communication. Whether you're communicating by written word, video, audio, or whatever, that thing you're trying to get someone to hear or understand? That's your content.

When leading the charge on POPS or company communications, it's important to think critically about what you're trying to say. This may sound obvious, but you'd be surprised by how many times people don't think about what points they're trying to land. You want "what you say" to be exacting to "what you mean" so there's zero ambiguity in the message. This adds to your credibility and confidence as a communicator, and your audience will grow to trust your communications more.

To do this:

1. Draft your message.
2. Choose your channel.
3. Have someone else review your message for clarity.
4. Eliminate nonessential fluff (trust us, there is some).

5. Lead with the important stuff; people have limited attention spans.
6. Practice giving your message (either by rereading as your audience, or speaking out loud for video or an in-person presentation).
7. Hit send.

How You Say It

Next, consider *how* you will deliver the message. Communication delivery can include any combination of tone, pacing, context, emojis, facial expressions, body language, and pitch. These things impact how your audience responds to your message, and whether they even hear it. For critical messages, it's important to keep in mind, in the words of Maya Angelou, "People will forget what you said, people will forget what you did, but people will never forget how you made them feel."

The words you choose, and how you deliver them is vital to success in people operations, to build trust and to maintain a safe and inclusive working environment. Pausing to think about the delivery can assuage frustrating situations, resolve some of the sting of a potential conflict, and help to create a foundation for employees to feel safe to provide critical feedback with one another so they can grow and excel.

Where You Say It

You've got your content, your positioning, and you've thought about delivery. The next thing to consider is the format of your message, or *where* you'll say it.

Message format can be as essential as tone or pitch when landing a message (see Figure 13.2). Some messages lend themselves better to certain channels. A notification of termination, for example, is better handled in an in-person discussion than through an email. A company event should be announced in an email rather than a phone call. In addition, different communication technology platforms carry inherently different meanings. A text is immediate, an email is formal, an in-person meeting is very personal, and video—well, video can be all of those things, depending upon how it's used.

When considering the right method of delivery, take into account how your employees naturally look for information. What are their communication preferences? Will you get more attention from them if you text them versus sending an email? Do this and your messages will be better received and are more likely to be consumed.

	Email	Blog	Intranet	Message (People Hub)	Zoom/ Webcast	Digital Signage	One-on -One	Meeting
Open Enrollment	X		X	X				
Cake in the Kitchen	X			X				
New Hire Welcomes	X			X		X		X
Quarterly Wins		X		X				
All Hands Meeting				X	X			X
Manager Office Hours				X	X			
CEO Message				X				
Performance Conversation				X			X	

FIGURE 13.2 An example of types of appropriate communication channels by topic.

Source: Zenefits, 2021.

Communication Tech Tips

People spend up to 80 percent of their work day in communications, between emails, meetings, and conversations (Zandan, n.d.). In HR, it could be more. You could spend your whole day (and weekend) answering one-off questions from employees or resending emails that you've already sent. But who wants to do that? It's more likely you'll avoid the HR-police typecast if half your job isn't sending nagging follow-up emails.

Instead, use technology to effectively scale your communications while giving your employees greater access to self-service help. The basis of this is providing important documentation in digital, available ways that employees can access at any time. This means cloud-based and mobile friendly.

One example of using technology to aid in communications is managing your employee handbook in the cloud. Post your employee handbook, complete with all your corporate policies, to the cloud once, and know that all your employees will have immediate access to it. Encourage them to bookmark the document and refer to it before they come asking the POPS team questions. Anytime there's an update to a policy, you can update your digital employee handbook once and seamlessly push it to your workforce for their acknowledgement through a digital signature. This is a *one-to-many communication approach*, or the ability for information to be posted in one spot while servicing unlimited people.

Technology-enabled listening is another way to digitally scale communications. Employee engagement surveys and pulse surveys (more on these in Chapter 15) are a one-to-many listening tool. Employers can ask their people for opinions on any number of topics, asking for feedback or soliciting ideas in a quick and complete way that allows the POPS team to recommend quick action to department or company leaders.

Another important part of communication is staying technically literate. Millennials and Gen Zers are the first of many generations who have relied on true technology-based communications for their entire lives. They are experts in mobile app platforms, they navigate between messenger apps freely, and they have a different expectation of things like emoji use and video communication. What age group is your workforce? What are their unique relationships with digital communications? Should this impact the ways in which you communicate updates, rewards, and recognition?

As a specific use case, emojis have been seen to improve the effectiveness and positive associations with corporate messaging particularly with younger audiences. These artful little pictures hold a lot of power, from allowing peers to show support to one another, to magnifying employee recognition, and contributing to a general positive vibe that is part of an enjoyable employee experience. So, although it's considered very informal, don't be afraid to use modern communication tools like emojis or gifs from time to time on the appropriate channels, if that is authentic to you, your leaders, or your company. Several studies that link emoji participation in the workplace to improvements across the business include:

- "Positive Work Culture and Using Emojis to Contribute to It" (Lalwani 2019)
- "Why Emojis May Be the Key to Employee Retention" (Kinni 2016)
- "The Communicative Functions of Emoticons in Workplace E-Mails :-)" (Skovholt, Grønning, and Kankaanranta 2014)

Measuring Success

The last part of a communication plan is measuring success. This can be tricky. But if you look obliquely at certain aspects of your business, you'll be able to ascertain data on your efforts. Here are a few ways to measure communication programs:

- **Survey active employees.** Survey employees before and after you introduce a communications strategy on how well they think the organization does in general with communications, how they feel their communications are with their managers or peers, and how much time they spend clarifying misunderstandings. Tracking this figure over time will provide a reliable dataset from which you can extrapolate the lost time or money from miscommunications. You can also survey employees after big meetings, after an important meeting, and so forth, to determine how well they absorbed the information.

- **Ask employees for feedback during onboarding and offboarding.** Solicit feedback on your communications process from new employees and employees ready to leave the company. These two groups generally provide more accurate and less politically correct responses on how you're doing as far as sharing appropriate information.

- **Quantify incoming questions, address, and measure results.** For example, if you get three questions a week on paystubs, after you implement a communication plan to address this gap in employee understanding, measure how many paystub questions you get after you have published the oft-requested information. If you did a good job, there will be fewer.

- **Review open rate for messages you send.** This is next level, as you may need specialized tools to explore email open rate, text receipts, or intranet page views or videos watched.

When you put it all together, your communications strategy should increase workplace productivity by providing clarity to employees on a number of fronts, increasing overall company communication competency, making POPS leaders and managers more accessible and responsive, and providing effective ways for employees to engage and connect with the business.

The Old HR Way: Lacks a relevant communications strategy and the means to validate its success. Human resource leaders are policy police, siloed, and operating apart from the rest of the organization.

The POPS Way: Develops a communication plan that drives the company values around communication as well as defining the cadence, tone, and channels for various internal company announcements. The POPS way engages employees, encourages people to treat one another as adults, and leverages tailored communication strategies to drive productivity.

PART IV

Unleash Your Workforce

CHAPTER 14

Performance Alignment

The moment each of your employees' individual efforts directly helps your business achieve its overarching goals is the moment your business starts humming.

If you've ever been there, you know what this looks like. Your staff arrive at the job, hang their coats, settle into their workspace, and know exactly what to do. Each tiny little aspect of work, which we all know makes up most of the work day, is aligned; a coagulating mass and strength that helps your business move mountains.

At the individual level, employees know how to thrive. They've been given the tools to excel at their work. They feel safe asking questions or offering ideas to their boss. And their individual goals have a direct and clear impact on the business's goals.

When we say "unleash your workforce," we don't just mean removing tasks that can be automated, although that helps. We mean creating an environment in which employees do their best work, unfettered by lack of clarity or unsupportive communication. It is an environment in which each tiny piece of work counts.

Traditionally, businesses relied on traditional performance management processes—like annual review cycles—to ensure employees were effectively contributing to the business. Once-a-year reviews identified both top employees and bottom-performers and rewarded them with either salary increases or course-correction plans, respectively.

These yearly events were stress inducing for everyone involved. Employees worked feverishly to build reports that reflect a year's worth of work for the one or two hours managers reviewed their work to justify whether the person would receive a raise, promotion, or termination. Leadership sweats out several weeks or months to complete stack-ranked analyses. And managers fretted over the inevitable requirement to fire people on their team. What was meant to boost productivity across the organization became a nerve-wracking time suck.

It isn't that the intention of the traditional performance review process was off base, per se. The goals of traditional performance management were valid: to recognize top performers and provide support for bottom performers. It's just that the old methods have become tarnished over time. People have started to fear the performance review. Companies have started to see performance reviews as a litigative shield to wrongful termination lawsuits where the point of documenting performance became to "cover your ass," not to aid in the professional development of your people. And, maybe most important, annual review cycles simply can't keep pace with to today's rapidly changing economy. We're living in an era marked by rapid and iterative change. Things like agile development and ever-shorter product life spans have promulgated well beyond software development and must be reflected in the way we manage people, too.

The result is that the traditional performance review is failing its intended purpose. Today, 58 percent of executives say performance management processes don't engage workers or drive productivity (Buckingham and Goodall 2015), and it's estimated that 70 percent of all international companies are actively moving away from traditional performance reviews (TruQu n.d.).

Yet it's curious. Even while giant companies are ripping out antiquated annual reviews, very few companies have done away with performance management outright. Netflix's former chief talent officer, Patty McCord did away with annual performance reviews and replaced them with honest conversations. Accenture replaced their annual reviews with a process that documents employee progress over time. That's because despite the fact that traditional performance reviews fall short of providing value, businesses still need a way to set goals and expectations, connect with staff to drive progress, identify performance gaps, and document employee underperformance.

Not only that, but employees *want* regular and consistent feedback. Seventy-two percent of employees say their performance would improve with "corrective feedback" (Zenger and Folkman 2014), and 68 percent of employees who receive accurate and consistent feedback say they feel more fulfilled in their jobs (Peacock 2016).

The point is, the concept of performance management shouldn't die. We're just at a point in time where employers need a new way to do it. Enter the Performance Alignment approach (see Table 14.1).

Performance Alignment is an employee performance framework that embodies an agile, open, transparent approach to employee development that aligns directly to the larger goals of the company. In a performance alignment model, you ditch the classic once-a-year performance evaluation in favor of more frequent and less formal conversations that help drive greater employee success across your business. It also sets teams up to

TABLE 14.1 Key differences between performance management and performance alignment.

Performance Management	Performance Alignment
■ Focuses on annual reviews and stack ranking to drive progress ■ Rigid, formal, and hierarchical	■ Focuses on frequent check-ins between managers and uses goal-setting and goal-adjusting to drive progress ■ Informal, often verbal, and handled with an "adult-to-adult" mindset

Source: Zenefits, 2021.

flex and change expectations in response to the business's needs more frequently than once per year.

While performance alignment isn't markedly different from performance management in concept, the nuances may be the difference between a fear-laden team and a confident, independent team. In this chapter, we'll go over the five pillars of a successful performance alignment strategy that will help you operationalize an unleashing of the workforce's potential:

Performance Alignment
1. Aligns to your overarching business goals and values
2. Occurs frequently and consistently
3. Is measurable and adaptable
4. Drives the intended actions
5. Treats your people as adults

Pillar 1: Performance Alignment Aligns to the Overarching Business Goals

The first thing you need to do is align each person's work to the larger vision by using cascading goals.

There are many models of cascading goals that could work for your business, and no one-size-fits-all approach. We'll go over a few versions of cascading goals that you could consider (V2MOMs, OKRs, BHAGs, "The Whats and The Hows"). The purpose is not to prescribe to you a certain way of managing your goals, but more to get your mind thinking about ways to construct goal-setting. Feel free to adopt these common cascading goals frameworks directly or adjust them to better fit your needs.

V2MOMs

Vision, Values, Methods, Obstacles, and Measurement, or V2MOM, is a cascading goal model developed by Marc Benioff, chair, chief executive officer, and founder of Salesforce. He says the V2MOM goal model is one of the biggest secrets to Salesforce's growth success, noting: "I've always thought our biggest strength is how we've maintained alignment while growing quickly."

This acronym works to frame these business areas:

- **Vision:** Defines what you want to do or achieve.
- **Values:** Your company's principles and beliefs that help you pursue your vision.
- **Methods:** The action items and tactical steps you need to take to get the job done.
- **Obstacles:** Anticipated challenges you'll need to overcome to achieve the vision.
- **Measures:** The ways in which you measure achievement.

The model can be used once by your leadership team and disseminated across the business. Or you could require each department, or even each individual, to draft their own V2MOMs that snap to the overarching goals.

Table 14.2 shows an example of a V2MOM.

OKRs

Objectives and Key Results (OKRs) are used at companies like Google, LinkedIn, Twitter, and Zynga.

To use OKRs, you develop two to three objectives and two to three key results that align to those objectives in a given window of time, classically one to three months. Upper management identifies the objectives, while individual teams spell out individual key results. Each key result is accompanied by a confidence interval, to keep employees motivated. The lower the confidence level, the harder it is to achieve the goal.

It looks a bit like Table 14.3.

BHAGs

Big Hairy Audacious Goals (BHAGs) is a cascading goal model coined by Jim Collins and Jerry Porras (2004) in their book, *Built to Last: Successful Habits of Visionary Companies*. BHAGs are long-term goals, we're talking in the 10–25 year time span, guided by your company's core values and

TABLE 14.2 An example of a completed V2MOM.

Vision
- Level the playing field for small business
- Remove obstacles to accessible healthcare
- Make work easy and exceptional for employees

Values
- In it together
- Act like an owner
- Empathy over ego
- Put the customer first
- Operate with integrity
- Innovation for the greater good

Methods
- Building the team—the right people, the right jobs
- Building the product—one code base for full product
- Delivering exceptional customer experience
- Accelerating growth with the right partners, channels
- Innovating product with analytics, AI and the unknown

Obstacles
- Execution—distribution to a massive market
- Complexity—product breadth/depth, multiple personas and buying motions
- Hiring—finding the right talent in the right locations
- Growth—expanding customer base

Measures
- Growth—100 new customers in each market, with <5% churn
- Customer Experience—20% improvement in Net Promoter Score (NPS)
- Operating Efficiency—30% improvement in customer lifetime value to customer acquisition (LTV:CAC) ratio
- Team—increase employee engagement and retention by 10% each

purpose. Just like its name, they're meant to be big and hairy and audacious. We're talking, Microsoft's "a computer on every desk" kind of big.

It may seem hard to imagine our world 10–25 years from now, but BHAG goals don't require certainty. They break the known and challenge impossibility. The hope is that, once the vision is disseminated across the organization, every tiny effort—which we all know makes up a majority of the day—moves the impossible closer to the possible.

The Whats and the Hows

The Whats and the Hows is an approach whose name pretty much describes how it works. The model aims to clarify *what* you need to get done, and *how* you're going to do it.

TABLE 14.3 Example of a completed Objectives and Key Results form.

Team: *Quality Control Team*
Objective: *The stated objective developed by management*
Time Period: FY22, Q1
- KR1: 80 percent confidence
- KR2: 50 percent confidence
- KR3: 30 percent confidence

Progress: The progress I've made so far. . .

	Week 1	Week 2	Week 3	Week 4
Month 1	*Weekly notes on what was accomplished that drove the KR . . .*			
Month 2				
Month 3				

Source: Zenefits, 2021.

In a Whats and Hows model, leadership identifies top-level business goals. Then, each team and person layers on their associated goals. These are the whats. Each what should come with an attached metric to assess goal achievement. After the whats are decided, each group then adds how they expect to complete the stated goal. The hows are geared to reflect some of the softer-skill values of the company that help describe how the business is oriented to drive its goals. This could be process design, operations, behavior, or values, among other things. It might also be the reduction of things, like meetings, or redundancies.

WHATS   What are you trying to accomplish?
What are the metrics that validate goal attainment?

HOWS   How is your business designed to achieve goals?
How do you expect your employees to handle themselves behaviorally to be in alignment with the goals?
Table 14.4 shows a completed example of the Whats and the Hows.

A General Note on Goal Setting

One of the biggest goal attainment killers is bad goal setting. Yes, there are good ways to write out goals, and yes there are bad ways. Good goals are SMART. They are Specific, Measurable, Achievable, Relevant, and Time-bound. Good goals specify what's intended to get done, by when. They

TABLE 14.4 Example of a completed the Whats and the Hows.

The What						The How
Business Goal	Metric	Team Goal	Metric	Individual Goal	Metric	Values, Process, Operations, Philosophy
Develop more innovative products	Get on the most innovative companies list	Create three new products this year Update five new features on our existing product this year	Delivery quota (Yes/No) Delivery quota (Yes/No)	Lead two new features project this month. Reduce the number of bugs reported by customers by 20 percent	Delivery quota (Yes/No) Number of bugs reported per feature release	We embrace a "fail-better" ethos in our company culture, which means new ideas are valued and rewarded even if they fail. We evaluate employees by their originality of ideas. We operationally support innovation by hosting an internal hack-a-thon each year that encourages new thinking and new teams.

Source: Zenefits, 2021

155

demonstrate the relevance or alignment to larger initiatives, and put a time cap on when it's expected to be completed.

Bad goals lack any one aspect of SMART goals, or they *add too much specificity*, limiting how a goal can be achieved. Let's look at both cases using a hypothetical example.

Let's say you are working on your social media goals and want to increase your Instagram followers. You write out your goal as follows:

Goal 1.0: To increase Instagram followers.

It's not yet good because we don't know how many Instagram followers you want to add, or by when. You make it SMART by adding key ingredients.

Goal 1.1: To increase Instagram followers *by 1,000 followers by the end of fiscal year*.

Now your goal is Specific, Measurable, Achievable, Relevant, and Time-bound. SMART! But, to continue the hypothetical example, while you were thinking about Instagram you got excited about a new video tactic that you think will achieve the results you're looking for, so you throw that in there too.

Goal 1.2: To increase Instagram followers by 1,000 followers *through engaging video content* by the end of fiscal year.

Whoops. You've overdone it. By specifying the tactic "through engaging video content" you've made your goal too specific. If video content doesn't do the trick to gain Instagram followers, you miss your goal. You don't want to miss the goal because you were too explicit on how you'd achieve it. If video content doesn't work to earn followers, there are myriad other ways that could: carousel posts, giveaways, increased engagement with other followers, hashtag strategies, and so forth. A better way to write the same goal would be to drop the "through engaging video content," and just leave it as: "To increase Instagram followers by 1,000 followers ~~through engaging video content~~ by the end of fiscal year." That way, you keep "how the goal will happen" out of the picture, but it's still SMART. This provides room for multiple failed approaches on the way to success.

Final Goal: To increase Instagram followers by 1,000 followers by the end of fiscal year.

Help coach staff and your company on how to set good goals when rolling out any new goals, and be sure to have a review stage where goals are edited for alignment, achievability, and effectiveness. Note too, it's okay if goals change throughout the year or quarter. It's actually good. Adjusting goals as they reflect the needs of the business and market is a good way to keep you working on the right stuff.

Try It Out!

Choose a framework from above and build out cascading goals.

Are there models that work better for smaller companies rather than larger ones? Is there an orientation that makes more sense for your people or leadership? Are your goals SMART? Remember there's not a one-size-fits-all method. The point to make sure you have goals that are actionable, can be communicated and cascade for alignment.

Pillar 2: Performance Alignment Occurs Frequently and Consistently

The next pillar of performance alignment is the regularity of communications between managers and employees. This is *how* and *when* managers and employees are expected to sync up and talk. It doesn't need to be a formal process with a specific agenda, in fact it shouldn't be! Much of performance alignment culture is the informal, approachable tone it sets. Communications are safe and approachable. With regular touch-bases between managers and employees that reaffirm an open-door environment, employees gradually become more comfortable sharing the honest (often tough to hear) opinions that make your business better. Here's a cadence we'd recommend:

- **Weekly one-on-one conversations.** Managers and direct reports discuss hot topics, obstacles, or frustrations that impact immediate projects to help get stuff done quicker—face-to-face.
- **Monthly one-on-one conversations.** Managers and direct reports connect on more operational issues such as team cohesion, processes, or collaboration—face-to-face.
- **Quarterly peer-reviews.** Peers evaluate one another on performance, attitudes, behavior, team dynamics, how an individual is performing, and the value they bring to the team—HR technology or other digital form.
- **Semi-annual performance alignment.** Bi-directional review between managers and direct reports—HR technology or other digital form.

Developing a regular rhythm for performance check-ins slowly reinforces the performance culture you want to seed throughout your teams.

Pillar 3: Performance Alignment Is Measurable and Adaptable

The third key pillar to a performance alignment is that it's measurable and adaptable. If your cascading goals were SMART from the outset, it's likely already measurable. But here is the other key to performance alignment: adaptability.

Traditional performance management processes tended to be rigid. Goals were set once and unchanged. A performance alignment approach bends and twists in sync with the changing work needs. Yes, you'll need to track individual and team performance against goals, but you also need to be introspectively aware of whether stated goals are reflective of the driving concerns of the business at any given time. If business goals change, so should employees' goals, and so should the relative expectations of goal achievement within that time frame.

In practice, judging the appropriateness of existing goals and changing them is more the job of managers, not a POPS team. But you need to coach managers to embrace adaptive goal setting. Teach them how to be more concerned with the overall health of the business rather than simply ticking goals just to achieve them.

If there are significant changes to the business (such as changes to leadership, changes to the macroeconomy, or restructuring of teams) or its goals, managers need to reassess the relevance of their goals, and make adjustments accordingly. Basically, there are two outcomes: (1) employee-level goals *will also* need to change, or (2) employee-level goals *won't* need to change.

If employee-level goals need to change, managers should connect with their direct reports during ongoing informal verbal conversations to inform them of the changing priorities. Together, they can talk through how this impacts each employee's individual goals or projects, and set new goals when required. Document the new goals in writing, clearly explain the expectations, and BOOM—you're back in alignment. It's as easy as that.

If employee-level goals don't need adjusting, individual goals remain, and it's then valid to measure employees' performance against those goals.

- To what extent did the person/team meet their goals or not?
- Is this the first time the person/team has achieved or missed their goals?
- Has the person been given an opportunity to correct their work and have they adjusted or improved?

Document and track answers to the preceding questions in your HR system of record on the singular employee record discussed in Chapter 6.

Tracked performance provides a clear picture of employee and team productivity. Similar to traditional performance management processes, this can help inform raises, promotions, or terminations.

Remember, too, often lagging performance isn't an indication of a bad employee, it's an indication of bad motivation by the company, or miscommunication of the role. Your job is to be investing in the employee experience that drives high performing teams. So, coach your managers to be genuinely interested in *why* employees are underperforming, so that they can find solutions and make progress midstride. Train managers to "look beyond the number" and get curious about the softer, more human, aspects of their teams. This is people work. Here are some examples of questions a manager might ask: Is there a team tension? Is there a lack of motivation? Are people overworked? This information should inform what's talked about at regular check-ins to talk with underperforming employees.

If and when lagging performance persists (either in performance or behavior), tell managers to document it! Written documentation of missed marks is not meant to be a way to protect you from litigation. It's meant to be a tool for employee growth and business alignment. It's true that most managers are afraid they will offend their employees if they provide negative feedback, but remember most employees (57 percent) actually prefer "corrective feedback" to "praise/recognition" (43 percent). They feel it helps them do a better job (Zenger and Folkman 2014).

So again, coach your managers to unshackle fear a little bit. Help them *share* constructive criticism *early on*. Provide positive feedback when they do. Too often, we see that managers don't reach out to HR until they have a big enough problem that they need help in firing an employee. At that point the managers don't have any documentation that shows there's been a persistent problem, or they've tried to solve the problem on their own first. This makes the situation unclear. Don't let it get to that point. Uncharged verbal communication coupled with appropriate written documentation will diffuse and fix most performance problems and is the adult—POPS—way to manage people.

If you still are struggling with underperformance, or missed marks of any kind, your employee handbook should clearly stipulate the consequences.

Pillar 4: Performance Alignment Drives the Intended Actions

The fourth pillar to a performance alignment is that it drives the intended actions. The key here is clarity. It's easy to unintentionally drive the wrong actions. We mentioned this briefly in Chapter 12 as it related to incentives. If you recall, a marketing promotion didn't align to the sales teams' compensation plans and resulted in sales avoiding hot leads. But the same thing can be true more holistically across your business. Let's use a quick hypothetical example to illustrate this.

Say you're a manufacturing company. Your documented annual goals are to diversify your product lineup by 5 percent and decrease spending by 10 percent. To align to these core goals, your company needs to focus on creating new products with a good market fit, without adding operational costs.

Good performance alignment would reward efforts for product innovation that required little to no operational costs—things like free market research. Development of new products given your existing infrastructures include operational changes that reduced costs.

Poor performance alignment would reward any innovation that required a lot of operational costs. Things like new requirements for new machinery or significantly more human capital.

To avoid mistakenly driving the wrong outcomes, go through a mental exercise and ask yourself how employees might interpret documented goals. Ensure they are clear and driving the intended actions. Clarity means every team and individual understands how their role and expectations fit into the larger company goals. Clear expectations, processes, rewards structures, and consequences help your employees make good decisions and keep your employees' actions aligned.

Pillar 5: Performance Alignment Treats Your People as Adults

How you conduct your performance alignment process is almost as important as building the plan. You must treat your people as adults, that's pillar number five. Treating employees as adults means you see them as humans and equals. You understand that we are all dealing with more than just work in our lives. You recognize, and respect, that we each come with a unique perspective. Appropriate tone and conduct will communicate this. Consider this statistic: 92 percent of employees agree that "negative (redirecting) feedback, if delivered appropriately, is effective at improving performance" (Zenger and Folkman 2014). That means even if you present a critical piece of feedback with the right demeanor, your employees will appreciate it and improve their performance.

Here are some best practices for people teams and managers to ensure they're treating their people as adults:

- **Be open, honest, and show genuine concern for success.** Every worker will have some area that could use even minor improvements. Although it may be uncomfortable, and every person responds differently to criticism, it's necessary for helping a worker establish success within your organization. Be open and honest, and assure them that your feedback is there to help them hone their strengths and talents for future career success.

- **Connect in-person (or Zoom call with video on).** Although it may be emotionally easier to deliver any bad news or negative critique over some kind of medium, it should always be done face-to-face either in person or over live video (Lazzareschi 2018). This allows for easier, more direct communication, where nonverbal communication (like facial expressions or body language) is invited.
- **Embody the value of the company in your presence.** Hard conversations are the most important time to demonstrate leadership and loyalty to your company values.
- **Provide clear direction and positivity.** At the end of the day, people do not like to walk out of an employee evaluation feeling as if they didn't get the direction they needed, or as if they've just been reprimanded. Even if your employee has serious improvements to make, most people thrive on positive reinforcement and actionable steps on how they can improve.

Putting It All Together, Rolling Out the Plan

To recap, to help unleash your workforce to its greatest capacity, consider a performance alignment process that includes cascading goals that align to the broader business goals, occur frequently and consistently, are measurable and adaptable, drive the intended actions, and treat your people as adults.

Adopting a performance alignment strategy instead of classic performance management can reduce fear and stress around performance reviews, and open pathways for clear, open, respectful communication. Done well, you'll get independently productive teams that are confident in working together to drive business goals.

The Old HR Way: Traditional performance management uses annual review cycles to track and monitor employee performance.

The POPS Way: Performance alignment uses cascading goals and regular verbal conversations between managers and employees to get the whole business "rowing in the same direction."

CHAPTER 15

Closing the Engagement Gap

As we've mentioned throughout this book, highly engaged workers drive more productivity. They're not tethered; they're unleashed. Whether they improve your product, service, employee collaboration, or brand reputation, engaged workers make a positive impact wherever they go.

The problem is, many businesses fail to engage their workers. Only 40 percent of US employees are actively engaged in their work, while 13 percent are "actively disengaged" and the remaining 47 percent are "not engaged" (Harter 2020). This could be due to poor leadership, toxic work cultures, failing to find and leverage authentic motivators in your rewards and recognition, or even something as benign as companies not knowing how to get the most from their workforce.

But it's crucial that companies engage their workers if they're serious about increasing employee productivity. Highly engaged workers add revenue, shareholder value, and aids in the resilience of a business during hard times. This means engaging employees isn't just a lofty HR goal, it's a bottom-line factor for your business.

But how do you pull this off, particularly if you're already wearing a ton of hats and managing a million things to keep the business afloat? It may seem like there would never be enough time in the day to add something as abstract as employee engagement. But that's the short HR view. The long-term POPS view understands hiring top talent, and engaging those people is the key to competitive sustainable advantage.

Perhaps it's easiest to look at how *not* to engage workers. Here's a simple way to do that: Never ask them questions, never hear their opinions, don't appreciate their work. That seems pretty obvious to most people. So, the opposite would be true, too if you *do* want to engage workers: Ask them questions, hear their opinions, and appreciate their work. But if you're looking to get a little more granular in your approach, we're with you. Let's go.

Ask Questions

Employees will feel valued and more engaged in their work when their opinions are genuinely heard, so ask them questions. You'll remember this important step from Chapter 11, too, where we advised asking employees questions to understand what motivates them. Good news, this works to engage people, too! Get curious about your people as people and as assets to the business: what motivates them, what discourages them, what are they excited about, what do they fear? What business ideas do they have? Where do they see process gaps or opportunities? What do they think about the direction of the company?

The trick here is to make sure employees feel safe to engage authentically back with you. The last thing you want is to pepper someone with questions, only to have them lie to you because they're afraid of retaliation. Instead, build a safe, inclusive work culture over time by consistently and repeatedly asking questions that reward honesty. Recognize not all people care to share in the same way, and make room for different methods of receiving employee feedback. Here are a few:

- **Anonymously:** Build surveys (or digital suggestion boxes) that anonymously capture feedback.
- **Identified:** Allow employees to provide known feedback to one another.
- **In person:** Talk with employees or managers one on one.
- **In small groups:** Provide digital forums (like Slack channels, intranets, or digital office hours) where people can ask/answer questions in a small group format.

Take time to listen to employee ideas about the business and continually work to establish your business as the kind of employer that cares about its people and their opinions.

Assimilate Answers

It's not enough to just listen to ideas if you never act on them. Failing to incorporate ideas will leave you seeming disinterested, which leads to distrust over time. Instead, look to assimilate employees' thoughts into the fabric of your business where you can.

Here's a good fictional example of how one employee's suggestion, and it's quick adoption by the employer, improved the overall business.

Dorian, a retail sales rep, worked the floor at an outdoor and camping shop. He suggested to his manager that shift schedules could be sent digitally in an email instead of posting them by hand each week and pinning them to the staff lounge. He said it would be helpful to all retail reps because they could have earlier access to their schedule and be able to get shifts covered more easily without having to go into the shop. The shift manager saw the value, and the change was made the next month. Over the next three months, several employees mentioned that the process was improved, and that finding someone to cover a shift was easier. Dorian was recognized for his idea by being named employee of the month.

What's particularly great about this example is that Dorian was recognized for his efforts. If the company made it out to be their own idea, Dorian may have felt slighted. Moreover, fewer employees would feel encouraged to share their own ideas, for fear their ideas would be stolen. Don't be an idea-stealer. Stoke the fire of idea generation by assimilating new ideas from your people into larger initiatives, and give credit where credit is due. This will demonstrate to employees that your company genuinely cares about its people: their ideas, their contributions, their efforts, and that you can't do it without them. In this way you'll encourage greater employee engagement.

Develop Employees

Employees will see you as truly interested in them, not just as cogs in a wheel but also as people, when you develop their success both for your company and the professional world at large. You want them to be successful at your company, and in any future world they pursue. This positions your company as inherently valuable to the individual and deepens the sense of mutual benefit in your employment terms.

To demonstrate your care at this level, invest in the career growth of each team player based on their needs. Provide coaching, teaching, mentorship, and access to resources that employees can use directly in their roles within your company, but that are also transferrable to other companies. These don't need to be expensive; in fact, they can be free. Here are a few low- to no-cost ways to achieve this:

- Mentorship programs inside your company
- Employee-hosted "lunch and learns" to teach new skills
- Giving people time off to attend school
- Education or continued learning stipends
- On-the-job skills training

You'll come up with the best strategies for your unique workforce, but the key takeaway is that you demonstrate your value for the personal development of each employee for the present and future. This will encourage greater employee engagement.

Reward Great Work

Employee rewards and recognition are the positive feedback loops employers provide for outstanding employee achievement. We've already touched on the relationship between rewards and recognition as an aspect of incentives and compensation planning in Chapter 12 and as part of your Motivation Matrix development in Chapter 11, but it's important to reiterate the importance of reward and recognition programs here too because frankly you won't have engaged employees if you don't recognize them for their efforts.

According to a 2013 *Harvard Business Review* survey of 568 US executives, employee recognition is the single most important factor in contributing to employee engagement (72 percent), yet a majority of employees (60 percent) say their managers don't provide frequent enough praise for good work, and 53 percent say their good work is never recognized (Harvard Business Review Analytic Service 2013).

Even a small boost in your employee rewards and recognition programs can have a big impact on your employee engagement.

Here's how to do it: Reward employees for outstanding work that moves the business in the intended direction. They can be formal or informal, and should be used every time your business or management wants to highlight a job well done. Don't worry about perfection here. It's better to provide consistent rewards as close to real time as possible. Although employee-of-the-year designations can be reserved for once-yearly crownings, studies have shown that more frequent, timely recognition can foster 14 percent greater employee engagement. Simple kudos, shout-outs, or Slack emojis are a great way to provide this kind of immediate feedback.

Your rewards program should be unique to your business and employees, but here's a quick list for easy reminders:

- **Make them public.** Public rewards receive more attention. Encourage your top performers to share their distinctions both internally and externally on social media.
- **Make them timely and frequent.** Designate one tangible or digital item that signifies great work, and give them to your team when they do good work.
- **Make them specific.** Make your praise specific to the person and work that you're looking to highlight. This will feel more personal to your workers and reinforce the values or actions you're looking to drive.

■ **Don't overthink it.** Giving someone recognition for their efforts can be as simple as "thank you" or "I appreciate you" or a shout out on a company email. Little acts of praise will go a long way. And will absolutely contribute to a more engaged workforce.

Measure Engagement

If you've made it this far, you're already doing the right things. You're listening to people's ideas, assimilating them into your business, coaching your employees to become better professionals, and rewarding good behaviors. You'd think these efforts would lead to greater employee engagement, but you shouldn't just assume it; you should measure it.

Although an increasing number of companies are interested in improving their employee engagement, very few are effectively tracking employee engagement with data, and fewer still are evaluating how they level up to business goals. Be among the stand-out companies that can quantify employee engagement.

Here are the two things to measure:

1. **To what extent are your people engaged?** Measure the percentage of your total workforce that is engaged, as well as how engaged they are on a five- or seven-point scale.
2. **Does engagement lead to productivity within the business?** Measure the percentage of your workforce that is engaged over time, and whether changes in engagement rates correlate with improved attainment of other goals.

Let's look at each of these through a practical lens.

To answer the first question, most companies rely on some sort of employee engagement survey that allows them to track the change of employee engagement over time. We're going to dive deeper into employee engagement surveys later in this chapter, but at a high level, employers should be interested in tracking total engagement rates as well as the strength of that engagement over time. One question can capture both sets of data.

The following statement reflects how I feel about my job:

I feel highly engaged in my work.
I feel engaged in my work.
I feel neutral about my work.
I feel unengaged in my work.
I feel highly unengaged in my work.

You would measure the percent of people who feel highly engaged or engaged as your total percent of engaged workers, and the total of people who feel unengaged or highly unengaged as the total percent of unengaged workers. Each level would define the extent of engagement.

Answering the second question—*Does engagement lead to productivity within the business?*—is much harder. You'll need to analyze data in more sophisticated ways such as tracking the relationship between employee engagement and revenue, customer churn, revenue growth, customer satisfaction (or Net Promoter Scores), and market share. To do this, you'll need to track very specific metrics with employee engagement surveys and overlay them on business performance metrics. If there are key milestones of change within the business, such as a new CEO or new product launch, POPS leaders will use these to assess whether the milestone made an impact on the workforce, too. A correlation analysis is the best way to measure these bivariate (two variable) or multivariate (multiple variable) analyses.

But since it's all based on data around employee engagement surveys, let's start there.

Types of Engagement Surveys

There are two different styles of engagement surveys. The *pulse survey*, a short employee engagement survey that is sent regularly, and the *employee engagement survey*, a robust employee engagement survey that POPS leaders typically send out once or twice a year.

Pulse Surveys

Use pulse surveys to get quick, real-time feedback from your organization. They're great for assessing employee reactions to certain milestones or events in the business like appointing a new CEO, or launching a new product. You could survey your staff before and after each key event to understand how your organization feels about the change. The same response-based pulse survey could be used to determine how people react to new PTO policies, new snacks in the office, a change to roles or responsibilities, or changes to the rhythm of the business.

Employee Engagement Survey Models

Employee engagement surveys are longer questionnaires that take a deep dive into the health of the organization. Unlike pulse surveys, these aren't quick check-ins. They are thoughtfully designed surveys that occur only once or twice a year that inform key business decisions. The key here is to measure what matters by building a survey that is consistent, and make sure your questions can inform actionable change.

Take slow, considered time when building your surveys. You need to build one survey that gives you the insights you're looking for that also remains relevant over time. You want many of the questions you use the first time to be used consistently over a multiyear span. This is because consistency is critical for data analysis. Data gets wonky if you don't ask questions in the same way, or don't ask the same questions at all, between surveys. You want insights to be clear and easy. You don't want to spend a lot of time data munching. So, slow down and design your survey so that responses are easily actionable and resilient. Also, you need to be careful what you ask for. If you know your employees are clamoring for something you absolutely cannot provide, don't ask the question. Otherwise, you will be sure to disappoint them when you don't address the issue.

There are many models for measuring employee engagement, which can inform your own benchmarks or indices. We'll recap a few here.

KENEXA'S EMPLOYEE ENGAGEMENT INDEX (EEI) According to the Kenexa Research Institute, which studies workplace performance, an employee engagement index can be scored based on four key categories:

- Pride
- Satisfaction
- Advocacy
- Retention

DELOITTE'S "IRRESISTIBLE" EMPLOYEE ENGAGEMENT MODEL A research team at Deloitte studied employee engagement indicators for five years, landing on five major elements (and 20 supporting strategies) that make a business "irresistible" to work for (Bersin 2015). Those are:

- Meaningful work
  - Autonomy
  - Select to fit
  - Small, empowered teams
  - Time for slack

- Hands-on management
  - Clear, transparent goals
  - Coaching

- Invest in management development
- Modern performance management

- Positive work environment
  - Flexible work environment
  - Humanistic workplace
  - Culture of recognition
  - Inclusive, diverse work environment

- Growth opportunity
  - Training and support on the job
  - Facilitated talent mobility
  - Self-directed, dynamic learning
  - High-impact learning culture

- Trust in leadership
  - Mission and purpose
  - Continuous investment in people
  - Transparency and honesty
  - Inspiration

EMPLOYEE NET PROMOTER SCORES   Employee Net Promoter Scores (eNPSs) are a simple, but effective, metric that simply consists of asking employees if they would recommend working at your organization to friends, colleagues, or family.

To calculate your eNPS, first include the question: "I would recommend working at this organization to friends, colleagues, or family" on your employee engagement survey. Employees will rank their agreement on a 0–10 scale. People who score six or less are classified as "detractors," 7–8 are considered "passives", and 9 and 10 are considered "promoters." Subtract the detractors from the promoters, and you will have your organization's score.

A negative score tells you that employees, on the whole, don't recommend your organization as a place to work, whereas a positive score shows good employee engagement and positive affiliation with the company.

MERCER'S "WHAT'S WORKING" EMPLOYEE ENGAGEMENT INDEX   Mercer (n.d.), a leader in HR consulting, surveyed 30,000 people in 17 countries to find 12 core dimensions of work that have strong correlations to employee engagement, and lumped them into an employee engagement index built of five statements.

The 12 dimensions are:

- Work processes
- Quality and customer focus
- Communication
- Work/life balance
- Job security and career growth
- Teamwork and cooperation
- Ethics and integrity
- Immediate manager
- Performance management
- Rewards (compensation and benefits) and recognition
- Leadership and direction
- Training and development

The What's Working Index measures employee responses to the following statements:

- I feel a strong sense of commitment to this company
- I am proud to work for this company
- I would recommend my organization to others as a good place to work
- I am not considering leaving this company in the next 12 months
- I am willing to go "above and beyond" in my job to help this company be successful

The preceding models should be seen as informative and educational. You can choose one of the models to inform your process, or start from scratch on your own theories of employee engagement. Regardless of which modality you choose, the important things to remember are that employee engagement surveys need to be actionable and repeatable. Favor question framing so that you get quantifiable answers when possible. Question framing can even be presented as a response to a statement, as long as it is measuring engagement in a way that helps you further your goals. And, again, take your time building these surveys. We can't stress this enough. It often takes people teams months to design the questions.

Empirical Measurement of Employee Engagement

Empirical data means data based on observation or experience. It's used to verify the truth or falsity of a claim. Rolling out employee engagement surveys is a first step to understanding your employee experience. But sometimes relying on survey data alone can lead to misunderstandings. For example, employees are sometimes afraid to speak their minds honestly in surveys, even if they're anonymous. Or, employees might not see the value in taking a survey, so they rush through the answers without careful consideration. To balance any bias in engagement surveys, best-in-class POPS teams track empirical data points, too.

The following are examples of empirical measurements that can help you track employee engagement:

1. Employee Turnover Rate

Employee turnover rate is the measurement of the number of employees who leave an organization during a specified time period, typically one year. It's an important data point to track because consistently high turnover rates could be an indication of greater problems such as management, values, or collaboration.

2. Absenteeism

Absenteeism is the rate at which people don't show up for work, or show up late, without good reason, as measured by the average number of days taken off by your employee base, and then looking for anomalies. High rates of absenteeism suggest disengaged workers who don't want to put in effort.

3. 90-Day New Hire Success

Most turnover happens in the first 90 days, so be particularly objective in monitoring these first three months. Look at the rates of new employee 90-day failure, as well as employee engagement with onboarding content. If your employees are failing right out of the gates—as calculated by leaving the company or not getting up to speed quickly enough—this can indicate gaps in your organization. You may have a poor onboarding process, lack of training, lack of managerial and team support, or a bad hiring fit.

A Note on How You Track Employee Engagement Data

You could read all this data collection, tracking, and monitoring as big brother-ish, but don't. In the data-empowered world of people operations, we aren't looking to track employee data to fault find or catch people red handed. Instead, we're using data to be better informed about the organization as a whole. Remain inquisitive about the business objectives and employee performance at the personal level and you won't be led astray. Instead, you'll be hyper attuned to situations that are causing problems, and you'll be better prepared to make necessary changes in real time to improve work experience.

Try It Out!

Build Your Own Employee Engagement Survey!

You can adopt any of the foregoing models to inform your employee engagement thinking, but at the end of the day you'll need to build the actual survey. Here are some general categories and questions that could make up an engagement survey. Keep in mind these questions are examples only and should be adjusted to better fit your organization's needs.

1. Individual engagement

- I am compensated fairly for the work that I do.
- I am proud to work here.
- I would recommend this organization to friends and colleagues.
- I feel motivated by my role, team, or workplace.
- I feel supported by my team.
- I see myself working here in five years.
- I am excited by my work.
- I know what is expected of me.

2. Team dynamics and trust

- I feel valued by my manager and team.
- I trust my colleagues and management team.
- I enjoy working with my team.
- I feel that the goals of the company are aligned with my own.
- I trust the leadership of this company.
- I feel that my team is effective.
- I trust my colleagues to do their jobs well.
- My team helps me complete my work.
- I know who I can turn to for help.

3. Diversity and inclusion

- I feel included and that my opinions are met with inclusivity.
- I feel we hire and value a diverse workforce.
- My colleagues respond to nonconforming ideas with compassion and inclusivity.
- I respond to nonconforming ideas with compassion and inclusivity.
- I am afraid to speak my mind.

4. Technology and resources

- I am given the proper time and resources to do my job well.
- I feel that I have been trained properly for my role.
- My team and company have access to the technology or tools that we need to get the job done.
- Our technology and tools are sufficient to get the job done.

5. Recognition and career development

- I am recognized for my work.
- I am valued by my team and organization.
- My efforts are recognized fairly.
- I am supported to advance my career.
- My people team and manager provide career development pathways.
- I receive regular feedback.
- My performance feedback is appropriate and forward-thinking.

6. Understanding long-term goals and company vision

- I believe this company will be successful in reaching their goals in the long term.
- My leadership team is effective.
- I believe in the mission and values of the company.
- If it were my money and opportunity, I would invest in this company.
- I understand the company's long-term goals.

7. Empirical data

- Turnover rates.
- Absenteeism.
- 90-day new hire success rates.

Iterate How You Work

Employee engagement surveys and data are only as good as the action you take on them. Often, we see companies trying to do too much with engagement data by either asking too many questions or promising too much change. The worst thing you can do is to require your staff to fill out a bunch of survey data and then do nothing. Leaving your people, who may have spent real consideration and time answering each question, wondering, "What ever became of that survey we took?"

To keep your datasets manageable and actionable, clearly define what you want to measure, build surveys and data collection that measure those things, and then have a clear action plan for communicating with staff the results of the surveys and your intended action plan.

First, decide to what degree and how you'll share the results of the surveys. Some companies have a full transparency model where they share all the results with all people. Others take a more curated approach where managers view a certain slice of the data and employees see another, more limited, view. Either way, present the information to the entire workforce with a company announcement or email so that employees can look at the results individually.

Then, help your company understand how the leadership interpreted the results. What was different from last year? What was the same? What does this tell you about your trajectory and the happiness of your people? Where is there room for real change?

Finally, communicate your action plan. Your people team should work with the CEO and other key leaders to identify a few core insights from your survey and then build action plans for the company and specific departments.

Closing the Gap

Your people build your business when you let them. Keep a highly engaged workforce by asking employees questions, listening to their responses, integrating their ideas into your company, and measuring engagement over time. Ultimately your goal is to have unengaged people become more engaged, retain employees who are already engaged, and close the gap between the number of people who feel connected to their work.

The Old HR Way: Cares about employee engagement but doesn't have a standard process for encouraging it, measuring it, or making changes to the business. Lacks a measurable connection to employee engagement and business results.

The POPS Way: Leverages a systematic process for encouraging employee engagement, adjusting the business, and measuring outcomes. Can demonstrably prove the value of employee engagement on business objectives, and has the leadership team on board with investing in ways to promote greater engagement across the business.

CHAPTER 16

Creating a Diverse, Equitable, and Inclusive Workplace

Is this issue of diversity and inclusion in the workplace just a buzzphrase that's going to peter out in a few months or years? We don't think so.

A massive number of Millennials and Gen Zers are entering the working world. Generation Z alone, defined as people born between 1996 and the newly emerging Generation Alpha, represents 61 million people, a group that's bigger than Generation X and two-thirds the size of the Baby Boomers. These individuals come from a world vastly different to that of their parents. They've never known the world without internet or smartphones, and they have immediate access to content made from anywhere. This gives them a vastness of perspective, thoughts, and worldly opinions unobtainable by previous generations. They're ready to work hard and be loyal, but they have some new expectations about how the world of work should work. Namely, they expect positive day-to-day work experience that interacts fluidly with their nonwork lives and demand social equity and inclusion for ideas and people. In fact, according to Handshake's 2019 survey of 14 million college students and alumni from more than 800 universities across the United States, two thirds of students and recent grads said they'd only work for an employer that's built "an inclusive company culture" and provides "a sense of belonging to employees from all backgrounds" (Handshake 2019).

Gen Z has shifted the focus on social causes, too. Unlike Millennials, who felt that climate change was the number-one social issue of the times, Gen Zers feel social justice is the number-one social imperative, according to The Center for Generational Kinetics (2020).

This corroborates an anecdotal encounter we had with a recruiter from a top tech firm in Silicon Valley. After picking up a shared Uber with this recruiter back in 2019, we struck up a conversation. She was coming back to Silicon Valley after a tour of Ivy League schools. We asked her what she found was the most important factor top graduates sought when considering job opportunities, and she said plainly: "Diversity and inclusion. It's by far and away number one."

Diversity, equity, and inclusion (DEI) are the understanding and valuing of the different perspectives, experiences, and backgrounds that make each person unique. This includes but is not limited to an individual's race, ethnicity, gender, age, religion, disability, and sexual orientation. All these attributes contribute to someone's personality, skill sets, experiences, and knowledge. Diversity, equity, and inclusion are about encouraging people to bring their whole self to work, and facilitating real change in systems that were prone to bias, discrimination, or intolerance.

But it's not just the younger generations' care that's giving DEI a rise in prominence. DEI is continually connected to lifts across the business according to analysts who study business performance. For instance, DEI-focused companies report 2.3 times higher cash flow per employee, a 19 percent increase in revenue compared to less diverse management teams (Lorenzo et al. 2018), and are 1.7 times more innovative (Bersin 2019). Additionally, movements like the #MeToo movement and the Black Lives Matter movement pushed DEI issues onto the main stage of national politics, the news, social media, and everyone's Sunday dinner table. All this together is amounting to a surge of attention and resolution to create real and lasting change in our business culture and identities.

It may feel imperative, then, to launch a DEI strategy today(!), right after you finish reading this chapter. But hold on.

Before you do, it's important to first have an honest pulse check to discover "where your company is at," says Kari Girarde, Head of Community and Internal Communications at Zenefits. "Ask yourself, is your company ready for a systematic change or is this simply an HR effort in this moment?"

Girarde, who over the course of her career has launched several Engagement, Corporate Social Responsibility, and DEI programs in companies ranging from 150 to 6,000 employees, says the reason that you need to do a quick pulse check before you introduce DEI efforts into the fabric of your company is because it's something that can take years to build and prove value from. The last thing you want to do is start weaving DEI activities into your culture, only to have your company see it as mere HR window dressing or worse, inauthentic. Similarly, you don't want to create something that is not supported by senior leadership and, thus, doomed to fail. Instead, you'll want to assess where your company is and then drive awareness in the short term, while building an ongoing evolution as you thread programmatic change throughout your entire organization.

Basically, there are two types of situations small businesses face when spearheading DEI shifts. If you're lucky, you work at a company that already values DEI and has made it a priority in their values. POPS leaders in these companies might find it easier to infuse shifts in company culture into everything they do and get immediate and appreciative feedback. The other case is that you work for a company that hasn't considered DEI or is apprehensive around prioritizing it. We're not trying to sugarcoat things here. Yes, there are still many companies that question the value of DEI initiatives, despite the growing evidence of its benefits. If you work for one of these companies, you'll need to work harder and spend more time proving the value of DEI in subtle shifts over time. If this is your situation, consider what steps you can take today that will begin to sow change. For example, you could promote corporate social responsibility (CSR) activities that support underrepresented groups, reword your job postings to attract a wider pool of talent, ensure a diverse interview team to promote diverse hiring, or support employee-led affinity groups. These are just a few examples. We're sure you'll think of more. Challenge yourself to think of ways to drive depth in your culture and promote diversity and inclusivity. Consider holding office hours to discuss these ideas with employees and involve them as champions, as you all work together to bring workable solutions forward. Small, morally accurate steps don't need to cost a lot of money, or any money for that matter. Implementing small and free tactics that gradually grow over time *will* alter the make-up of your workforce. In turn, you'll be able to prove the value of diverse, equitable, and inclusive practices to the business' bottom line.

Eventually, and when your company is ready, you may establish larger moral stances on hiring for diversity and inclusion, and you'll be able to validate the success of DEI efforts by tracking metrics against specific, agreed upon goals. When you've reached this point, begin formalizing your DEI viewpoints by documenting your philosophy and vision.

Documenting Your DEI Philosophy and Vision

What your business stands for as it relates to humanitarian and social responsibilities helps inform your DEI philosophy and vision, which should be included in your DEI statement.

A *DEI statement* is a simple, clear statement that lets employees, customers, and communities know what you believe, who you are, and what you stand for as it relates to social-justice issues. It acts as a moral compass as you develop and implement your DEI strategy and your employees adjust their behaviors. As with all POPS strategies, take time to ensure your DEI statement bolsters the mission or purpose of the company, and reinforces employee productivity.

Start by asking yourself and your leadership team:

- What are your company values? Do they expand to diversity, inclusion, and equality?
- Have you addressed race, gender, identity, sexual orientation, age, disabilities, and anything else important to your culture?
- Why do you want to create a DEI statement?
- How are you going to take action?

Here's our Zenefits company DEI statement as an example:

At Zenefits we are leveling the playing field—for everyone. No matter who you are, where you're from, how you think, or who you love. We believe you should be you. Be who you want to be. Be your best self. Be human. We are united with our customers and our employees in standing for what is right. We will acknowledge the truth. We will always strive to be better. We will listen, but we won't be silent.

Once it's drafted, publish your DEI statement in an easily accessible cloud-based platform that employees can refer to at any time, on any device. That could mean you publish it internally on an intranet, externally on a webpage, or on each job-post listing. We've even seen companies publicly post their DEI perspectives on Instagram in an effort to connect with employees and customers. Whether they are a customer or future employee, a public DEI statement gives people a sense of who they are doing business with and gives them a choice.

You need to ensure your leaders are committed to DEI by discussing the DEI philosophy with your leaders and ensuring they are on board and accountable. Whether you're committing to DEI for the first time or recommitting to it, no cultural shift will be as effective without support from the top. Ask your CEO to copresent on the importance of driving a diverse and inclusive workforce, whether that's through email, all-hands meetings, or simple announcements to the company.

It's important that senior leadership comes together as a united front and remains consistent over time to the ideas you put forth. You can't just bring in a DEI professional who gives a rallying speech and think your work is done. Your employees need to hear directly from the senior leadership team how your commitment to diversity is real and the extent to which it impacts jobs and expectations. For most companies, this means communicating that everyone is expected to support a culture of diverse, open-minded thinking, and reminding employees that engaging in behaviors that do not support safety and inclusivity is strictly unacceptable. If it helps you communicate the message, we like the analogy one Society for Human Resource Management (SHRM) article used to describe what DEI really means ". . . diversity is inviting different kinds of people to a party; inclusion is asking everyone to dance; equity is asking everyone to help to plan the party and then valuing and utilizing their input" (Falcone 2020).

Some people in your organization will struggle to understand what diversity, equity, and inclusion means. They might struggle with how to identify and acknowledge it, and some might attempt to prevent it. This is where more formal education programs come in. There are two routes you can take here. If you have the budget available, you could pay for professional training programs wherein third party professionals help broach uncomfortable subjects such as racism, institutionalized discrimination, and unconscious bias and teach better practices. If you don't have the budget, you can create a similar, but free DEI training program from within your POPS department. One way you can do this is to pull together a powerful slide deck that teaches employees about unconscious bias, workplace discrimination, and how things like race, age, gender, and diverse backgrounds impact the ways we each view the world, our work, our colleagues, and people in general. Either way, aim for your training to do more than teach employees about DEI key terms. Give practical advice about how to combat discrimination in the workplace, how to work with diverse teams, how to create spaces where everyone can be heard, how to work with nonconforming opinions, how to excel as a team, and how to report issues that they see if people are behaving outside the values of your organization.

Creating Subtle Shifts in Culture

Once you have a vision, leadership support, and a way to educate employees on the value of DEI in the workplace, you can start implementing subtle changes into the fabric of your business to create a more diverse and inclusive path.

One practical approach to becoming a more diverse workplace is to recruit more diverse candidates. Diversity recruiting is about hiring the best person for the team, and valuing the unique perspective that women, LGBTQs, and people of color (PoC) bring to the company. Here are some tips to help you improve your recruiting process so that everyone feels welcome to apply:

1. **Make sure job ads are diverse and inclusive.** This can include both where you post ads and what you include in your copy. For instance, are you using gendered pronouns (he/him) or gender neutral pronouns

(they, them, ze, hir)? Does the job require a college degree if experience can be substituted? Is your job listing accessible to the seeing or hearing impaired?

2. **Create diverse interview panels.** This not only shows that you have diversity in your workplace, but you also value the opinions of those employees. Bring in people from various backgrounds and tenure, and ensure that they showcase the values you've set forth as a company. For instance, people should not be afraid to be themselves in an interview setting.

3. **Create an employer brand that consciously values diversity.** Celebrate women, people of different ages, people of different ethnicities, people with disabilities, LGBTQ, and cultural events on your website and on social media in a way that's authentic and accurate to your brand.

4. **Hire diverse candidates in significant numbers.** It's not enough to have one "token" Black, Indigenous, or people of color (BIPOC) member on your team. That's a quick way to offend your employees and create a real distrust of your values. Instead, bring in equitable numbers of diverse candidates for all positions at all levels. And hire significant numbers of diverse workers.

5. **Develop, retain, and promote for diversity and inclusion.** Invest in your diverse workforce by treating all diverse employees as full and equal team members. Develop, retain, and promote people of all backgrounds in significant numbers. Consider tying an element of performance and compensation to your DEI values and goals.

6. **Adapt your business to fit the needs of your employees.** As you increase the representation of diverse people in your business, you'll need to adjust your workplace to adapt to their professional and sociocultural expectations, instead of asking them to adjust to yours. If you're truly listening to the motivations of your employees in an honest way, where employees feel safe to share their needs and opinions, this will become a natural part of your business cycle.

Another practical approach to stitch DEI into the fabric of your business is to review your holiday schedule as a way to celebrate diversity in your business. Which holidays does your company formally recognize, and how are employees permitted to celebrate? Here are some ways you could rethink your company holidays to be more inclusive:

1. **Choose various cultural holidays to recognize to diversify an Anglo-American perspective.** There are many cultural holidays that can be recognized in a variety of ways, including Chinese New Year, Hanukkah, Ramadan, Diwali, Juneteenth, and many more.

2. **Offer a flexible holiday schedule where the employee chooses the holiday they want to celebrate.** This provides support for individuals who do not follow a mainstream sociopolitical or religious construct for holiday schedules, and it removes the burden on HR to guess which holidays are important to the majority of workers.

3. **Encourage cultural education.** Recognizing holidays doesn't always have to be a paid day off. Empower employees to share and celebrate different cultural holidays.

A final practical approach would be to look at behavioral conduct both inside your company and out. Internal codes of conduct involved how employees interact with each other, such as how meetings are conducted, or how decisions are made. External codes of conduct refer to how the business represents itself to its customers, to the greater public, and how it spends its money. Here's a bit more on that:

1. **Internal conduct.** Employee conduct looks at how your employees interact with one another. There are many ways to look at how employees interact with one another to root out problem areas and redefine good habits. This could include everything from how meetings are conducted to the language people use with one another. Is it inclusive? What kind of language do people use? Is it sympathetic to people's needs or does it include stereotypes and slurs? Address meeting culture, too. Are remote workers included in meetings given links to conference room meeting invites? Are minority holidays respected when deadlines are being made? Do you ask project participants for their opinions and truly listen and give their ideas fair consideration? And what about employee habits within the lifecycle of a business? What happens when women announce a pregnancy?

2. **External conduct.** This refers to how your brand is being represented outside of the company. If your brand is truly integral to its DEI mission, it must put its money where its mouth is. How businesses arrive at profitability are unique to each company, but systemic problems that perpetuate social injustice are embedded in how business happens. For example, when you're buying marketing ads are you ensuring they're posted to diverse, representation friendly media outlets? Do your images and graphics depict multicultural people? What about programmatic spending on Google, Facebook, and YouTube? Often, algorithms will automatically *direct advertising dollars to the highest highest-performing ads*. Are you overriding algorithms to show representational depictions of minority groups?

Evaluate your success creating inclusive conduct through employee surveys, exit interviews, stay interviews, or—if budget allows—third-party analysis.

If social justice is really going to be righted, we need to think beyond roll call. Yes, we need BIPOC represented fairly in hiring and in leadership positions. But we also need to think about how larger systems (such as internet algorithms and accessibility) prolong injustice, and we need to actively work to jettison systems that hinder progress. To put it frankly, what is your company doing with its money to offset the imbalances of social justice?

Big problems often require big solutions. Luckily, businesses encounter opportunities to ignite change every day on both large and small scales. The rise of remote work, for instance, which was accelerated by COVID-19, resulted in a large-scale epiphany by employers that sounded something like "Hey! People actually can be productive when working remotely!" This remote work realization, impacting both the employer and the employees, will likely have profound effects on DEI in the workplace, too. Viewed from the employer perspective first, remote work untethers businesses from their locations. With virtually enabled hiring, managers are empowered to draw from larger geographic pools of candidates, because employees can suddenly be located anywhere. Apart from the obvious benefit of hiring more skilled people, this also calls into question whether headquartering a business in an expensive city—once known to draw most skilled, but also most affluent and privileged people—represents an advantage anymore. Business owners could headquarter and hire in cheaper cities, thus driving down overhead costs, opening the option for more diverse hiring, and creating more powerful and skilled teams. Viewed from the employee perspective, as businesses unshackle ties to certain cities, individuals living in less expensive areas have a greater chance of being a successful candidate for jobs.

Here's an example. A single parent living just 80 miles outside of downtown San Francisco might not have been able to manage a full day of interviews at a high-growth tech company in 2019, despite being really close to one of the biggest tech hubs in the world. Those 80 miles might have meant significant childcare costs, dependence on a car, and the costs of parking and eating in a city. Any one of which could have been prohibitively expensive. Fast forward to 2021, with virtual interviews and remote work becoming the norm, that same parent can not only nail the interviews from their living room, but also complete their work without having to relocate or take on greater costs of living.

In at least two ways—namely, socioeconomically and geosocially—the rise of remote work has theoretically leveled the playing field for greater

DEI. But COVID-19 is just one example of an event that gave us the opportunity to move our society in the right direction. As leaders in business and the future of work, people ops practitioners must *continue* to seek change and hold each other accountable for driving greater social justice within our respective centers of influence. There are no limits to how work cultures can be designed to steer toward greater social equality. It could come through recruiting, hiring, developing, promoting, educating, spending, documenting, advocating, or more. If DEI is important to your company, you'll find a way. The one key we'd recommend, regardless of your approach, is to remain steadfast. Cultural change is not easy. DEI efforts aren't some program that can start and stop. To have an inclusive culture, you must practice what you preach—all day, every day—in everything you do. Gradually, and together, we will shift. And while DEI efforts may feel like a hard sell in your company today, as you roll out subtle cultural changes that embrace diversity and inclusion, you'll see clear gains in greater innovation, greater profits, and happier—and more productive—employees for anyone who questions you.

The Old HR Way: Lacked a formal DEI policy, doubted the impact a diverse and inclusive workforce could have on the bottom line.

The POPS Way: Understands that embracing DEI means positioning the company to better attract, recruit, and retain top talent. Understands that younger generations seek social justice as the number one most important thing our world needs to work on, and seeks employers who embody acts of change. Commits to developing a DEI philosophy that permeates work culture through employee conduct and brand conduct. Holds itself and others accountable to creating change inside centers of influence.

CHAPTER 17

Making Remote Work, *Work*

The rise of remote work was gaining in popularity well before the pandemic hit. A not-so-hushed rise of distributed workforces, aided by an increasing number of virtual work tools, was taking hold. Recruiters were attracted to the prospect of hiring talent without the constraints of geography. And business owners liked finding top talent in low-cost-of-living regions. Human resources thought leaders even named the expansion of remote and distributed teams as the number-one work trend in 2019 (Suzuno 2019). That was a trend they expected would continue to gain strength in 2020. But when COVID-19 hit, the adoption of remote work exploded at a speed and scale no one could predict. It became one of most drastic changes to work we've witnessed in modern history. And now it's a topic we can't avoid when talking about employee experience and workforce productivity.

Indeed, Gallup reported that at the pandemic's peak, 51 percent of US working adults moved to at-home offices to avoid spreading the virus. And though that number fell to 33 percent by December 2020, early research suggests that the shift to remote work will be a lasting phenomenon, particularly for highly paid jobs that require higher levels of education (Brenan 2020).

Researchers at the University of Illinois and Harvard Business School estimate that 16 percent of American workers who once worked from offices will permanently switch to at-home work, at least two days per week. A "dramatic and persistent shift in workplace norms around remote work" with "implications for companies, employees, and policymakers alike," said Christopher Stanton, an associate professor at Harvard Business School and lead researcher on the project (Senz 2020).

So the question now is not *if* remote work will be a part of the future, but to what extent? And for those companies that *choose* to offer remote work options post pandemic, the question is how can people ops design work cultures where people remain productive regardless of where their employees are located? Luckily we have pandemic-induced datasets to pull from—as a kind of global case study—to inform our decisions.

Here are some things we learned right away.

One, remote work productivity varies by industry. Industries that have a greater focus on computer-oriented tasks report an easier switch to remote work, and, often, increased levels of productivity. Information companies, like technology, telecommunication, or media reported the least loss of productivity due to remote work caused by the pandemic, while administrative jobs reported the highest gain in productivity (a 49 percent increase, per Senz 2020).

Two, remote teams need certain infrastructure to be successful. Employees need access to critical tools and resources, such as internal databases, inventory management systems, or client records, to perform core job requirements. Even simple things like clocking in and out or logging meal breaks need to be remote enabled to keep business in compliance with federal and state regulations.

Three, remote work *isn't* a great option for certain industries. Companies with high levels of customer interaction or hands-on production don't work well with a remote work model. Accommodation and food services companies reported a 49 percent loss in productivity when forced into remote work conditions due to the pandemic. Transportation and warehousing services reported a 38 percent loss. Although there may be certain jobs at restaurants or manufacturing facilities that could work from home, it might not work for the sector at large. So how will you know if remote work options will be good for *your* business?

Knowing If Remote Work Can Work for You

Well, you won't until you try it and measure its impact. But there are a couple of ways to rough out an estimate.

A quick mental assessment is a good place to start. What is the make-up of your business? According to pandemic analyses, roles that have a high dependency on computers and low dependency on physical products or people tend to pull off remote work best. Some roles actually *improve* in performance. Do you have a high percentage of workers who might actually be aided by remote work options? Or do you have a large requirement for person-to-person jobs and manual labor?

You can also ask employees for their opinions, directly. If you can't talk to each person in your company one-on-one, run a quick pulse survey to ask folks if they'd like to work remote (Yes/No)? If so, how many days per week would they want to work remotely (1–5). And how productive do they think they would be (on a five-point Likert scale from very productive to very unproductive). If you ask why people want to work remotely, you might glean some other important information that could inform in-person work policies too. For instance, according to research by Upwork, an online network of freelance workers, when asking what about remote work employees liked during the pandemic, "no commute" topped the charts (49.0 percent), followed by the "reduction of non-essential meetings" (46.3 percent), "less distractions than in the office" (41.2 percent), and "increased productivity" (32.2 percent). Only 1.9 percent said "nothing has worked well" (Ozimek 2020).

There are also costs to consider. What are the financial implications of switching to a more remote work scenario? Cost savings could include decreased rent obligations, fewer office supplies, or less reliance on certain perks like commuter benefits or parking passes. Additional costs could include things like an uptick in software licenses for core software-as-a-service (SaaS) infrastructure, remote work stipends to create in-home workstations that work for employees, and increased hardware costs for certain job required tools like keys, lab equipment, or other hard goods.

If, by your estimation, the benefits of remote work outweigh the costs, we say go for it! You'll be able to measure the impact of the change in your performance metrics over time to validate or invalidate whether remote work gives a boon to your particular business. But indicators from the COVID-19 remote work experiment seem positive. The next question is, how do you help set the bar of remote work excellence? And we'll spend the remainder of this chapter focusing on exactly that.

You're Going Remote! Now What?

Once you've determined to add remote work as a formal option for your employees, it's time to get down to the brass tacks of how to pull it off—really well. Again, COVID-19 has helped. Society has played witness to both the successes and failures of remote work, giving us a nice blueprint to work from. Let's look at what it tells us.

You Don't Need to Limit Your Remote Work Policy to a One-Size-Fits-All Approach

Because you're acting in the best interest of the company and not discriminating against certain workers, you can specify which teams or individuals have remote work options. And, you can decide how much remote work is permitted. Many companies are finding success with a hybrid remote work solution, where employees work remotely two to three days a week and come into the office two to three days a week. People work in different ways. We learned that sometimes too much remote work can lead to mental distress. People miss the face-to-face connections they have with their peers and long to connect outside of virtual conference rooms. A hybrid approach gives a nice balance for in-person dialog, and at-home focus. Executed well, hybrid remote policies allow companies to reap the benefits from all sides: increased remote work, optional office work, and decreased overhead costs.

People Work Hard, No Matter Where They Are, When They Are Engaged

Many employees took their newfound remote-work freedom and went somewhere. They went to their hometowns, they went to Mexico, they went to the mountains. And guess what? They were still productive! What used to be some companies' biggest fear—people sneaking away on vacations, trying to make it look like they were working on the company's dime, but were really slacking off somehow—were largely debunked. Engaged employees worked as many hours (or more) with their remote freedom. Plus, many grew to value their employer and job more. Keep your employees engaged in or out of the office. Try introducing fun Slack channels where people of similar interests can chat and make friends. Or reminding people of the value of each person's work through good goal setting, regular check-ins, and employee recognition programs. Keeping employees engaged will ensure the ball won't get dropped.

Remote Work Does Not Mean Your Employees Can Move

The IRS doesn't care if people travel around for long periods of time, but they care if you move. Paying state income taxes is an important part of tax compliance. If employees move, your tax burden as an employer changes, which may or may not be something you're willing to do. Remind workers that moves must be cleared by management in order for the company to stay on the right side of the law.

People Need Good At-Home Working Environments

Energy levels, posture, ergonomics . . . these things all affect people's productivity. If you think your remote employees can perform at the same level when working in a cramped kitchen with half a dozen roommates or children running around, well you're wrong. Help remote workers design effective workspaces by managing common challenges of remote offices. Here are a few suggestions that have been shown to boost employee productivity:

- Distinguish working hours from nonworking hours with housemates
- Consider the layout of your workspace
- Designate specific office zones
- Ensure your office space gets lots of natural sunlight
- Improve the ergonomics of your desk space with books to prop up screens, or pillows to adjust your seating height
- Create opportunities for movement in the day, like walking around the house between meetings

Employers Are Responsible for Paying for All Hours Worked of Which They Either Know or Have Reason to Believe Were Performed

The FLSA has very strict standards on employee pay. The federal law requires that employers pay their employees for all hours worked, whether required by the employer or that an employer allows an employee to perform even if not requested. This can include situations in which an employee works outside his/her scheduled time without the employer's permission, but the employer knows or has reason to know the employee is working. "Remote work by nonexempt employees can pose a challenge with regard to ensuring employees are paid for all time worked, as the traditional workday may be blurred in a remote environment," according to a 2020 article by Christine Townsend of law firm Ogletree Deakins.

Set Clear Remote Work Expectations in an Updated Employee Handbook

Clear, documented expectations make remote work satisfying and productive. Did you know two-thirds (67 percent) of American workers find their employee handbooks "useful" and almost half (41 percent) have referred to it within the last six months? With changing work policies and federal regulations, our employees need our help navigating what's expected of them. The best way to clearly communicate new expectations, rules, and consequences is by communicating your expectations verbally and documenting them in an employee handbook that lives online for all to access. Here are a few specifications you might consider:

DEFINE WORKING HOURS The most successful remote teams measure outcomes, not hours, but clarity is important. Define working hours for each role and employee type. And be upfront about them. What are the minimum and maximum hours permitted for each role? Which days of the week are people expected to be available? Does this job require East Coast hours? Does it require attendance at a weekly all-hands meeting? Take measure of what you need from your employees for success and let them know.

DEFINE COMMUNICATION AND RESPONSIVITY EXPECTATIONS We know that some roles are more collaborative than others, and many mission-critical roles rely heavily on communication. Formulate your expectations for responsiveness based on role-specific requirements, but with the understanding that the entire business needs focused time to do its best work. If you rely on, or are used to, a highly collaborative team or work scenario, consider asking employees to respond to "lite requests" within two hours, and more detailed ones within three hours.

Or perhaps it makes sense for you to run fully asynchronous work, like the 100 percent remote team at Doist, the tech firm behind productivity app Todoist. Doist's ethos on communication is that employees are generally expected to reply within 24 hours. The company says this helps them maintain high levels of productivity as employees are empowered to disconnect and dedicate focused time to work. It also helps keep those across time zones included as individuals respond when they can (Doist 2020).

ADDRESS ACCESSIBILITY AND SECURITY All remote companies need to have strong accessibility and security measures in place. Be explicit and communicative about who can access what and from where. Consider the following:

- **Software-update requirements:** Have a policy requiring employees to keep software up to date on all the devices they're accessing on the company network or from email.
- **Virtual private networks (VPNs):** Provide a professional-grade VPN for employees to use.
- **Full-disk encryption:** Make sure physical devices that contain sensitive information are fully encrypted, so even if it's stolen, your business is safe.
- **Good password hygiene:** Prompt employees to change their passwords every six months with requirements for strong passwords that include an uppercase letter and at least one symbol.
- **Log out policies:** Mandate that employees log out when the device is not in use—always!
- **Smart use:** Be clear about expectations for company property or devices that have access to the network, such as putting computers in the trunk of the car and not leaving devices unattended in public.

Remote Work Could Change Your Hiring and Onboarding Process

Some people work better than others in remote offices. If you're looking to fill a remote position, consider adding interview questions that address the candidate's ability to perform job duties at home based on their personality and work preferences. How do they feel about self-starting projects? How do they feel about virtual communication? Are they okay working on asynchronous schedules?

You'll also need to reconsider your onboarding process. In the old days, onboarding happened at the place of work, the new hire often got a buddy to help orient them with the business and its people. Now, people are left to their own devices: computers, virtual productivity tools (such as Slack, Microsoft Teams, etc.), and email. People operations software walks people through each step of the onboarding flow, from new hire paperwork, to direct deposit set up and benefits enrollment. If you want every "i" dotted and every "t" crossed, you'll want to automate your onboarding through tech.

The Future of Remote Work

The way we work has forever changed. Younger generations, drawing from vastly different experiences, have transformed it. Technology has evolve it. And we recently watched as the enormous socioeconomic experiment of the COVID-19 pandemic changed it. As leaders in business, we need to pivot. Though we don't yet know to what extent, the shift to remote work will continue to expand, first to industries that tend to be more computer and desk oriented, and then to other industries as technology advances.

Addressing whether remote work works for your business will be up to you, the nature of your business, your leadership, and the desires of your staff. But we hope with lessons from COVID-19 that companies with aspirations to unleash a remote workforce your company can do so successfully right out of the gates.

The Old HR Way: Wasn't sure if remote work was possible. Considered hypothetical examples of remote work or hybrid work solutions, but remained concerned about the feasibility of such plans.

The POPS Way: Leveraging insights from the mass assimilation of remote work due to COVID-19, leaders feel emboldened to incorporate remote work opportunities to more aspects of their business. POPS leaders can now focus attention less on whether remote work works, and more on how to make it work best in class.

PART V

The Future of People Operations

CHAPTER **18**

The Rise of the CPO: Building a Modern People Ops Team

We know that while some people reading this book are people team leaders themselves, while others are business leaders trying to get a grip on the modern modalities of HR. Regardless, this chapter includes context on both what to consider for first timers and some updated thinking on what to focus on, for those growing in the role. We'll jump into how to build a people ops team including who to hire, and in what order.

To meet your organization's unique needs, you need an owner to harness the best set of strategies, programs, operations ideas, and tools offered in this book. Depending on where your business is on the POPS Maturity Model, that person might need to fit POPS into an existing role as CEO or as finance or operations lead. But if you have the flexibility, we've also included some frameworks to consider in building your POPS organization from the ground up.

We'll start at the top.

Once a new C-suite title catches on, it can spread throughout the US economy in a hurry. Laszlo Bock became Google's first head senior vice president (SVP) of people operations about a decade ago. He demonstrated that the company would benefit from a more ambitious, data-driven approach to all sorts of talent-related topics, beyond what a traditional HR function could provide.

"Dozens if not hundreds" of other companies peeked into Google's approach to see if they ought to be trying something similar, Bock recalls. "I hope many do reverse engineer it! Companies that get this right perform better and have happier people." (Anders 2019).

Today, the overall hiring growth rate for CPO jobs tops 32 percent a year. Don't think of this new title as merely a fancy name for traditional human resource functions. CPOs in the past few years have uprooted toxic cultures, worked directly with the CEO to define key goals, and advised on acquisitions. And their role—building great employee experiences that unleash potential has become more critical. The start of the pandemic in 2020 highlighted this crucial need for agility, which will continue to be a business requirement.

So far, software and tech companies are leading the way in adding CPOs to their executive teams, but as you'd surmise from the rest of this book, their potential for impact is huge for any business sector.

Ideally, you should bring in the most strategic people operations person you can afford—as soon as you can. This hire will help build out the foundational programs to set up your business to grow.

What a POPS Pro Should Bring to Your Business Plan

A smart business plan should be bolstered by a strategic people plan. That input is crucial to laying the foundation for the growth of your business and your team.

A strong people operations partner should help you think through the "scaffolding" for your scalable organizational structure. Key tenets should include provisions for each stage of growth including:

- The right leadership team
- The best talent and key roles
- Organizational structure
- Management process and systems
- Culture

If you delay hiring a people professional until you have 200 or more employees, you could actually put your business behind in terms of missed opportunities. For example, hiring or keeping the wrong talent in key positions can create downstream problems in productivity, morale, and even legal issues.

An experienced people professional can mitigate these risks with a focus on bringing in the right talent for your company early on and help your business grow and thrive with the right culture from day one.

We recognize that one challenge for smaller businesses is justifying the investment for a senior people person when you already have a tight budget. Successful people operations professionals garner a good salary, commensurate with their value. According to ZipRecruiter.com the salary for this role ranges from $73,000 to $261,000. This is contingent on the size and location of the company and the amount of experience required.

If you are in a business poised for significant growth, then it's a smart strategy to "overhire" in the people role to help ensure smart, sustainable growth strategies, foundations, and guardrails.

Ironically, fast (but ineffectively supported) growth has been the undoing of many great business ideas. In the small business realm, companies like Zynga games, Crumbs Bake Shop, and Wise Acre Frozen Treats are all cautionary tales of growth at all costs. Our own company—the fastest-growing software company in 2015—also lost its footing for a time before resetting with a strong focus on the right values, the right culture, the right business model and infrastructure.

It's also important to be objective about where your organization is on the POPS Maturity Model, when setting expectations for your CPO or people team. We get it: if you pay for a strong leader, you want all the benefits that come with advanced mastery.

Who doesn't want to be in a *Best Places to Work* ranking, or do 360-degree reviews, or have a solid mentorship program? But a good CPO will help you determine the *right things to do first*. Strategy, grounded in reality and tied to key business objectives will benefit you most and help focus your business on the right building blocks at the right time.

In addition to knowing *their* business function, a strong people ops practitioner ought to know *your* business. Your people partners will understand your business model, path to profitability, funding and investors, resource allocation, products, customer experience, employee sentiment, and motivations.

That foundation will accelerate their ability to build your business with the right resources and within the necessary constraints.

Unlike the misconception that an HR person is a "people pleaser", the CPO should be "the truth teller"—unafraid to say the unpopular thing. The CPO needs to look at everything through the people lens and share the unvarnished, data-supported truth in order to drive better listening, faster action, and recovery, as well as overall organizational resilience.

As we mentioned, it is important at the beginning of the engagement with a people leader or team to have an objective assessment of your business's POPS maturity. Likewise, it's important to align the right behavioral style of POPS leaders to fit your short- and longer-term business needs.

For example, high growth businesses with new products or business models might do best with a CPO that self-identifies as a builder: someone who thrives on creating from a blank slate and who does well in ambiguity. For that type of business, leaders have the opportunity to continue to reinvent their careers, trying on new skills and ownership.

POPS STAR

Amy Dalebout's first day at her job as VP of People and Culture at MotoRefi turned out to be the first day the whole company went remote, due to COVID-19. In the next seven months, she helped the team grow from 65 to 160. Amy would tell you, this wasn't "a happy accident."

A seasoned business executive with operations, change management, and people-programs experience, Amy quickly dug into the tech company's business, culture, and team to build out a measurable, flexible People and Culture Roadmap. This strategic plan is aligned to company goals, metrics, and values to help inform and focus the right work and priorities. And Amy leverages technology for greater impact; in fact, MotoRefi is running at the "Scaling" level on the People Ops Maturity Model.

For her fast-growing business, one of Amy's key success metrics is the Employee Net Promoter Score (eNPS), which gauges an employee's willingness to recommend the company to peers and potential employees. Amy's roadmap prioritized remote employee engagement, employee benefits, and development to keep her smart staff motivated and willing to recommend new hires.

In the process of building a highly functioning remote team, she's powered a high eNPS and nearly tripled the organization. That includes her first few hires for her People and Culture team, to help ensure the People and Culture team continues to review, assess, and flex their roadmap plan to best meet the needs of the business.

If your business is proven and stable, and if you have a consistent business model, adding POPS teams that are natural optimizers or maintainers might be the best fit. These are the type of people who are motivated to add to existing foundational elements. A POPS leader who is a builder might be great for a year or two at this kind of business but will likely outgrow your company in terms of their interest.

In fact, your CPO should help you create a succession plan for every member of your executive and high-performer team, including the CPO's own role. Short term, it makes the function stronger to have a team member in development to collaborate on key company initiatives. And longer term, it sets the business up for better continuity. It might sound counterintuitive, but especially in a small business, succession planning should include planned and emergency successor options. Sometimes, the planned

The ROI of POPS

There is a direct correlation between successful organizations and those that employ the right POPS leaders and strategies. On average, they have significantly lower turnover and better hiring, which is important because turnover can cost 33 percent of total salary to replace each person. They also have better organizational development and improved business longevity. In the next chapter, we'll take a closer look at how properly measuring people ops can improve an organization.

successor might not be ready when you need them, and you'll need to consider an outside candidate.

The POPS Organization

Now that you have an idea of the right POPS leader for your people function, what about the team?

Well, here's the truth, for the majority of small businesses: the team is often a team of one. Therefore, mindset and behaviors are nearly as important as skill sets and experience. Therefore, it's imperative to do the analysis and make the case for hires that best meet the needs of the company, not only the role.

Keith Hammond at *Fast Company* wrote an article in 2005: "Why We Hate HR," which we talked about in Chapter 2. Unfortunately, that mindset is deep and pervasive. You don't need a party planner, or cheerleaders, but you do need those who understand and are passionate about building employee engagement and experience to drive business. And they'll need to help ensure appropriately calibrated, cascading goals, and values that are woven throughout the culture, to support in making the hard decisions.

When it comes to selecting the right person or people for your POPS program management, you need to think long term. Regardless of whether an individual stays with you five or more years, the choices they make could impact your business for years beyond their tenure.

That's great news if you make the best hiring decisions. With the right foundational and compliance decisions early on, it will be much more efficient to grow the right talent pipeline to fuel the evolving needs of your business. In turn, the POPS team can spend time developing your managers. This will be key in helping to advance your business from one level of

TABLE 18.1 List of responsibilities included in people operations.

Included	Optional	Excluded
Essentials	Training	Accounting
Employee records	Facilities/workplace	Corporate IT
Policies & documents	Office management	External
Hiring & onboarding	Community relations	communications
Time & attendance	Workplace technology	Pet projects
Payroll	Corporate social	
Benefits	responsibility	
Culture & productivity		
Listening & feedback		
Internal communications		
Engagement & wellbeing		
Talent Management		
Recruiting		
Performance management		
Learning & development		
Succession planning*		
Alumni program*		
Strategy		
Workforce planning*		
Organizational structure		
Extended workforce		
strategy		
Remote work operations		
Compensation strategy		
Diversity, equality, &		
inclusion		
People Ops measurement		
People Ops technology		

*typically at larger companies
Note: this varies from company to company, and by stage. When it comes to organizational design, larger companies sometimes break out responsibilities into subteams such as Talent or Culture and Talent.
Source: Zenefits, 2021.

maturity to the next. You'll need the bulk of the company on board with tools and training to manage everything from policy to culture to performance alignment.

However, when you make the wrong choices, the repercussions, such as neglecting to classify employees properly, could lead to dissatisfaction, turnover, and FLSA violations with long-term ramifications.

POPS Hiring Checklist

1. Be crystal clear on your hiring strategy.
   Clearly define the role. Know what it is you'd like to see accomplished in the next 12–18 months. Understand what skills are needed to round out your team or the department. And be honest on the how—what is the culture or value-add you need to ensure that this team will work and be superproductive?
2. Craft a set of interview questions that will uncover a POPS mindset. Consider these attributes:
   - Openness, curiosity
   - Willingness to try new things
   - Hands-on builder
   - Growth mindset
   - Comfortable with change and ambiguity
   - Strategic and tactical
   - Decision oriented
   - Flexible and knowing when to make exceptions.
3. Determine their level of comfort with technology.
   The modern world of work requires the use of technology to support the business and enhance the people experience. Make sure they are comfortable and eager to use technology, and learn about new tools to increase their effectiveness.
4. Ensure alignment around ownership.
   POPS teams can easily become subsumed (and distracted) by requests and suggestions from others. Your POPS team should not be there to do managers' jobs for them; rather, they should focus on building frameworks to empower your managers and employees.
5. Your POPS leader should have—and welcome—diverse experiences.
   Context switching from assessing talent, to developing a hiring "brand" on social media, to developing benefits plans, to coaching leaders are often all in a day's work for small business POPS pros. Explore your candidate's experience, and look for a varied background and a can-do attitude.

Tips on Team Building

In the ideal world, you'll bring in a new team with great POPS-level acumen and behaviors. But in the real world, you will likely have to look at your existing team to see if you can level up people who are already great assets to your organization. Then determine the risks/reward of changing them from their current roles—even if it is part-time to start.

For example, do you have people in HR support roles, such as someone doing data entry on time tracking, or keeping employee records up-to-date for compliance or benefits?

We're big advocates for hiring from within and giving interested employees the opportunity to stretch and learn. But the key is setting fair and honest expectations and assessment. In reality, people who are the right fit for an organization at one time might not be the best fit later.

Expectations need to be very clear: outline the role and develop a measurable project to test their acumen. Then, frame out the time, training, check-ins, and assessment to determine if this transition will work.

What could be perceived as kindness to keep someone on that isn't great for a role is actually just the opposite. We've all kept that person we liked, and we're all, in hindsight, sorry that we did. POPS people do the right expectation setting and aren't afraid to make hard decisions that power the company. If you have to let people go, you do it fairly, help them make the transition, and don't make it weird.

When you get the right person or people in the role(s), the best development is on-the-job learning through stretch projects. Talk to them about what you need and also ask, when they've got some wins under their belt: "What else do you think we need? Do you want to lead it?"

On our Zenefits team, for example, our recruiter took on employer branding and social media programs, our POPS specialist pulled together the framework for a global handbook, and another member of the team created remote open office hours to augment great new programming for our diversity, equity, and inclusion initiatives.

Once you've assigned interesting projects to your team, empower them to do the work without micromanagement: let them make mistakes and learn. By offering your new or existing open, flexible, and curious POPS people a healthy amount of responsibility, trust, and regular check-ins/accountability, you build on to the behaviors that will engage them even more.

Ultimately, a strong POPS person or team will continually assess your organization for trouble spots.

For example, during the COVID-19 pandemic, mental health and well-being escalated quickly as people managed personal health, family care, children learning online at home, and business uncertainty. Good POPS teams recognized the problem, found and regularly assessed data from surveys, weekly manager check-ins, exit interviews, and turnover statistics to monitor, find trigger points, and recommend remediation and follow-up to keep employees engaged and leadership informed. (see Figure 18.1)

According to a brand report by the Starr Conspiracy, "Like it or not, employers play a role in the physical, mental and financial well-being of their employees. The response to this reality will have the most significant impact on the employer brand (positively or negatively) in the next few years" (Starr Conspiracy 2020).

So, make sure your business is proactively responding to employee concerns by focusing on the whole person, not just the work they do for you.

The POPS team is your organization's front-line workforce. They build the framework to understand and adjust for optimal employee well-being which delivers optimal business impact. Although they shouldn't be treated

FIGURE 18.1 The many aspects of employee well-being.

Source: Adapted from Starr Conspiracy, "Brandscape 2021: Workplace Wellbeing," December 2020, https://brandscape.thestarrconspiracy.com/brandscape-2021-workplace-well-being/#/new-reality.

any differently from than any other team, they ought to be grounded in preventative self-care.

Arianna Huffington, who founded Thrive Global in 2006 after her own well-documented burnout at the Huffington Post, said that people leaders ". . . have become the most important professionals within an organization. I'm sure you're all finding it easier to convince the CFO and the CEO that spending on your employees and your own well-being and resilience is essential for the bottom line."

She advocates that taking time off is an investment in leadership. We agree. Put on your own oxygen mask first. But don't confuse that with being the parents of your organization.

The Old HR Way: Hire for competency in learning, staying aware of and abiding by rules, from compliance to the company handbook. Good at upholding traditions and established ways of doing things. The team is likely to include data entry, tracking, and managing. Look to create, define, and own the culture. Candidates join "because I'm a people person."

The HR team was known as the caregivers of the company. They were always the people with the candy bowl, everyone's mother.

The POPS Way: Far less administration focused and more automation and data focused. Use data rather than "gut feel" to inform insights, power actions, and gauge impact. Skills are likely to include data analysis and an understanding of how to prioritize programs to help the business. Look to curate, not create, the culture. Top candidates join "because people are the most important advantage of a business."

POPS is all about ensuring a powerful experience with the company to build your business and unleash your people's potential. Your POPS is not your mom.

CHAPTER 19

Measuring People Ops

Today, metrics are an essential part of any high-performing team. People ops is no exception. Want a seat at the table? Data is your ticket. You'll need more than just spreadsheets of raw information, of course. You need insights, analytics, and a point of view.

Data helps uncover insightful workforce trends, ranging from the business impact of recruiting processes to departmental performance and employee engagement. It helps show where you're overspending and surfaces risks. It also gives teams actionable ways to improve based on real-world, tangible data.

People ops teams can use workforce analytics to help business leaders unlock higher performance and growth. A consistent review of your team's morale, for example, enables you to proactively spot employee red flags like disengagement. In turn, you'll be able to mitigate the impact of these risk factors. These could include things like a drop in sales productivity, a poor customer experience, or a lagging supply chain.

In this chapter, we explain which people metrics to track and how to use them in leveling up your processes to gain richer insights into the people who make up your business.

From Gut Instinct to Data-Driven Decisions

Measuring the workforce is no easy feat. It's not like a supply chain. People are complex and fluid. The world of human relations is based on many qualitative factors, and quantifying these can be challenging. But with the right internal processes and tools at your disposal, it can be done.

One of the benefits of people operations, which we've alluded to continually throughout this book, is the digitization of more processes, which improves data capture and the ability to make smarter decisions. By tracking, logging, and analyzing more employee touch points, you can surface more insights, trends, and recommendations.

POPS STAR

As the digitized "first responders" to roadside assistance, the HONK Technologies team of customer care personnel are the human interface to stranded motorists. In turn, HONK's technology finds the closest service-provider partner in the area to deliver faster, better roadside assistance. Therefore, Rob Snodgrass, HONK's VP of people and talent, is laser-focused on building and measuring an empathetic employee experience, to support an empathetic customer and partner experience.

People operations technology plays a key role in keeping the HONK team engaged and measuring the impact on the business.

"Now our people can see their pay stubs, benefits balances and total hours worked; our managers can see attendance, schedules and performance reviews; and our executives can see the cost of benefits, functional productivity from total hours worked, retention and ramp times. And everyone understands where all the information lives: in Zenefits," adds Rob.

Data is the bridge that connects people operations to the business strategy. And, as we mentioned, it's paramount in the move from HR administration to people operations. Organizations look to people operations for strategic direction based on their data-driven decision-making approach. This reduces the emphasis on top-down subjective management styles and gives people teams the power to influence business decision-makers for the better. No longer simply the disciplinarians resolving office disputes, people teams now have a greater impact across all areas of the business. These include:

- Business direction
- Organizational structure
- Company mission and goals
- Productivity measures

People Analytics: Metrics That Matter

People analytics is the process of collecting and analyzing data across the employee lifecycle for the purpose of improving an organization's overall workplace performance. This process is also sometimes called workforce analytics, or talent analytics.

Identifying which metrics to track is the first step in building an effective, data-driven people operations team. It's not enough to simply know what was happening. You also need to know why, and—in a highly optimized workplace—what could happen next.

To do this, people teams must develop a comprehensive measurement and reporting strategy, one that coexists with the entire business.

Some of the core components to people analytics include:

- *Operational reporting:* a collection of basic historical data used to identify and reflect on what has happened in the past. An example of this would be a headcount or turnover report.
- *Advanced reporting:* more sophisticated reports, usually including additional data sources, which identify trends that directly impact decision-making. Examples include employee engagement and well-being scores.
- *Strategic analytics:* statistical analysis and modeling of reports to proactively identify business opportunities and vulnerabilities. Examples include diversity scoring and its impact on the business, detailed employee turnover analysis, and benefits benchmarking.
- *Predictive insights:* prediction of future outcomes and scenarios based on strategic analytics, data models, and scenario planning—empowering decision makers with actionable insights for rapid, data-driven decisions. Examples include projected salary costs and forecasted retention rates and costs.

How to Track Your Progress

As you progress across the People Operations Maturity Model, your ability to make decisions based on data improves. This goes for the people team, executives, and any business decision maker. You and your team can move faster, with more confidence. This also builds credibility within the organization.

Following are some examples of the types of metrics tracked at each stage of maturity.

Level 1: Chaotic

At this level, you're likely tracking things manually. Data needs to be created from manual sources (which is painful), dug up from original sources such as your employees, or exported from various systems. It takes minutes, if not hours, and insights are pretty basic. Executives, managers, and employees typically need to come to you in order to get the information. Common metrics at this stage include:

- Headcount
- Salary
- Turnover
- Absence
- Time off
- Hiring costs
- Training expenses

Level 2: Reactive

At this level, you've digitized some basic processes and have a better under-standing of your workforce. This provides quicker access to some basic metrics and the ability to drill down into more specifics. Some information still needs to be pulled from manual sources and a lot of spreadsheets are involved. It still takes minutes—and sometimes hours—to complete most queries. Common metrics at level 2 include:

- Headcount trends (insights by type, location, department, location)
- Compensation breakdown
- Overtime expenses
- Paid time off accrual and liability
- Voluntary and involuntary turnover rates
- Time off details
- Workforce expense details
- Time to hire

Level 3: Moderate

At level 3, you've digitized the majority of your processes and have access to more data. Challenges center around aggregating and reconciling data across sources and systems—and keeping it all in sync. You have a line of sight into core workforce trends and things such as time, pay, and ben-efits. You can access most of these in seconds from a dashboard on your computer or smartphone. Everything is updated in real time. More sophis-ticated analysis, such as trends reports and comparisons, takes more time and effort. At this point, you're starting to surface more valuable business insights. Common metrics at this level include:

- Workforce insights (starts, exits, promotions)
- Tax, wage and labor distribution
- Turnover causes and costs
- Benefits utilization trends
- Benefits cost breakdown
- Speed to open enrollment
- Time to productivity
- Ability to slice, dice, and drill down

Level 4: Scaling

At this level, core processes are completely digitized and integrated. You no longer have to spend time on aggregating and integrating data sources. For the most part, you have one view of the truth at your fingertips from a variety of purpose-built dashboards. This frees you and your team up to focus on more strategic people analytics—things such as the employee experience, engagement, and well-being. You're also starting to run trends and do benchmarking to see how you're doing compared to peers and market comparables. These insights are valuable to your executive peers and all people managers. Common metrics here include:

- Fluid workforce composition trends (full time vs. part time vs. contingent)
- Compensation changes and trends
- Employee engagement
- Performance alignment
- Salary benchmarking
- Benefits benchmarking
- Diversity and inclusion breakdown

Level 5: Mastery

Finally, at level 5, you're getting predictive. You're leveraging trends and benchmarks to identify business risks and opportunities. You're able to model future scenarios, anticipate challenges, and surface insights to decision makers. Data is accessible on demand in seconds, often being pushed to you proactively in the form of alerts, nudges, and scheduled reports and analytics. When you're making a job offer, it tells you it might not be accepted because the salary is lower than the market rate for that position. You can predict lower turnover rates due to recent changes in your benefits offering. You're turning insights into a competitive advantage. Metrics at this stage include:

- Employee well-being
- Team well-being and burnout
- Employee engagement details
- Workforce productivity
- Forecasted retention rates
- Potential employee flight risks
- Diversity, equality, and inclusion benchmarks
- Peer cost benchmarks

Whether you are operating at level 1 or level 5, the fundamental enabler and driver of this evolution is technology. Without the right tools at your disposal, capturing data points and gathering real-time insights into workplace metrics, and then turning them into action, isn't feasible. We'll discuss this more in the next chapter. In summary, armed with data, you and your team can make smarter decisions, faster. You're on your way to strategic people operations.

CHAPTER 20

POPS Technology

Technology has changed almost every aspect of our personal and professional lives. Just think how dramatically things have changed over the past decade or so. Tasks that took hours, now take seconds. Information we used to chase down is pushed to us at just the right moment. AI, autopilot, and robots are helping us accelerate through life.

What about HR technology? Up until recently, have you ever heard an employee say I love this HR system? Has your HR system of record pushed meaningful workforce insights or suggestions to you at just the right time? We hope so, but probably not.

In this chapter, we'll share the shortcomings of legacy approaches to legacy HR technology and some common pitfalls to avoid. We'll then describe how to make the leap from HR administration to people ops when it comes to choosing technology, and how it can benefit your business.

The Shortcomings of HR Technology

Here's the issue. Yesterday's HR systems were built for the old way. They were designed for yesterday's workforce, and yesteryear's approach to managing it. They were built for HR, not people ops. Here are a few specific problems with traditional HR, payroll, and benefits systems:

- **Built for processes, not people.** Legacy systems were built for administrators, not the employees and end users who have to interact with them every day. Most of these tools are for tracking employees, not making life easier for them or empowering them to do their best work. Work technology should be as easy and fun as everyday consumer apps like Instagram, Google, and Uber. Users should enjoy using them, not loathe it.

- **Too limited.** Some small businesses start with accounting and payroll software and subsequently try to extend those applications to broader people-operations needs such as scheduling, time tracking, and employee engagement. The problem is accounting and payroll systems weren't built as all-in-one HR solutions. They either lack key functions like engagement surveys and employee well-being, or they have a clunky integration with other software providers.
- **Too complicated.** There are thousands of enterprise HR applications, but they're overly complex and expensive. You can't even try many of them before you buy. They take big budgets and teams just to get up and running. Then they need to be integrated and maintained.
- **Outdated.** Systems built decades or even years ago fail in many ways. They lack mobility for the deskless workforce, and are too reliant on on-premise hardware rather than mobile apps. They also don't effectively support contractors or gig workers; instead, they focus primarily on W-2 employees. They don't include collaboration, engagement, and feedback tools to improve employee productivity. And they lack data points and predictive insights.
- **Create disparate systems.** There are thousands of HR and "talent management" applications. There are hundreds of recruiting, or "talent acquisition" applications alone. If businesses choose software al-a-carte to fulfill certain needs, they can end up with a hodgepodge of disparate systems that run disjointedly.

A Better Way

A better way to approach HR technology is to invest in technology that works the way your business works: integrated, connected, and designed to create an employee experience that drives productivity and happy customers.

People operations technology is all-in-one HR software that connects your employee and business data to drive seamless people management, from payroll and benefits to paid time off (PTO) and performance reviews. Embracing people operations technology (see Table 20.1) enables companies to shift their focus and priorities. It all starts with the employee experience.

Below you'll find a comprehensive list of HR functions that have a technology associated with it. How many systems are you using at your business to manage these tasks? Ideally, you're running as few software solutions as possible to keep overhead costs down and uniform data management high.

TABLE 20.1 HR technology landscape.

HR TECHNOLOGY LANDSCAPE

Core HR Systems: Legacy approaches to managing payroll and HR (the old way):
- Accounting (some do very basic payroll and payments)
- Payroll
- Human Resource Information System (HRIS)
- Enterprise Resource Planning (ERP) systems *large enterprise companies*
- Time & Attendance, or Workforce Management (includes scheduling, clock in/out, PTO)
- Compliance

Talent Acquisition: If you're doing a lot of recruiting, consider these applications:
- Recruitment Marketing
- Sourcing and Candidate Relationship Management (CRM)
- Applicant Tracking System (ATS)
- Digital Assessments
- Video Interviewing
- Onboarding

Talent Management: Niche applications for discrete needs across the employee lifecycle
- Performance Management (goal tracking, 360 feedback, performance reviews)
- Learning & Development
- Compensation & Benefits
- Employee Surveys & Engagement
- Recognition & Rewards
- Workforce Analytics

Productivity Tools: Employee listening, communication, and productivity tools
- Surveys
- Collaboration
- Remote work tools
- Asynchronous communication
- Reporting & Analytics
- Other

Source: Zenefits, 2021.

Design a Great Employee Experience

Today's most successful companies are focusing on the employee experience—including their HR software choices—and turning it into a competitive advantage.

Although it might seem strange to connect POPS technology with the well-being of your employees, the evidence is overwhelmingly supportive of the notion. Employees increasingly want transparent access to their personal and business information. That means they want on-demand access to pay information, benefits, role expectations, company vision, and more. And, they want this information to come in the form of a modern digital experience that they've come to expect: mobile friendly, in an app, available 24/7, no human gatekeepers of information.

With the right technology choices, like Zenefits' all-in-one People Operations Platform, this is possible. Employees gain instant access to all the HR data that is permitted for them to see, anytime of the day, and from any device. Employers drive a trusting relationship by providing transparency to things that matter to employees. And the entire employee lifecycle is documented and reference-able through digital, ongoing records of performance feedback, coaching, and guidance entered into the system from managers and peers. What's more is that technology that was built to put people before process includes the soft aspects of company culture that we all know drive happy workers. Apps within the platform might feature stress and burnout issues through self-diagnosis quizzes and reference materials. Employees can learn about common workplace problems and self-teach solution strategies on their own time. And peer-to-peer communication apps help boost collaboration and productivity across teams.

Remove the Need for the 9–5, Empower Asynchronous Work

People operations technology recognizes that humans aren't hostages to schedules. Even if you're running a regular cadence of performance reviews, POPS technology provides a documented space where employees can solicit or request feedback from peers or managers at any time. They can jot notes that are pertinent to their roles inside the app, where managers can see and review the comments in real-time.

With the right technology in place, companies find it easy to manage teams in the office, in remote offices, or in hybrid scenarios because core aspects of people management are no longer tied to designated HR reps in a corner office. Rather, HR comes with all employees, through their mobile devices, and answers questions immediately. This empowers consistent work environments across asynchronous work hours and different employee types.

Improve Employee Listening, Collaboration, and Communication

It's true, as your company grows, managing communication gets more complicated. Adding locations, different time zones, and distributed work environments exacerbates the challenges. The quicker you scale, the more difficult this becomes.

Systems can bring people together in a virtual work environment and maintain a consistency in communication that will be familiar across your workforce no matter where they are. This is critical to scaling culture and productivity. People ops technology can help facilitate this in a major way. CEOs and people leaders can push important messages and announcements to all—or only to certain employees—through mobile push notifications or "listening" to employee needs through engagement surveys as we covered earlier. Again, all of this is from a single place (see Figure 20.1).

Embrace the Fluid Workforce

People operations systems must meet the needs of the fluid workforce to drive more efficiencies in a project-based Information Age. But what does this actually mean?

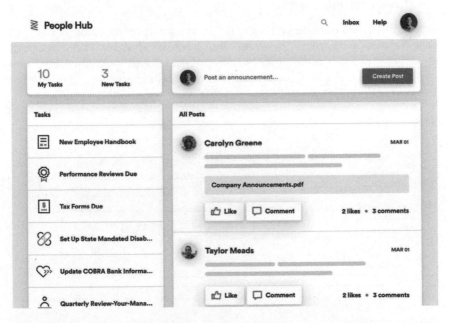

FIGURE 20.1 With people operations software, employees can collaborate with one another, and people teams can send out important information.

Source: Zenefits, 2021.

POPS technology needs to be able to keep up with this dynamic workplace trend. It should be able to classify and document every worker properly, including contractors. Top people platforms mitigate the ability to treat contractors like employees where it's inappropriate (or illegal), such as doing formal performance reviews (see Figure 20.2). On the other hand, tracking time and managing payments and taxes for contractors is an imperative. They differentiate when benefits, like telemedicine and ACA-alternative insurance plans are eligible for employees, and may even offer contractors unique health insurance options since they don't qualify for typical insurance plans.

These sophisticated employee data systems are best when an intuitive interface makes it easy for each employee to navigate his/her individual HR needs, provisioning just enough information for each person without inundating each of them with information that isn't relevant. A good system leaves employees feeling like it's easy to access information anytime, anywhere.

Proactive Compliance Guidance

There's been an exponential increase in compliance regulations over the past couple of decades. There are hundreds of changes every year and it's difficult to keep track of all the federal, state, and local laws. Overtime requirements, minimum wage, the FMLA, Consolidated Omnibus Budget

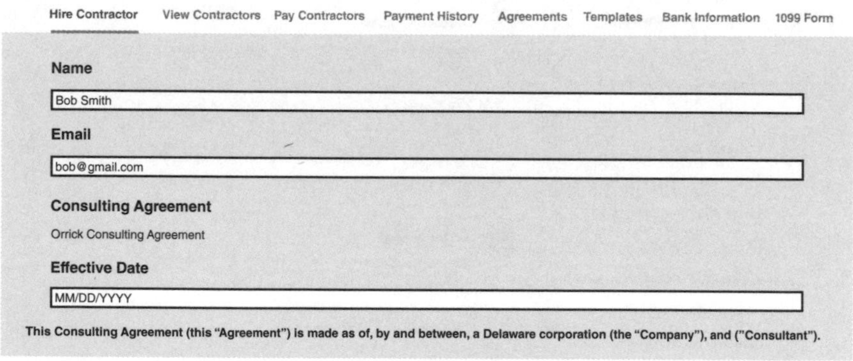

FIGURE 20.2 An example of a consulting agreement provided for a 1099 employee in the Zenefits app.

Source: Zenefits, 2021.

Reconciliation Act (COBRA), and taxes are fluid and complex. The ACA alone is over 20,000 pages long. It's especially difficult for small businesses that lack large HR compliance teams.

The good news? The more you digitize and track touch points across HR, payroll, and benefits, the more you can keep informed and alerted of potential risks. The best people operations platforms include safeguards and deadline alerts. They help you monitor compliance status and set custom reminders unique to your business. Systems can automatically send mandatory notices and calculate things like COBRA payments. Built-in overtime safeguards can send employees reminders to take required breaks and lunches. They also include a library of regulation updates, templates, and tools so you can stay on the right side of compliance (see Figure 20.3).

Automate Everything, All in One

If it's not abundantly clear by now, the key is to choose and implement technology solutions that bring all your workforce data under one roof—a single application that your entire staff and POPS professionals use together. The best solutions on today's market are natively built, meaning a software application that is built on a single code base so there is no lag time between systems or technology decencies that could leave your business out of key information. It means one app, one login, one user experience, and one database. The beauty of this is a new level of automation made possible by everything being combined, freeing up time for POPS leaders to focus on employee advancement, not paperwork. A new hire can set up their contact information, fill out their I-9, set up their direct-deposit preferences, enroll in benefits, and set up their Slack and Gmail accounts all in one workflow, in minutes, from their smartphone, by themselves. Before they even start work (see Figure 20.4).

The following applications can be automated and managed all in a single application and workflow:

- Hiring and onboarding
- Employee profiles
- Digital documents
- Org chart
- Scheduling
- Time tracking (clock in/out) w/geo-location
- Time off (PTO management, approvals, accruals)
- Benefits (automated shopping, enrollment, deductions, administration)

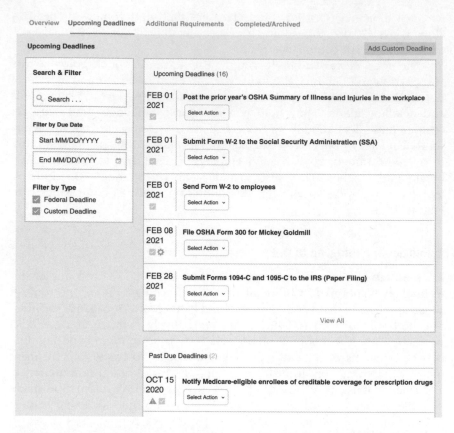

FIGURE 20.3 An example of the Zenefits Compliance Assistant, a digital feature that alerts businesses of federal compliance deadlines for HR, benefits, and payroll.

Source: **Zenefits, 2021.**

- Flex accounts (HSA, FSA, commuter cards, and claims)
- Payroll and taxes
- Performance management (goals, reviews, check-ins)
- Compensation benchmarking
- Employee engagement
- Employee feedback and pulse surveys
- Employee well-being (track and monitor stress, anxiety, etc.)

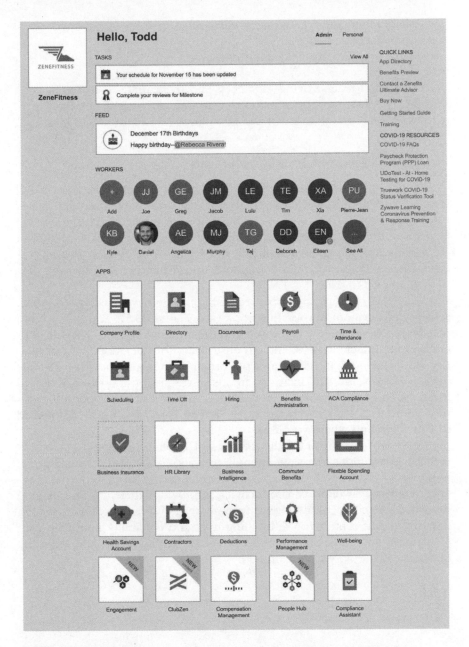

FIGURE 20.4 A snapshot of the Zenefits all-in-one employee dashboard.

Source: Zenefits, 2021.

- Collaboration and communication feeds
- Compliance assistance
- People analytics, insights, and trends

In addition to improving efficiency and the employee experience by having all of these processes automated in one place, digitizing them captures additional data points that can be analyzed and turned into insights.

Increase Intelligence with Data-Driven Insights

Traditional approaches to HR technology meant rudimentary use of digitization and information silos. Analyzing data was time consuming and often error prone. There were often manual steps involved like aggregating benefits utilization and trend data. In many cases it didn't exist at all. For example, employee engagement and well-being levels with year-over-year comparisons? It also required continuous updates and rework to keep data in sync and up to date.

With the right people ops technology, you have easily accessible, reliable information at your fingertips (see Figure 20.5). You can have a 360-degree view of every employee and the entire workforce. This includes contractors. It includes cost and expense data. It includes operational metrics like headcount, turnover, and performance trends. It includes strategic insights like diversity and inclusion trends across key business functions and locations. Most importantly, it includes leading indicators of your key business priorities. Data is always up to date in real time. Insights can be pushed to you when and where you like.

These are just a few of the benefits of moving disjointed legacy HR technology solutions to a single people operations platform. By making the transition, you'll be well on your way to enhancing your employee experience, improving workforce productivity, improving efficiency, and making more data-driven decisions. You're winning over your employees by putting them front and center. You're building trust and credibility internally with your board and leadership team. And you're helping build and scale the business. Where do we go from here?

FIGURE 20.5 An example of a Business Intelligence report including data on turnover, workforce diversity, employee compensation, and more.

Source: Zenefits, 2021.

CHAPTER 21

Turning POPS into a Competitive Advantage

The world has changed a lot over the past hundred years. We've come a long way since farms employed one out of every two workers. The work itself has changed. The reasons why we work have changed. The workforce has reinvented itself. Technology has—and will continue to—disrupt and reinvent work. The workplace is changing beneath us, fast-tracked in many ways by response to the COVID-19 pandemic.

The rapid digitization of the workplace and broader economy will continue to accelerate. This will create new challenges, but also new opportunities, a new level of data, insights, and possibilities.

Now a bigger change is necessary. A change that impacts every employee, worker, and company on the planet. A change to the ways in which work gets managed. A change to the relationship between a company and its people. A change to the vision, principles, and purpose of human resources as we knew it. This change is much needed, and overdue.

We hope this book has provided you with some inspiration. We hope it has motivated you to challenge the status quo of HR. We hope that it has provided you with a blueprint for change and useful tactics, best practices, and examples for a new way forward with POPS.

As you embark on the journey to people operations, we encourage you to keep business priorities in focus. Everything in people ops needs to be tied to evolving business objectives and priorities. People ops initiatives, insights, and KPIs should be leading indicators for those of the business. They should surface real business opportunities and risks. Measuring these priorities is the only way to show progress and demonstrate value. This is foundational to becoming more operationally forward.

There are a few key takeaways from this book.

First takeaway: embrace automation. It delivers a better people experience, empowering employees and workers of all types to have the modern consumer-like experience they're accustomed to. It removes process bottlenecks, empowering them to find their own answers and do things on their own, in a secure, controlled environment. Automation reduces time, costs, hassle, and variance. It reduces the risk of errors. It increases data capture and helps facilitate valuable insights for faster decisions. And, finally, it frees you up to focus on more important work.

Second takeaway: put your employee experience first. Every company invests in their customer experience. But it's employees that deliver that experience. As organizations recognize that their people are their ultimate asset, they're investing in a unique and compelling people experience. They're focused on employee motivation. They're providing employees with modern technology because they know it's critical to success and productivity. They're listening to their people and, more importantly, acting on their feedback. They're investing in employee engagement, collaboration, and well-being—and becoming great places to work.

Third takeaway: unleash your workforce. With technology in place, you can move from paperwork to people work. Embrace the Pareto principle and focus your time on the 20 percent of activities that drive 80 percent of organizational value. Liberate your organization from low-value busywork. Make this true for you, your people team, and your entire workforce. Design organizational programs, systems, and rituals that help elevate team engagement and productivity. Design rapid feedback and listening cycles. Keep a close pulse on employee sentiment. Measure and monitor productivity.

Make this the charter of people operations at your company. Communicate your vision, roadmap, and progress. If you're doing all this well, it will show. And, of course, you'll be measuring it along the way. You can see it in feedback from employees, peers, and leadership. You can see it in your eNPS and engagement scores. You can see it in your Glassdoor rankings. And, you can feel it. You're becoming a great place to work, an employer of choice in your industry, category, and geography, or wherever matters to you.

There is no doubt about the value of people to every organization. There is no doubt that people are a company's greatest asset and biggest driver of success. There is also no doubt that there has never been a better time for a better and more modern approach to empowering people. This is the purpose of people ops. We wish you all the best on your journey to POPS.

Digital Tools and Resources

We're happy to share our library of free digital resources and tools for business leaders and POPS practitioners.

To access the many tools and templates referenced in this book, visit www.zenefits.com/pops-extras

Bookmark this URL! This consistently updated site is your one-stop shop for free HR tools, checklists, and templates to make your job easier.

For a free POPS Maturity Model assessment, visit www.zenefits.com/pops-quiz

This free online tool helps POPS leaders self-assess their departmental sophistication, revealing strengths and weakness in their processes. Use this tool to up-level your people ops and create a better employee experience.

Get POPS Certified! Visit www.zenefits.com/pops-academy

Whether you're an accidental HR leader or a seasoned pro, the POPS Academy provides the knowledge and best practices to take your craft—and company—to the next level. Get certified on the concepts in this book, from high-level strategies to practical examples, and learn how to progress across the stages of the POPS Maturity Model.

Glossary

Absenteeism: the rate at which people don't show up for work, or show up late, without good reason, as measured by the average number of days taken off by your employee base

Advanced reporting: sophisticated reports, usually including additional data sources, which surface trends that directly impact decision-making. Examples include employee engagement and well-being scores

All-in-One HR: the notion that all aspects of HR, including workforce management, payroll, and benefits, are built into one native technology solution

Applicant Tracking Software (ATS): a popular automated recruiting tool that modern people teams use. They allow you to easily manage the application and hiring process by keeping a database of applicant information

Benefits: any additional advantage an employer gives to its employees, including both monetary and nonmonetary perks such as health insurance, paid vacation, equity, flexible work arrangements, life insurance, commuter benefits, remote work stipends, and more

Brand perception: the perceived feeling a consumer has about a brand

Candidate profile: a list of qualities and attributes of your ideal candidate based on market research and current employee data

Cascading goals: goals that are arranged so that they pass from one level of an organization to the next while ensuring alignment between different layers in the organization

The Cloud: any product or service delivered via the internet

Communications strategy: an explicit plan that outlines the process of communications inside a company, this can be both internal and external

Compensation philosophy: a formal statement that explains your moral position on pay, while providing a framework for pay consistency

Data insights and analytics: the knowledge and trends that a company gains from analyzing an aggregated set of data points

Data lake: a digital storage repository that holds a vast amount of raw data in its native format until it's ready to be used

DEI statement: a simple, clear statement that lets employees, customers, and communities know what your company stands for as it relates to social justice issues

Democratized data: free and available access to data without running into gatekeepers

Empirical data: data based on observation or experience

Employee motivation: the level of energy, commitment, and creativity that employees bring to their jobs every day

Employee Net Promoter Score (eNPS):   gauges an employee's willingness to recommend the company to peers and potential employees

Employee onboarding: the process of getting a new hire in compliance with new hire paperwork and ensuring they have the tools, training, and resources needed to do their jobs well

Employee record: a document that holds important details about each employee and their employment situation

Employee turnover rate: the measurement of the number of employees who leave an organization during a specified time period, typically one year

Engagement survey: a robust survey sent to employees, which covers a wide variety of topics, including engagement, contentment in one's job, employee well-being, and more

Fair Pay Philosophy: a system of thought that believes one's pay should match one's merits, tenure, and skill sets, remaining unbiased by age, gender, race, religion, or prior relationships, and is competitive with other similar roles in similar geographic areas

Fluid workforce: the dynamic nature of workers that includes contractors, gig workers, and part time workers—in addition to full-time employees—to drive more efficiencies

Guardrails: intelligent interventions designed to prevent damaging actions or avoid unintended consequences

Health insurance benefits: a specific category of benefits that usually include medical, dental, and vision insurance

Hoteling: a method of office management in which workers dynamically schedule their use of workspaces such as desks, cubicles, and offices. It is an alternative approach to the more traditional method of permanently assigned office seating

HR automation: the use of computers and technology to perform human resourcing work with minimal assistance by humans

HR system of record: a singular, cloud-based application that holds all of a company's workforce data, including employee records, HR, compliance, payroll, and more

Monetary perks: work benefits that are paid out in money, like equity, bonuses, or profit sharing

Motivation: the general desire or willingness of someone to do something.

Natively built software features: when software features are built within a company's primary code base

Nonmonetary perks: work benefits that are not paid out in money, such as flexible work hours, paid time off, or career opportunities

Nudges: gentle, digital reminders

One-to-many: the ability for information to be posted, displayed, or sent from one spot while servicing unlimited people

Operational reporting: a collection of basic historical data used to identify and reflect on what has happened in the past

Pay equality: similar pay among different groups

Pay equity: fairness of one's pay proportional to their job, taking into consideration any monetary disbursements: salary, incentives, bonuses, etc.

Pay rates: the amount each worker is paid per hour, week, project, year, or pay period

Pay schedules: the combination of a pay period and a pay date that defines how often employees get paid

Pay type templates: premade rules and definitions affixed to the various pay types

Pay types: the recurring pay scenarios your company uses frequently

Payroll deduction: a reduction of income from an employee's earnings

Payroll service: payroll services are offered by a third-party company that specializes in payroll

Payroll software: an application specifically designed to streamline and manage employee payments

People analytics: the process of collecting and analyzing data across the employee lifecycle for the purpose of improving an organization's overall workplace performance

People operations (people ops, or POPS): a human-centric business approach that emphasizes workforce empowerment to drive growth

People operations technology: all-in-one HR software that connects employee and business data to drive seamless people and workforce management

People Ops Maturity Model: measures the extent to which an organization's people operations is driven by established and documented best practices, processes, standards, and metrics proven to drive business outcomes

Peoplework: the work that seeks to empower people to do their best work

Performance Alignment: an employee performance framework that embodies an agile, open, transparent approach to employee development that aligns directly to the larger goals of the company

Personally Identifiable Information (PII): any data that can be used to identify an individual

Plan mapping: the preconfiguration of health insurance rules for situations like employees not selecting or defining coverage

Predictive insights: the prediction of future outcomes and scenarios based on strategic analytics, data models, and scenario planning

Privacy and security: the safeguarding of data and users of data in a digital system

Programmatic advertising: using technology to automatically upload your job description to targeted websites based on your predefined job requirement

Pulse survey: a short employee engagement survey that is sent regularly

Regression analysis: a mathematical way of sorting out which of the variables among a set of variables has an impact on an outcome

Salary benchmarking tools: salary data for specific jobs in specific geographic regions

Self-service: when people can access information and perform common tasks on their own

Strategic analytics: statistical analysis and modeling of reports to proactively identify business opportunities and vulnerabilities

User permissions: definitions that determine who can access what information in a given software platform

Workflow automation: an orchestrated and repeatable set of activities

References

Akerlof, George A. and Yellen, Janet L. 1990. "The Fair Wage-Effort Hypothesis and Unemployment." *Quarterly Journal of Economics* 105 (2): 255–283.

Anders, George. 2019. "We Found 57 Routes into the C-suite. If you're a Problem-fixer, Step Right Up." LinkedIn, December 5. https://www.linkedin.com/pulse/we-found-57-routes-c-suite-youre-problem-fixer-step-right-anders/.

Baldoni, John. 2009. "New Study: How Communication Drives Performance." *Harvard Business Review,* November 19. https://hbr.org/2009/11/new-study-how-communication-dr.

Bersin, Josh. 2015. "Becoming Irresistible: A New Model for Employee Engagement." *Deloitte Review 16,* January 27. https://www2.deloitte.com/us/en/insights/deloitte-review/issue-16/employee-engagement-strategies.html.

Bersin, Josh. 2019. "Why Diversity and Inclusion Has Become a Business Priority," updated March 16. http://joshbersin.com/2015/12/why-diversity-and-inclusion-will-be-a-top-priority-for-2016/.

Bock, Laszlo. 2015. *Work Rules! That Will Transform How You Live and Lead.* New York, NY: Hachette Book Group.

Bolden-Barrett, Valerie. 2017. "Just Two Payroll Errors Can Cause 49% of Employees to Start Job Hunting." HR Dive, June 7. https://www.hrdive.com/news/just-two-payroll-errors-can-cause-49-of-employees-to-start-job-hunting/444377/.

Brenan, Megan. 2020. "COVID-19 and Remote Work: An Update." *Gallup,* October 13. https://news.gallup.com/poll/321800/covid-remote-work-update.aspx.

Buckingham, Marcus, and Ashley Goodall. 2015. "Reinventing Performance Management." *Harvard Business Review,* November 16. https://hbr.org/2015/04/reinventing-performance-management.

The Center for Generational Kinetics. 2020. "The State of Gen Z 2020: Gen Z as Consumers, Influencers, and Trendsetters." https://genhq.com/wp-content/uploads/2020/10/State-of-Gen-Z-2020-Consumers.pdf.

Chamberlain, Andrew. 2015. "Why Is Hiring Taking Longer? New Insights from Glassdoor Data," June 18. https://www.glassdoor.com/research/time-to-hire-study/#.

Collins, James C., and Jerry I. Porras. 2004. *Built to Last: Successful Habits of Visionary Companies.* 3rd ed. New York, NY: HarperCollins.

Collins, Jim. n.d. "First Who—Get the Right People on the Bus." Accessed January 2, 2021. https://www.jimcollins.com/article_topics/articles/first-who.html.

Curry, Andrea. 2020a. "How Small Business Employees Really Feel About Their 2020 Benefits and Perks." *Workest* (blog). Zenefits, October 8. https://www.zenefits.com/workest/how-small-business-employees-really-feel-about-benefits-and-perks/.

Curry, Andrea. 2020b. "Surprise! Majority of Small Business Employees Feel Engaged at Work During COVID-19." *Workest* (blog). Zenefits, August 10. https://www.zenefits.com/workest/surprise-majority-of-small-business-employees-feel-engaged-at-work/.

DesRosiers, Haley. 2018. "3 Key Benefits of Integrated Timekeeping and Payroll." *American Payroll Association*, November 2. https://www.americanpayroll.org/news-resources/apa-news/news-detail/2018/11/02/3-key-benefits-of-integrated-timekeeping-and-payroll.

Doist. 2020. "The Pyramid of Remote Team Communication Tools." *Ambition & Balance* (blog), Doist. Accessed December 28, 2020. https://blog.doist.com/remote-team-communication-tools/.

Doshi, Neel, and Lindsay McGregor. 2015. *Primed to Perform: How to Build the Highest Performing Cultures through the Science of Total Motivation.* New York, NY: HarperCollins.

Duval, John. 2018. "How an HCM System Can Improve Productivity for HR, Part Four: Payroll." Fuse Workforce Management Human Resources and Payroll Blog, May 15. https://www.fuseworkforce.com/blog/how-an-hcm-system-can-improve-productivity-for-hr-part-four-payroll.

Emergence Equity Management. 2018. "The Rise of the Deskless Workforce." Emergence Equity Management. http://desklessworkforce2018.com/.

Falcone, Paul. 2020. "Viewpoint: Make This Checklist Your DE&I Launching Point." SHRM, October 5. https://www.shrm.org/resourcesandtools/hr-topics/behavioral-competencies/global-and-cultural-effectiveness/pages/viewpoint-make-this-checklist-your-dei-launching-point.aspx.

Ferguson, Grace. 2020. "How Much Does Small Business Health Insurance Cost?" *Workest* (blog). Zenefits, January 13. https://www.zenefits.com/workest/how-much-does-small-business-health-insurance-cost/.

FMI. 2013. "FMI's 2013 Incentive Compensation Study." *FMI Quarterly*, December 6. https://www.fminet.com/fmi-quarterly/article/2017/12/five-steps-innovative-compensation-strategy/.

Gaille, Brandon. 2017. "19 Employee Motivation Statistics and Trends." BrandonGaille.com, May 20. https://brandongaille.com/17-employee-motivation-statistics-and-trends/.

Gartner. 2020. "Gartner CFO Survey Reveals 74% Intend to Shift Some Employees to Remote Work Permanently." April 3. https://www.gartner.com/en/newsroom/press-releases/2020-04-03-gartner-cfo-surey-reveals-74-percent-of-organizations-to-shift-some-employees-to-remote-work-permanently2.

Girod, Chris, Paul Houchens, Dave Liner, et al. (2020). "2020 Milliman Medical Index." Milliman, Inc., May. https://us.milliman.com/-/media/milliman/pdfs/articles/2020-milliman-medical-index.ashx.

Glassdoor. 2020. "50 HR and Recruiting Stats That Make You Think." https://b2b-assets.glassdoor.com/50-hr-and-recruiting-stats.pdf

Gonzalez, Elizabeth. 2020. "A Guide to Benefits Administration for Your Business." The Blueprint. *The Motley Fool*, August 10. https://www.fool.com/the-blueprint/benefits-administration/.

Hammond, Keith. 2005. "Why We Hate HR." *Fast Company*, August 1. https://www.fastcompany.com/53319/why-we-hate-hr.

Handshake. 2019. "Handshake's Campus to Career Report: Early Career Trends to Watch in 2019." https://go.joinhandshake.com/rs/390-ZTF-353/images/Handshake-2019-Campus-to-Career-Report.pdf.

Hannon, Kerry. 2020. "It's a Terrible Time for Small Businesses. Except When It's Not." *New York Times*, December 14. https://www.nytimes.com/2020/12/14/business/smallbusiness/small-business-start-ups-entrepeneurs.html.

Harter, Jim. 2020. "U.S. Employee Engagement Hits New High After Historic Drop." Gallup, July 22. https://www.gallup.com/workplace/316064/employee-engagement-hits-new-high-historic-drop.aspx.

Harvard Business Review Analytic Service. 2013. "The Impact of Employee Engagement on Performance." *Harvard Business Review*, September 13. https://hbr.org/resources/pdfs/comm/achievers/hbr_achievers_report_sep13.pdf.

Hasan, Syed Zia-Ul. 2017. "To What Extent Is Money a Motivator for Employees?" ResearchGate. https://www.researchgate.net/publication/316421509_To_what_extent_is_money_a_motivator_for_employees.

Horowitz, Ben. 2014. *The Hard Thing about Hard Things: Building a Business When There Are No Easy Answers*. New York, NY: Harper Business.

Hussain, Amar. 2019. "4 Reasons Why A Remote Workforce Is Better For Business." *Forbes*, March 29. https://www.forbes.com/sites/amarhussaineurope/2019/03/29/4-reasons-why-a-remote-workforce-is-better-for-business/.

IBM. n.d. "Building a Human-centered Organization: Breaking down Insights from 7 Years of Research and Application." Accessed December 24, 2020. https://www.ibm.com/design/thinking/page/hco.

Jobvite. 2019. "2019 Recruiting Benchmark Report." https://www.job-vite.com/wp-content/uploads/2019/03/2019-Recruiting-Benchmark-Report.pdf.

Kinni, Theodore. 2016. "Why Emojis May Be the Key to Employee Retention." *MIT Sloan Management Review.* June 23. https://sloanreview.mit.edu/article/tech-savvy-why-emojis-may-be-the-key-to-employee-retention/.

Kohn, Alfie. 1999. *Punished by Rewards: the Trouble with Gold Stars, Incentive Plans, A's, Praise, and Other Bribes.* Boston, MA: Houghton Mifflin.

KPMG International. 2018. "Rise of the Humans: Digital and Human Labor and Its Impact on the Global Workforce." https://assets.kpmg/content/dam/kpmg/xx/pdf/2018/10/rise-of-the-humans-combined.pdf.

Lalwani, Puja. 2019. "Positive Work Culture and Using Emojis to Contribute to It—The Week of May 6, 2019, on HR Technologist." *HR Technologist*, May 10. https://www.hrtechnologist.com/articles/digital-transformation/positive-work-culture-and-using-emojis-to-contribute-to-it-the-week-of-may-6-2019-on-hr-technologist/.

Lazzareschi, Bella. 2018. "The Shift in Performance Management." *Workest* (blog). Zenefits, February 12. https://www.zenefits.com/workest/shift-performance-management/.

Leinwand, Allan. 2017. "Five Tips for Introducing Intelligent Automation to HR." *Forbes,* November 16. https://www.forbes.com/sites/forbestech-council/2017/11/16/five-tips-for-introducing-intelligent-automation-to-hr/?zd_source=hrt.

Lettink, Anita. 2019. "No, Millennials Will NOT Be 75% of the Workforce in 2025 (or Ever)!" LinkedIn, September 16. https://www.linkedin.com/pulse/millennials-75-workforce-2025-ever-anita-lettink/.

Lorenzo, Rocío, Nicole Voigt, Miki Tsusaka, Matt Krentz, and Katie Abou-zahr. 2018. "How Diverse Leadership Teams Boost Innovation." Boston Consulting Group, January 23. https://www.bcg.com/en-us/publications/2018/how-diverse-leadership-teams-boost-innovation.

Lund, Susan, James Manyika, Liz Hilton Segel, André Dua, Bryan Hancock, Scott Rutherford, and Brent Macon. 2019. "The Future of Work in America: People and Places, Today and Tomorrow." McKinsey Global Institute, July. https://www.mckinsey.com/featured-insights/future-of-work/the-future-of-work-in-america-people-and-places-today-and-tomorrow.

Manyika, James, Susan Lund, Michael Chui, Jacques Bughin, Jonathan Woetzel, Parul Batra, Ryan Ko, and Saurabh Sanghvi. 2017. "Jobs Lost, Jobs Gained: What the Future of Work Will Mean for Jobs, Skills, and Wages."

McKinsey Global Institute, November 28,. https://www.mckinsey.com/featured-insights/future-of-work/jobs-lost-jobs-gained-what-the-future-of-work-will-mean-for-jobs-skills-and-wages.

Mercer. Employee Engagement Index. https://www.mercer.com.

Murlis, Helen, and Peggy Schubert. 2001. "Engage Employees and Boost Performance." Hay Group. https://home.ubalt.edu/tmitch/642/Articles%20syllabus/Hay%20assoc%20engaged_performance_120401.pdf.

Murthy, Vani. 2014. "The Consequences of Willful Failure to Pay Payroll Taxes." *Journal of Accountancy*, June 1. https://www.journalofaccountancy.com/issues/2014/jun/20149645.html.

Nucleus Research. 2018. "Guidebook: Zenefits." December 5, 2018. https://nucleusresearch.com/research/single/guidebook-zenefits/.

O'Donnell, Riia. 2020. "How Do I Offer Health Insurance to My Employees?" *Workest* (blog). Zenefits, November 5. https://www.zenefits.com/workest/how-do-i-offer-health-insurance-to-my-employees/.

Osterhaus, Erin. 2015. "How Software Can Reduce Payroll Losses from Time Theft." *Software Advice,* April 23. https://www.softwareadvice.com/hr/industryview/time-theft-report-2015/.

Ozimek, Adam. 2020. "The Future of Remote Work." *Upwork,* May 20,. https://www.upwork.com/press/releases/the-future-of-remote-work.

Peacock, Amelia. 2016. "Over 30% of Millennials Unhappy with Their Job and Plan to Quit Within Six Months." *Clutch,* December 7. https://clutch.co/press-releases/millennials-unhappy-plan-to-quit-6-months.

Pijnacker, Lieke. 2019. "HR Analytics: Role Clarity Impacts Performance." *Effectory,* September 25. https://www.effectory.com/knowledge/hr-analytics-role-clarity-impacts-performance/.

Pink, Daniel H. 2011. *Drive: The Surprising Truth about What Motivates Us.* New York, NY: Penguin Publishing Group.

Rynes, Sara L., Barry Gerhart, and Kathleen A. Minette. 2004. "The Importance of Pay in Employee Motivation: Discrepancies between What People Say and What They Do." Wiley Online Library. John Wiley & Sons, November 17. https://onlinelibrary.wiley.com/doi/abs/10.1002/hrm.20031.

SBA Office of Advocacy. 2018. "Frequently Asked Questions," August. https://www.sba.gov/sites/default/files/advocacy/Frequently-Asked-Questions-Small-Business-2018.pdf.

SCORE. 2014. "Work With Me, People! Statistics on Small Business Human Resource Trends," April 21. https://core.score.org/resources/work-me-people-statistics-small-business-human-resource-trends

Senz, Kristen. 2020. *"How Much Will Remote Work Continue After the Pandemic?" HBS Working Knowledge,* August 24. https://hbswk.hbs.edu/item/how-much-will-remote-work-continue-after-the-pandemic.

Shahzadi, Irum, Farida Khanam, Shagufta Nasreen, Syed Shahzaib Pirzada, and Ayesha Javed. 2014. "Impact of Employee Motivation on Employee Performance." *European Journal of Business and Management* 6 (23): 159–166. https://doi.org/https://doi.org/10.7176/EJBM.

Sheetz, Michael. 2017. "Technology Killing off Corporate America: Average Life Span of Companies under 20 Years." CNBC, August 24. https://www.cnbc.com/2017/08/24/technology-killing-off-corporations-average-lifespan-of-company-under-20-years.html.

Society for Human Resources Management (SHRM). 2017. "Average Cost-per-Hire for Companies Is $4,129, SHRM Survey Finds," May 19. https://www.shrm.org/about-shrm/press-room/press-releases/pages/human-capital-benchmarking-report.aspx.

Skovholt, Karianne, Anette Grønning, and Anne Kankaanranta. 2014. "The Communicative Functions of Emoticons in Workplace E-Mails: :-)." *Journal of Computer-Mediated Communication 19 (4)*: 780–797. https://doi.org/10.1111/jcc4.12063.

Smarp. 2019. "What Is the True Cost of Poor Employee Communication?" (blog), April 30. https://blog.smarp.com/what-is-the-true-cost-of-poor-employee-communication.

Smartsheet. 2017. "Automation in the Workplace 2017." https://www.smartsheet.com/sites/default/files/smartsheet-automation-workplace.pdf.

Starr Conspiracy. 2020. "Brandscape 2021: Workplace Wellbeing." December. https://brandscape.thestarrconspiracy.com/brandscape-2021-workplace-well-being/#/new-reality

Sullivan, John. 2018. "HR, We Have A Problem: Up to 80% of Employees Don't Trust Us." *TLNT,* August 27. https://www.tlnt.com/hr-we-have-a-problem-up-to-80-of-employees-dont-trust-us/.

Suzuno, Melissa. 2019. "Top 2019 Talent Trends: The Remote and Distributed Workforce." *Greenhouse* (blog). https://www.greenhouse.io/blog/top-2019-talent-trends-the-remote-and-distributed-workforce.

TIME. 1961. "Business: The Automation Jobless." February 24. http://content.time.com/time/subscriber/article/0,33009,828815-1,00.html.

Todd, Robb. 2020. "How Long Your Small Business Will Last, According to Data." *Fundera*, November 18. https://www.fundera.com/blog/small-business-survival.

Townsend, Christine Bestor. 2020. "U.S. Department of Labor Issues New Guidance on Remote Work." Ogletree Deakins, August 28. https://ogletree.com/insights/u-s-department-of-labor-issues-new-guidance-on-remote-work/.

TruQu. n.d. "12 Eye-Opening Statistics About Traditional Performance Reviews" (blog). Accessed December 26, 2020. https://truqu.com/en/blogs/12-eye-opening-statistics-about-performance-reviews/.

Upwork. 2017. "Freelancers Predicted to Become the U.S. Workforce Majority within a Decade, with Nearly 50% of Millennial Workers Already Freelancing, Annual 'Freelancing in America' Study Finds." October 17. https://www.upwork.com/press/releases/freelancing-in-america-2017.

US Department of Justice (DOJ). 2018. "Employment Tax enforcement," May 1. https://www.justice.gov/tax/employment-tax-enforcement-0.

US Department of Labor (DOL). 2008. "Fact Sheet #21: Recordkeeping Requirements under the Fair Labor Standards Act (FLSA)." Revised July. https://www.dol.gov/agencies/whd/fact-sheets/21-flsa-recordkeeping.

US Department of Labor (DOL). 2020. "Wage and Hour Division Data." https://www.dol.gov/agencies/whd/data.

US Immigration and Customs Enforcement (ICE). 2019. "Form I-9 Inspection Overview," August 19. https://www.ice.gov/factsheets/i9-inspection.

Wiles, Jackie. 2018. "Peer Feedback Boosts Employee Performance." Smarter With Gartner, May 11. https://www.gartner.com/smarterwithgartner/peer-feedback-boosts-employee-performance/.

Workfront, 2020. "State of Work 2020." https://www.workfront.com/sites/default/files/resource/file_pdf/2019-09/sow-report-2020.pdf.

Yello. 2020. "2020 Interview Scheduling Statistics and Trends: A Recruiter Survey" (blog). https://yello.co/blog/interview-scheduling-statistics/.

Zandan, Noah. n.d. "How Much of Our Workdays Do We Spend Communicating?" *Quantified Communications* (blog). Accessed December 26, 2020. https://www.quantifiedcommunications.com/blog/how-much-of-our-workday-do-we-spend-communicating.

Zenefits, 2020. "Employer Health Benefits Report." https://www.zenefits.com/wp-content/uploads/2020/08/benefits-benchmark-report.pdf.

Zenger, Jack, and Joseph Folkman. 2014. "Your Employees Want the Negative Feedback You Hate to Give." *Harvard Business Review*, January 15. https://hbr.org/2014/01/your-employees-want-the-negative-feedback-you-hate-to-give.

Acknowledgments

We want to thank the many people who made this book possible.

To our customers, for your stories and successes, which are helping us draft the future: Adryon Ketcham, Amy Dalebout, Beth Anne Wilhelm, Caylen Coxall, Eric Edelson, Jodie Heal, Kyla Hanaway-Quinlan, Michelle Liggett, Mike Boyadjian, Monica Haley, Nigel Barry, Paulina Song, Rob Snodgrass, Ross Thomason, Sarah Shepard, and Tori Soler.

To the Zenefits teams for their continued support. Let's be clear—this book was a total team effort. Without them this book would not be possible: Andrea Curry, Ankur Patel, Brittany Goodliffe, Christian Flaten, Danny Speros, Didi D'Errico, Doug Sechrist, Irmarie Berdecia, Kari Girarde, Jean Lee, Rob Stevenson, and Scott Blankenship. And last, but definitely not least: an extraordinary thanks to Jean Spencer, one of the masterminds—and master editors—behind *People Operations*. Thank you. We're truly in it together.

To the many brilliant minds who are making people operations technology real: Zenefits product managers and engineers. And finally, to the Zenefits team—past, present and future—for advancing our mission of leveling the playing field for small businesses.

To our editors and support from John Wiley & Sons, whose guidance kept us on track: Mike Campbell, Kelly Talbot, and all the other editors and professionals who were involved.

About the Authors

Jay Fulcher A serial entrepreneur, Jay Fulcher is passionate about leveling the playing field for America's small businesses through strategic use of technology. Jay's successful track record includes CEO and executive roles at both public and private technology companies including Zenefits, Ooyala, Agile Software, PeopleSoft, and SAP. A seasoned business operator, he's built organizations with a focus on people—with ample opportunity for play, purpose, and potential. Jay's perspective on entrepreneurship has been featured in CNBC, Bloomberg, *Forbes, The Wall Street Journal,* Yahoo Finance, Fortune Healthcare Summit, *South by Southwest, Money 20/20,* and more. In addition to his current role as chairman and CEO at Zenefits, Jay is an active board member and advisor. Outside of work, Jay is an avid outdoorsman, sports fan, and enjoys spending time with his family on their ranch.

Kevin Marasco Kevin Marasco's built his career at the intersection of technology and the future of work. Three times over, Kevin has scaled start-up, private, and public software companies past 1,000 percent growth, including HR technology companies HireVue, Taleo (acquired by Oracle), and Vurv Technology. As unconventional and curious as he is passionate and humble, Kevin serves as Chief Marketing Officer at Zenefits. He also serves as a board advisor, start-up investor, and venture advisor. Ultramarathon runner, surfing enthusiast, and father of two, Kevin is also a sought-after speaker and guest on business, marketing, and work tech podcasts and media sites.

Tracy Cote Tracy Cote built her career in people operations by helping demystify the practice in corporate and university settings. Tracy's smart, empathetic—but also direct and relatable—leadership approach has resulted in strong, scalable businesses, supported by strategic people experience programs. Her work has garnered Best Place to Work accolades at companies including Zenefits, Genesys, MobiTV, Inc., and Organic Inc. She currently serves as an advisor at Zenefits and the Chief People Officer at StockX. Tracy is a media and podcast regular, with her insights appearing in *Forbes, Huffington Post, The Wall Street Journal,* and LinkedIn Live. A working mom, she is also a vintage glamper, tiki drink enthusiast, and maker of her own skincare products.

Index

A

absenteeism 172
A/B test 135
accessibility, remote work and 192
advanced reporting 209
Affordable Care Act 219
agility, as small business advantage
all-in-one HR 55
American Payroll Association (APA)
    81, 84
American Society for Personnel
    Administration (ASPA) 20
analytics, data insights and 57–8
Analyze step to building motivation
    118, 120
Angelou, Maya 142
Applicant Tracking Software (ATS)
    78
artificial intelligence (AI) 6
Ask step to building motivation
    117–18, 119
assimilate answers, engaged
    workers and 164–5
at-home work environments 190–1
automate administration/
    compliance step of POPS 30
automation; see also HR
    automation: federal/
    state tax filing 86; health
    insurance benefits (see
    health insurance benefits

automation); hiring/
    onboarding, e-signatures
    and 73; state economic
    security 86; technology and
    all-in-one 219, 220–2; time
    and pay (see time and pay
    automation); workflow 55

B

Baby Boomers 177
background checks, hiring/
    onboarding and 73
benefits, defined 91
Benioff, Marc 152
BHAGs cascading goal model
    152, 153
Big Hairy Audacious Goals
    (BHAGs) 152, 153
biometrics 84
Black, Indigenous, or people
    of color (BIPOC) 182
Black Lives Matter movement 178
blended teams 9
Bock, Laszlo 32–3, 197
bottom-up *vs.* top-down work
    environment 17
branding, HR and 23–4
brand perception 23
buddy punching 84
budget, compensation strategies
    and 127–31